# A Single Step

# A Single Step

A MEMOIR

Heather Mills McCartney

WITH PAMELA COCKERILL

An AOL Time Warner Company

Warner Books Edition



Originally published in Great Britain under the title *Out on a Limb*
(copyright © Span International, 1995, 1996; text copyright ©
Pamela Cockerill, 1995, 1996).

Warner Books, Inc., 1271 Avenue of the Americas, New York, NY 10020

Visit our Web site at www.twbookmark.com

An AOL Time Warner Company

Printed in the United States of America

First Warner US Printing: October 2002
10 9 8 7 6 5 4 3 2 1

ISBN 0-446-53165-0
LCCN: 2002109816

This book is dedicated to the many people I love—I wish I could have mentioned you all. To my brother, Shane; sister Claire; wonderful friend Ruth; my best friend and loving husband, Paul; but most of all to my sister Fiona, whose devoted care helped me overcome my accident and make it through the darkest hours.

# *Foreword*

Over the years, many people have contacted me saying that reading of my experiences proved helpful in their own lives. One man even said it stopped him from committing suicide. Although I used to be very open about my life, accepting that for some it was inspirational, soon after I met Paul the situation changed. Privacy became so hard to find that it became really valuable to me and I virtually stopped answering press questions about myself. There are three reasons I am opening up my life again and writing this book.

The first reason is that the silent option I adopted after meeting Paul completely backfired on me. Instead of accepting that my respect for Paul and his family was important to me, reporters seemed to resent my decision, and wrote things that were either misreported or completely made-up. By last year so much rubbish was being written about us that I was finding it hard not to speak out and defend myself. It was Paul who suggested I should tell my own story.

I still might not have gone ahead if we hadn't heard rumors that an unauthorized biography about us both was being planned. That was the deciding factor. Unauthorized biographies can spread lies and gossip over which you have no control. People we know have suffered that way and I have no intention of joining them. By writing my own book, I can at least set the record straight. After they've read it, people can decide for themselves.

Finally, by far the most important reason for publishing this book is to help the people who have inspired me and changed the direction of my life—the amputee civilians, survivors of land-mine explosions, their families and friends. All the authors' net proceeds from the sales of *A Single Step* will go to the UNA Adopt-A-Minefield charity and its offshoot, Survivor Assistance.

*A journey of a thousand miles must begin with a single step.*

Lao-tzu (604 B.C.–531 B.C.),
*The Way of Lao-tzu*

# *Introduction*

The light was so bright it was hurting my eyes. For a moment it seemed to be the most important pain in my body, but then I became aware of other, more urgent pains—of a grating, stabbing sensation in my left side and of a tight clamp squeezing viciously at my hips. Somewhere in the background I could also feel a dull ache in my left leg but it was so slight compared with the other pains that I was barely conscious of it.

I had no idea where I was or how I had arrived there. And at that moment I didn't care. All I could focus on was the pain. As I stared up toward the ceiling, faces loomed and faded like ghostly masks. Familiar faces, uttering soft, jumbled words of comfort. Raffaele, Grandma, Ruth, and then, one by one the faces went, until there was only my sister Fiona.

She took my hand. "Heather? Are you awake?"

I grunted.

"You know what's happened, don't you?"

"I know it hurts."

"You've had an accident . . . a bad accident. But you're going to be all right."

"Oh." I was hardly listening. "Fiona, I've got to have something for the pain. Go and ask somebody, please."

Fiona shook her head. "They said you can't have any more painkillers because you've got some crushed ribs and your lung is punctured. The doctor explained when you asked yesterday. Don't you remember?"

"No." My mind was a total blank. "How long have I been here?"

"Three days."

"What happened?"

Fiona's voice came from far away. "A police motorcycle hit you when you were crossing the road. You were with Raffaele, though God knows why . . ." She leaned closer. "Do you really not remember? Raffaele said you were conscious the whole time."

I struggled to recall and memories began to emerge out of the haze.

The sun had been shining, that much I did remember . . . and putting the stereo in the boot of the Saab so it wouldn't get stolen . . . and setting off with Raffaele to walk to Kensington Gardens to feed the squirrels . . . and standing at the edge of the road waiting to cross . . . and the noise of police sirens . . . then after that . . . nothing. Total blackness.

I groaned.

Fiona leaned forward. "Where does it hurt?"

"Everywhere. My chest, my hips . . ."

"That's because you've broken your pelvis." She hesitated. "What about your leg? How does that feel?"

"It hurts a bit. Not as much as the rest of me though."

Fiona squeezed my hand hard. She was sitting behind me and I couldn't see her face properly. "Heather, there's something I've got to tell you. Someone's got to do it . . ."

"Tell me what?" I wished she'd stop talking. It was hard enough to cope with the pain without trying to hold a conversation.

Fiona came around to the side of the bed. Tears were streaming down her cheeks. "You've lost your leg, Heather. Your left leg. Below the knee. It's gone."

I stared at her, not taking it in. Not wanting to take it in.

Fiona choked. "I'm so sorry," she said. "They wanted to sew it back on but they couldn't. It was too badly damaged."

Fiona says I shouted out "No" when she told me that, but I don't remember. All I do remember is the black clouds swirling in on me again as I passed out and my mind floated away to another time, another place nearly twenty years earlier.

Mum had been wearing her new fur coat that night, a full-length dark brown mink that had cost a fortune (as Dad never stopped reminding her). It was typical of Dad to splash out on something flashy like a fur coat that would make people think what a big shot he was. It was a nice coat though. I can still remember the way it tickled my cheek and the sudden smell of Blue Grass perfume as Mum bent over to kiss me good night. She looked really excited. A night out at the opera was a big treat. Since we'd moved to the country she hadn't gone out much at all—Rothbury was miles from anywhere and Dad worked late most evenings.

Mum's hair was long and blond and she always wore it tied back from her face but that night, because it was a special occasion, she'd left a few curly wisps in front of her ears. Under the fur coat she was wearing a dark blue silk dress with a single string of pearls. Next to her, Dad looked slim and handsome in tuxedo and bow tie. I remember thinking proudly that they looked like film stars.

Dad was fidgeting to be off—he was always impatient, but that night he had a reason. They were late. He held the back door open. "Come on, Bea," he scolded. "The curtain goes up in three-quarters of an hour." Mum pecked Shane and Fiona on the cheek and scurried off obediently. At the door she turned to Joan, our baby-sitter. "Send them to bed, Joan, if they don't behave." Then she winked at me to show she was only joking.

For an hour or so after Mum and Dad left, Shane, Fiona, and Joan watched the telly in the lounge while I played with Ben in the kitchen. Ben was our Old English sheepdog. Dad had bought him for us just before we moved to Cockshott Farm six months ago and for me he was the best thing about living in the country. I used to take him for long walks through the woods behind the farm and he'd come back with goosegrass and burrs stuck in his coat that would take hours to pick out. Most nights, after Mum and Dad had gone to bed he'd sneak up the stairs and jump onto the end of my bed.

But that night Ben had grown tired of fetching his ball back and I'd left him snoring in his basket and gone back into the lounge to watch TV with the others. Fiona, who was only four, had fallen asleep on the settee and Shane was lying full length on the carpet watching an American detective program. When the news came on, Joan went into the kitchen to make herself a coffee, and while she was out of the room the phone rang.

"Get that, Shane, will you?" she called. But before Shane could obey there was a loud hammering on the front door. "I'll see to it," Joan shouted. "Just answer the phone, Shane."

Shane picked up the receiver but the TV was so loud he couldn't hear properly. He was still saying "What? What?" when the kitchen door opened and Joan led a policewoman into the room. A policeman followed her, cap in hand. I stared at them, puzzled. I don't remember feeling scared. I was too young to know that policemen meant bad news.

Shane stared too and held the receiver out to Joan. "It's something about a hospital," he whispered.

"I'll take it," the policeman said. "You two sit down." As he turned away and spoke quietly on the phone Joan gasped, "I'll fetch my mum," and rushed out of the room slamming the door behind her. All the commotion woke Fiona up and she looked as if she was going to burst into tears.

The policewoman came over and squatted down beside us. "Now, you're going to have to be very brave," she said. "Your mum and dad have had a bit of an accident in their car and they've had to go to hospital."

We gaped.

The policeman put the receiver down and came over. "Don't worry. I've just spoken to the ward sister and she says they're going to be all right. You'll be able to go and see them in a day or two."

Still we stared dumbly.

"We're going to arrange for someone to look after you while they're in the hospital," he continued. "Have you got any aunties or uncles who live nearby?" I shook my head. "What about your grandma and grandad?"

"They live in Brighton," Shane said in a small voice.

"All right, don't worry. We'll sort something out," the policewoman smiled. "Do you know where your mother keeps her address book?"

The police were still rummaging through Mum's desk looking for the book when Joan returned with her mother. Mrs. Wilson fired questions at them that they answered in solemn voices, quite different from the way they'd spoken to us. They were talking about Mum, I understood that much, and they were using strange terms like *hemorrhage* and *intensive care.*

I strained desperately to catch more. And that was when I heard the words that were to come back and haunt me twenty years later as the policewoman murmured to Mrs. Wilson, "I'm afraid it looks as if she's lost her leg."

Who was it said lightning never strikes twice?

# A Single Step

# Chapter 1

My very first childhood memory is of wandering through the meadow at the back of our house in Wales one hot summer's day when I was about four years old. I was so small I could hardly see above the long grass: I remember the buzz of insects all around my head and shiny buttercups brushing my face as I pushed my way through the field. But it wasn't the countryside that held my interest that day. I had another destination in mind.

My grandparents were staying at our house in Libanus for their summer holidays. If I shut my eyes I can still hear Grandma calling out from the back garden, "Where are you going, Heather?" Me yelling, "I'm going out to play!" Grandad's voice coming faintly back through the privet hedge saying, "Well, don't go far."

My memory gets hazy then, but Grandma often used to tell me the rest of the story. Apparently, two hours later when I hadn't come home everyone got worried and Mum, Grandma, and Grandad ran up and down the road knocking on doors asking if anyone had seen me. Libanus wasn't much bigger than a village and it didn't take long for them to check every house and work themselves into a state of panic. Mum went back to our house to ring the police while Grandma knocked a second time on people's doors asking them to check their garden sheds.

Then, at five o'clock, when Grandma was trudging back up the main street wondering what she was going to wear to my funeral, she suddenly saw one of the dummies in the Libanus dress-shop window move. Stopping to take a closer look she realized that the "dummy" was a small blond girl striking a statuesque pose and pretending to be a model . . .

Years afterward Grandma used to love to embarrass me by telling that story. "Heather always knew she wanted to be a model when she grew up," she'd say to my friends. "She started practicing for it when she was four."

But of course it wasn't true. At that age I didn't have any idea what my future held. Maybe it was just as well, because the rest of my childhood was hardly an ideal preparation for the world of the catwalk.

In this life there are some people who should never get married. There are also people who should never have children. My mum and dad belonged in both of these categories.

They had fallen in love at university when they were both eighteen, though which university and studying what subjects I never discovered. Communication with their kids was never one of my parents' strong points; in fact for a long time Mum and Dad's backgrounds were an almost total mystery to me. It was only years later, when I started to spend time with Grandma, that she told me about their childhoods and helped me understand why they became the sort of people they were.

Grandma wasn't actually my grandmother at all. She and Grandad had adopted my father when he was seven after finding they couldn't have children of their own. Dad's real mother was an unmarried girl of eighteen who'd died when he was small. By the time he went to live with my grandparents, Dad had been in and out of several foster homes.

"He was a bit unsettled by all that chopping and changing," Grandma told me once. "I don't think he ever believed he was with us to stay."

Dad grew up in Brighton where Grandma and Grandad had a grocery shop. Grandad was a mechanic for one of the Grand Prix teams but he'd bought the shop as a sort of insurance for their old age. While Dad was young, Grandma had to look after the shop on her own, which was hard work and probably explained why they didn't ever adopt a brother or sister for Dad.

"It took him a long time to come out of himself," Grandma told me. "He was a very quiet little boy when he was small." Though he can't really have been that "little" because he grew up to be six foot.

From very early on Dad was good at school, but what impressed the neighbors more was his extreme politeness. Apparently, as a young boy he'd always say, "Hello. How are you?" and shake hands solemnly when he was introduced.

For some reason, one story Grandma told me about Dad really stuck in my mind. It happened when he was about ten. Grandma had caught him one day setting fire to a spider in the cellar of their house: At the same moment as she yelled at him, it had exploded. He'd been so disgusted and frightened that he'd burst into tears and nothing Grandma said could console him.

"From that day on your father was always very kind to animals," she told me.

That was an understatement. He wasn't just kind to animals—he was crazy about them. When we were small, wherever we lived, there was always a dog or a cat around; at one time we even had a pet goose and a white nanny goat that used to run about the house and wake me up in the morning by licking my face. For a while when I was five or six, Dad worked for the RSPCA. I remember him once stopping the car by the side of the road to pick up an injured deer. He put it in the back of our Volvo estate car and brought it home to nurse it, and he was really upset when it died a few days later.

That childhood prank must have made a lifelong impact because Dad always kept a special place in his heart for spiders. When we were growing up he would never let us kill a spider but would always pick it up gently and put it out of the window.

"Spiders kill flies. They're our *friends,* Heather," he'd say. "You mustn't hurt them." Which, considering the way he behaved toward human beings, I always found a bit bizarre.

There was one other odd thing Grandma revealed about Dad. I grew up believing that Dad's name was Mark. It was what Mum called him and how all his post was addressed. But Grandma told me his real Christian name—the one his mother had given him—was John. She said he'd changed it when he was fifteen after a school trip. Grandma had been waiting for him at the train station and she'd got them to put a message out over the loudspeaker. "Will John Mills please go to the station entrance." When he got to the entrance there was a crowd of people with autograph books all expecting to see John Mills the actor. Dad didn't think it was funny. "He came downstairs that night and told us that from now on we had to call him Mark," Grandma said. "When I asked him why, he said it was because he wanted a name that was *his* so that when he made his mark in the world people wouldn't confuse him with anyone else." She smiled. "That's why he chose the name Mark I think."

Grandma always said that it was the first time she realized how ambitious her son was.

Dad was an achiever in everything he tried, and he tried most things: music (the banjo and guitar); photography (for which he won an *Evening Standard* award); and, of course, sport. Over the years he mastered jujitsu (a black belt); swimming (various medals); tennis, squash, mountaineering, and the pentathlon. In fact, you name it, he'd tried it. Whatever he took up, he had to be the best. You could forget all that nonsense about playing the game. For him the only thing that counted was winning.

Dad only ever mentioned his courting days to me once, when he told me that he'd met Mum during a mixed hockey match at their university. He was the captain of his team and she was the captain of hers and her team had beaten his. I remember thinking when he told me that, how getting beaten by a crowd of women wouldn't have gone down too well with Dad.

My mother Beatrice was also an only child but came from a very different social background from Dad's. Her father was a high-ranking army officer and she'd been born in India during the war and educated first in India, then at posh English boarding schools. Judging from the pictures in her photo album she was a stunning-looking girl with very long legs, fine blond hair, and the most incredible green eyes. By the time Mum went to university her father had retired from the army and the Finlay family was living in luxury in a big house in Scotland. As Grandma told it they weren't at all impressed when Beatrice came home from college with a cocky grammar school boy who called her Bea and whose parents ran a grocer's shop. Colonel Finlay thought Mark Mills was a most unsuitable match for his daughter and ordered her to break it off at once. But for the first time in her life Mum rebelled at being treated like one of her father's squaddies and there were tremendous rows. It must have been hard for Mum. It must have been even harder when her mother got cancer and her father blamed it on her, saying it was because of all the heartache she'd caused them. Mum went back to Scotland to nurse her mother, but after she died Mum dug her toes in and announced she was still marrying Dad. Her father never forgave her. He refused to go to the wedding and cut her off completely; in fact she only saw him once more in her life. So you couldn't exactly say Mum and Dad had the most promising start to their marriage.

After that it was downhill all the way. That's how it seemed to us anyway, stuck in the middle of it. I haven't much idea what happened in the years before Shane, Fiona, and I came along, except that Dad was in the army for a while—the Paras I think—which was where he took up rock climbing and doing the pentathlon. Perhaps he was still in the army when I was born—on January 12, 1968—because on my birth certificate, under place of birth, it says Aldershot. But by the time I was old enough to take in my surroundings, Mum, Dad, and I, together with my older brother Shane and younger sister Fiona, were living near Brecon in mid-Wales. To this day I don't know why we were living in an isolated place like Libanus, though it's near a big mountaineering center so perhaps Dad had something to do with that. But if he did he kept it to himself.

In fact the whole time we were growing up we rarely knew what Dad's job was. Whenever people at school, whose fathers were miners or farmers or salesmen, used to talk about what their fathers did for a living we were always at a loss to know what to say.

Sometimes I used to tell people my father was a vet. I must have thought of the idea because of all the animals he used to bring home. It was while we were living in Libanus that we had the white nanny goat that used to wake me up in the mornings. We also had Tigga, the huge striped cat, and, later, Ben, our lovely Old English sheepdog puppy who learned the Green Cross Code and used to see us safely to school each day. Ben was the only animal I ever saw my father mistreat, when he threw him in a river to teach him to swim. It wasn't a little stream, but a deep fast-flowing torrent. Ben's shaggy coat weighed him down and his head kept going under. I was so scared that I rushed at Dad and pounded him with my fists, screaming that Ben would drown, but Dad just laughed hysterically until I realized he was actually enjoying Ben's distress. He pinned my arms to my sides and made me watch until eventually Ben struggled to the shore, clambered out, and shook water all over us.

"See?" Dad said, grinning. "That's the way to learn. In at the deep end!"

Maybe he was right because, after that, Ben often jumped in the river on his own. But I never forgot the way Dad's famous compassion for animals once switched itself off.

I do have lots of happy memories of those years with the animals in Wales. I remember my first day at the little village school and looking out of the windows at the long-tailed Welsh sheep grazing just a few yards away. I remember sneaking at night into my mother's bedroom and dabbing her Nulon hand cream onto my podgy fingers in the hope that it would make them long and elegant like hers. I remember the sound of the wind howling around the Brecon Beacons while I was tucked up safe and warm in my bunk bed. Best of all I remember my grandparents coming up on the coach from Brighton to visit.

Grandma and Grandad were the kindest people I knew and always had time for kids. Grandad would play dominoes with us and bounce us on his knee and sing songs from *Mary Poppins.* On Saturday afternoon he would always sit down with me to watch the wrestling on TV. He used to get really carried away and would scream and shout at the television.

"You can't do that—that wasn't a proper throw," he'd bellow. I'd shake my head at him feeling very grown up. "Grandad, he can't *hear* you."

"Those bloomin' referees," he'd say, ignoring me. "They're useless. I could do a better job myself."

I'd laugh till it hurt. Dad had told me that wrestling wasn't a *real* sport like boxing, but Grandad used to take it so seriously.

Sometimes, after the wrestling, Grandma and Grandad would take us for a walk up on the hills where I'd play hide and seek with Ben behind the stone walls. After my adventure in the shop window, though, Grandma never used to let me out of her sight for long and our walks stopped being so much fun.

With us three kids and Dad to look after, being a housewife took up most of Mum's time while we were living in Wales. I don't think she was what you'd call a natural mother. Perhaps because of her own upbringing, she was never one for a lot of cuddling and hugging. But she was a good mother. I don't remember her ever hitting me, not even a slap, and our kitchen was always a lovely place to be in, full of the smell of home-baked bread and cakes. Mum always looked good in those days too, slim and pretty even after having three babies. With Dad's smooth good looks and our mops of blond hair we must have seemed an ideal family to outsiders. They could have used us for advertising shampoo or breakfast cereals.

But the reality was far from ideal. The reason was Dad. The trouble was you never knew where you were with him. One minute he'd be all sweetness and light, the perfect TV father, the next he'd be behaving like Attila the Hun. It only took the slightest thing to switch him from one personality to the other. Mum did her best to cater to his every whim, but it was never enough. Nearly every day Dad managed to find something to criticize and another excuse to explode.

Often it was the state of the house that set him off. He never did any housework himself but he insisted everything was kept spick and span, which wasn't easy with three small kids around. When a goat and an Old English sheepdog were allowed the run of the house as well, it was just about impossible. We got used to seeing Mum run around in circles when Dad was expected home, sweeping the floor, dusting the blinds, and fluffing up the cushions, but she needn't have bothered. He nearly always found something to pick on.

As well as being house-proud, Dad was a great one for routine. He couldn't cope with the slightest hitch or alteration to his daily timetable. Little things, like his supper not being ready when he came in from work, would send him off at the deep end. His temper when he was in his Attila the Hun mode used to absolutely terrify us. He'd yell, throw things, and belt Mum around the head—it didn't matter if we were there or not. Sometimes I really believed he was going to murder her. Once or twice I thought he was going to murder us too.

Shane came closest to being badly hurt. One day, when he was six, Dad caught him making a mess on the carpet with some crayons and he lost his temper and threw him against a window. It broke and Shane went straight through and cut himself quite badly. There was blood everywhere and Mum and Dad had to take him to the hospital to be stitched up. Dad got away with it, though. Shane told us that when the doctor asked how it happened, Dad said he'd fallen onto some glass in the garden.

Another incident I remember was when we were driving back home from Brecon one night and Fiona was carsick. Dad was always obsessive about his cars and kept them immaculate. He was so furious that Fiona threw up that he screeched to a halt and made all of us, Mum included, get out. Then he drove off, tires squealing, and we all had to walk home in the dark.

Mum used to cope with Dad's rages by going very quiet. I never remember her protesting or arguing with him. I suppose she thought it would just fan the flames. In some ways maybe her method *was* the best way to deal with him, because usually after a few minutes his anger would blow itself out and when he couldn't think of any more horrible names to call her he'd sit down and eat his supper. By the time Mum put his cup of tea in front of him he'd often forgotten what had sparked the row off and he'd be all bright and cheerful again so we could relax. Living with Dad was a bit like living on the edge of the volcano.

I must have been nearly six when Dad announced that he'd taken a job with the RSPCA and we moved up north to Alnwick on the Scottish borders. It was nice there, quite like Wales, but we didn't stay long. One day a furniture van turned up outside the house and without warning or explanation we were piled into Dad's new silver Volvo Estate and informed that we were moving to Cockshott Farm, Rothbury.

And it was at Cockshott Farm, six months later, that our lives were turned upside down when, setting off late for a show at the Newcastle Theatre Royal, and driving that same silver Volvo, my father overtook on a blind bend, crashed head-on into a lorry, and put himself and Mum into the intensive care unit of Newcastle General Hospital.

# Chapter 2

In the end, in spite of what the policewoman told our neighbor Mrs. Wilson that night, Mum didn't lose her leg. But it was a near thing. It had been almost severed in the accident and when she reached the hospital it was only hanging on by a tiny flap of skin and flesh. Miraculously the surgeons managed to insert a metal plate and reattach it, but they warned that she might never walk again except on crutches. They also said that she'd definitely never be able to dance or play tennis again, which were her two favorite hobbies. What was more important to Shane, Fiona, and me was the news that Mum wouldn't be well enough to look after us for several months.

Grandma had come up from Brighton straight after the accident and she stayed at the farm until Dad was discharged. The first day she went in to visit them both in hospital she left us at home with Joan, the baby-sitter, again. At teatime, when she came back in through the door, she was carrying Mum's fur coat over her arm and her face was furious. She didn't say anything to us but I remember hearing her stomp upstairs to hang the coat in the wardrobe, and then the sound of the wardrobe door slamming. I also remember feeling frightened. It was the first time I'd ever seen Grandma angry.

The next day Dad was released from hospital and when he arrived home with his head all bandaged up there was a big argument. I hadn't heard Dad shout at Grandma before. It was almost as bad as Mum and Dad's rows, but with a big difference—Grandma was shouting back. It was years later, when I was living in London, that Grandma explained what had made her so angry that day. She said that when she went in to visit her, Mum had recalled everything she could remember about the accident. She'd told Grandma that she'd been thrown out of the car and had been lying on the grass verge bleeding when Dad came over to her. But instead of giving her first aid, the first thing he did was to drag her new fur coat off her because he didn't want blood to get on it. Years later Grandma still got angry remembering it. My gran was funny like that. Some women don't get on with their daughters-in-law, but she and Mum were really good friends and Grandma hardly ever took Dad's side in arguments. Although she was his mother, she saw him for what he was.

I used to enjoy having Grandma around. We all did. We felt safe when she was looking after us, knowing she could stand up to Dad. She didn't smile much, in fact she often looked quite stern, but underneath she was kindhearted and Mum always knew if she called on her in an emergency she'd come up from Brighton to help out. At the time of the accident she must have been almost seventy years old, but she was still bouncing with energy and after dinner she always made time to play Scrabble with us or come out for a walk. I admired her ever so much. She was the sort of woman I wanted to be when I grew up.

Sadly, all too soon, Grandma had to catch the bus back to Brighton where she still had the shop to run and Grandad to look after. He'd retired by now but wasn't in very good health. Not long after she left, Dad announced that we couldn't afford to live at the farm any longer and days later we helped pile our furniture into a hired van and moved house once more. It turned out Dad had found himself a job at a detention center in a Royal Navy school at Seaton Sluice, north of Newcastle. He didn't tell us what the job was and none of us dared ask him about it. We hardly ever did ask him questions. Since as far back as I could remember, when it came to dealings with Dad, Shane, Fiona, and I had followed Mum's example and laid low, not saying anything that might rock the boat. After the accident, if anything, we kept even quieter because the slightest demand was likely to provoke an explosion.

Dad's new job came with built-in accommodation, a small house situated inside the security fence. It wasn't nearly such a nice place to live as Cockshott Farm, but I wasn't old enough to realize that having a rent-free house relieved some of my father's financial worries. All I did understand was that the move meant we had to get rid of Ben. That Dad did try to explain, saying that with his new job he wouldn't have time to look after a dog *and* us. In any case, he told us, pets weren't allowed at the center, so Tigga and the goat would have to go as well. They were passed on to the farm next door while poor Ben was given away to some people in Rothbury. The night he left I sobbed myself to sleep. It was one of the few times I remember crying in the whole time I was growing up.

Even with our pets gone, Dad found that coping with a new job, visiting Mum every day in hospital, and caring for three kids under the age of ten was too much for him to handle. So, a few weeks after we moved to Seaton Sluice, Fiona and I were taken into care. We never found out if it was Dad or Grandma who arranged it but to be honest we weren't that bothered. Being sent away to a children's home sounds traumatic but actually we quite enjoyed it. It was a nice children's home, a little countryside community with ruins nearby where we could play hide and seek. We had regular hot meals to eat too, which was more than we'd had at home since Mum had been in hospital, *and* we got 25p pocket money every Thursday. Best of all it was blissfully quiet in the home so you could sleep all night long and not be wakened by the sound of voices yelling and screaming.

Once a week Dad used to bring Shane, who was still at home, and take us to visit Mum in the hospital. She was slowly getting better but she'd lost a lot of weight and looked so pale and tired I hardly recognized her. The only part of her that hadn't changed was her hands. Even in hospital she still rubbed Nulon into them every day and filed and polished her nails so that when you saw her they were the first thing that struck you, laid on top of the bedsheets like china ornaments.

"At least I don't have washing-up hands anymore," she used to joke.

She wouldn't have to wash dishes for quite a bit. She hadn't even been allowed to walk yet, so it would be months before she'd be able to cope with looking after a home again.

I always felt uncomfortable going to see Mum in hospital. Not because of her leg—I was used to the scars now and I was fascinated by the skin grafts she was being given—but because of the way you were expected to behave. I wasn't used to people showing physical affection and I always squirmed when the bell rang for the end of visiting time and the other people in the ward bent over the beds to kiss their friends and relatives good-bye. Somehow I never seemed able to do that. Nor did Shane or Fiona. We used to mumble, "So long, then," and bolt for it.

One day when we walked into the ward we found Mum looking different. Her cheeks were all rosy and her eyes were red as if she'd been crying. She told us her father had been in to visit her. It was the first time she'd seen him since he'd disowned her when she married Dad. Someone had told him about the accident and he'd turned up with flowers and sweets wanting to bury the hatchet. He'd promised to return the next day when we were there. Shane, Fiona, and I were really excited at the idea of seeing a grandfather we'd never met. But he broke his promise. He never did come back and for the next few weeks when we went in to visit her Mum looked more ill than ever.

Eventually, nearly six months after the accident, the doctors let her come home to the detention center. She was walking on crutches by now, but officially she was still convalescing. However, that didn't last long. Once Fiona and I were sent back from the children's home she had to shop and cook for us again. Dad did nothing to help. To him housework was a woman's job, even if the woman in question was recovering from a traumatic accident.

It took Mum so long to hobble around that she didn't have much time left to spend on herself and the lovely well-groomed woman who used to be my mother was soon no more than a memory. At Cockshott Farm her dressing table had always been crowded with little pots of face cream but now I never saw her use them, and as the days passed she started to look more and more haggard and ungroomed. She hardly ever put on lipstick. The only beauty ritual she kept up was her hand care.

Every now and then, as if suddenly remembering the doctor's orders to let Mum take it easy, Dad would give her a day out in the minibus. This was an ancient vehicle belonging to the naval center and my father used it to take the lads who were on detention out on excursions. If there was room, and we weren't at school, he'd take one of us with him as well as Mum. I didn't enjoy the trips much. The cadets made me nervous—they were big and rowdy and some of them had tattoos—and on top of that Dad used to listen to the cricket on the minibus radio, which bored me to death.

I remember one of those trips in particular. It was raining and we were at the beach waiting for Mum and Dad to get back on the bus. They were taking ages—I think they'd gone to the toilets—and I'd rubbed a hole in the mist on the window to look for Mum. Suddenly I saw her limping on her crutches through the puddles in this blue woolen coat with her hair all wet and her face screwed up against the rain. She looked so ill and sad I hardly recognized her. Then one of the lads saw her.

"Oh, look," he laughed. "Here comes the miserable old bag now."

I was so hurt. I wanted to be brave enough to say, "How dare you talk about my mother like that!" Because she wasn't an old bag. She was beautiful. The only reason she looked the way she did was that she was unhappy. Even at the age of seven I realized that.

I knew why she was unhappy too. Since the accident, perhaps because of his bang on the head, Dad's rages had grown much worse. Often he behaved as if Mum was pretending to be ill just to annoy him. He'd suddenly hit her for no reason and even kick her crutches away. He started checking her housework: rubbing his fingers along the tops of pictures, searching for dust and inspecting the plates when she stacked them on the draining board. If they weren't as clean as he liked he would either hurl them on the floor or break them over her head. It was like living with a madman. Before the accident he'd been a cunning madman—he'd only shown his violent side at home. Now it had started to spill over in the outside world. One day, one of the naval cadets said something to annoy him and

Dad hit him so hard he knocked him out. Not surprisingly that was the end of his job.

We moved to a rented house in Seahouses, a small town on the Northumberland coast. I hated it. The air there always stank of fish and the rented house was a wreck, with no doors in the frames and plaster hanging off the walls. We stayed for two months, and then one day everything was packed up and we moved to Washington, ten miles south of Newcastle.

When you're older and used to traveling around the world, the places in England all seem close together, but when you're young and you drive somewhere for an hour it feels as if you've gone to a foreign country. To Shane, Fiona, and me, after the country villages we'd been living in till now, Washington was a foreign country. Once, years ago, it had been a small mining village. But over the years Washington had grown and all the other little villages around it had grown until they ran into each other. The whole place had become one big sprawling town, although all the areas were still known by their village names. We moved to a council flat in Sulgrave, which was one of these old villages. Our flat was in a low-rise development of dirty yellow bricks built around a central grassed courtyard. I went back there recently and the flats have all been sold off and done up and look quite nice. But then it was run down and vandalized with stairways that smelled of urine and a courtyard covered with piles of dog dirt. At night there were always kids running about and the sound of dogs barking and breaking glass.

Living there didn't help Dad's temper. He was always complaining about the noise and the neighbors and every night the flat echoed with his shouting. Although it was nice having Mum to look after us again, I often wished I was back in the children's home.

One of the things Dad grumbled about most was his food. I thought Mum was a brilliant cook but he'd criticize everything she put in front of him. Usually it was small things that set him off, like mashed potatoes with not enough salt, or a sponge cake that had sunk in the middle—Mum always had trouble getting her cakes to rise—but one unforgettable day she cooked chicken for dinner and when Dad started to carve it, blood ran out onto the plate. He stared at it as if she was trying to poison him. Then he swore and, picking up a chrome-legged kitchen stool, he started hitting her over the head with it. Mum fell on the floor and lay there with her hands over her head and he dropped the stool and started kicking her instead. Shane, Fiona, and I were all screaming by now, which maybe brought him to his senses. When he abandoned his attack Mum pulled herself up, sobbing, picked up her crutches, and hobbled into their bedroom.

There was a change in Mum after that, though it was hard to put a finger on what it was. She still didn't yell back at Dad or defend herself when he was violent, and she never, ever said a bad word about him to us. But her days didn't revolve around him anymore. It was as if that beating made her take a step back from her life and decide to change it. A few months afterward she enrolled at Newcastle University for a degree in psychology. I don't know why she chose psychology—unless it was to understand what made Dad tick—but whatever the reason, from that moment on she seemed to become a different woman. She was no longer the long-suffering doormat, but a more distant person who had less and less to do with us.

Even her appearance changed. She started a beauty routine again and pots of face cream appeared on her dressing table. She even began putting a dab of lipstick on before she left the house in the morning. After she'd been going to the university for a few months she took me with her one Saturday and we had lunch in the refectory. It soon became a regular date for the two of us. At Christmas she took me to a university dance and I talked her into buying me my first pair of high heels in honor of the occasion.

"They'll ruin your feet though," she warned. She was right. I couldn't dance a step in them and by the end of the evening I had blisters and a twisted ankle, but I was so happy. In high heels I felt grown up and I wanted to be grown up more than anything.

Mum's leg still hadn't healed completely but she was managing to walk without crutches now and that night she even tried dancing. Looking at her in her pretty black dress I saw her through fresh eyes. At home she still looked sad and tired but here among the other students, clapping her hands to the theme tune from *Zorba the Greek,* she looked like a young girl.

Dad wasn't happy about Mum going back to college and was jealous of the attention she gave her studies. He insisted she had to be home in time to make his dinner, so most evenings she would bring her psychology textbooks home with her to read after he'd gone to bed. Sometimes I used to flip through them, trying to make sense of the long words, and I noticed that inside all the covers she had written in her neat sloping handwriting *Beatrice Finlay-Mills,* which puzzled me. Mum had always written her name as plain *Beatrice Mills* before. But even when she explained that Finlay had been her maiden name I didn't realize the significance. I would have had to be a few years older to recognize that the name change was a warning of things to come.

# Chapter 3

With all the house moving of the past three years, my own education, as well as Shane and Fiona's, had been always stopping and starting and I'd never been a star pupil at school. But our stay at Usworth Grange Primary School in Sulgrave lasted longer, and after a few months I'd settled in and begun to enjoy my lessons and get good reports. Some of the teachers asked me what I wanted to be when I grew up. It was something that hadn't crossed my mind until then, but I started to give it a lot of thought. By the end of my first year my mind was made up. I was going to take lots of exams, go to university like Mum, and become a doctor. But not any old doctor. I didn't want to spend my time treating crying babies and spotty kids like Dr. Philips did at our local surgery. I had grander ambitions. *I* wanted to be a plastic surgeon.

It was Mum's leg that had given me the idea. Since she'd been discharged she'd been going back to Newcastle General Hospital every few months for skin grafts. Sometimes she'd take me with her and I used to talk to the plastic surgeon who was treating her. He was a nice man who answered all my questions patiently and I was fascinated by his tales of how he could change people's bodies—making scars like Mum's disappear and rebuilding chins and noses. I thought to have that power to alter someone's appearance must be wonderful.

But the odds were stacked against me. Waterloo Court, Sulgrave, was an ideal training ground for the professional classes. And I was a perfect candidate for being led astray. I was no longer at the center of Mum's life, and I never had been at the center of Dad's, so I had little supervision at home. Consequently, it didn't take me long to get in with the gangs of kids running around our courtyard and to start running wild. After school we'd get up to all sorts of mischief. One of our favorite pastimes was breaking down the door into the drainage system that ran under the flats and going "sewer trudging" in our wellies, screaming when rats ran across our feet. Afterwards we'd climb up the fire escape stairs and go running all over the flat roof of the courts. Then, when we got tired of that, we'd play "Knockie nine doors"—hammering on people's front doors one after the other and shouting rude things, then running away. One of our neighbors across the court was an old man called Stan who was totally bald and horrid looking and we'd knock on his door and yell, "Stan, Stan, dirty old man. Washes his willy in the frying pan," then run like mad. We were so cruel . . .

When we moved to Sulgrave, money was tight and for Christmas and birthdays that first year we got clothes as presents instead of toys. I wasn't happy about that and I started to look around for ways to make pocket money. I thought first of doing odd jobs but there wasn't a great demand for window cleaning or car washing in Waterloo Court. Then one day the answer came to me. At school in needlework class I'd made loads of little tapestry pictures from wool and cardboard. Why didn't I sell some of these masterpieces to our neighbors?

Waterloo Court was one of ten neighboring blocks of council flats, each built in the same courtyard design. That weekend I trudged around all ten blocks, knocking on doors and asking whoever answered if they wanted to buy one of my pictures. There weren't many takers; in fact most people didn't even answer the door. I'd reached Wellington Court and, after going all along the first landing without success, was just about to move up to the next one when one of the doors opened and a tiny Yorkshire terrier ran out yapping. A middle-aged man with graying hair peered around the door.

"Yes? Can I help you?"

I recited my set piece. "Would-you-like-to-buy-a-tapestry-for-10p?"

"Why don't you come in and show them to me, my dear?" he invited. Forgetting all my mother's warnings about wicked strangers I followed him in and sat on his settee next to the Yorkshire terrier and showed him my samplers. He told me I was very clever, and to my delight said he'd buy them all. As he counted the money out of a purse, I saw he had a finger missing on his right hand. I couldn't help staring at it—not in horror as most kids might have done—but wondering if a plastic surgeon could fix it . . .

As he handed me the money I saw from his face he'd noticed my interest in his finger stump and I felt myself blushing. He smiled and sat down next to me, putting his chin on his damaged hand so I got another good look at it.

"What's your name then?"

I told him.

"What a pretty name. Tell me, Heather, do you like sport?"

I nodded, still feeling embarrassed for staring. "Oh, yes, I love swimming."

"Really?" He smiled. "That's quite a coincidence. I'm a swimming instructor. Would you like me to teach you?"

Rather late in the day, I remembered Mum's lectures and repeated what I knew she'd expect me to say.

"I'll have to ask my mum and dad first."

"Better still, why don't *I* ask them?" he suggested.

Mr. Morris came around that night. Dad was out but Mum invited him in and made him a cup of coffee while he told her how he could improve my swimming. He was charming and funny and I could tell she liked him.

"Heather's got just the right build for swimming," he said. "In a few months she could be entering competitions." I could see Mum's eyes light up. She'd been into sports herself before her accident and was always telling Shane, Fiona, and me to take more interest in games at school.

When Mr. Morris told her he was the manager of the local swimming pool she agreed he could give me lessons. "Maybe it'll keep her out of mischief," she said, giving me a look that said she knew more than I thought about what I got up to around the Court.

After that, I went for swimming coaching once a week. Not only was Mr. Morris the local pool manager but he was a very good swimming instructor. Up till then I'd just been able to swim breaststroke but he taught me to do crawl and backstroke as well as how to dive. I didn't much like it when he used to get into the pool and put his arms around me, but I didn't think twice about it. After all, what other way was there to make sure I did my strokes properly? Margaret, the girl who lived in the next-door flat, started coming with me for lessons and, before long, our times were good enough for us to enter competitions. We both did well in local swimming galas. Being a couple of years older than me, Margaret was a slightly stronger swimmer, and I noticed that it was Margaret and not me who used to keep getting called into the manager's office. I didn't think much of it at the time. I thought it was to do with the swimming medals she'd won.

Then one day in the summer holidays Mr. Morris told us there was a competition coming up at Darlington. He said that as it was a three-day gala we would have to travel there the day before and stay for three nights. I was thrilled, and couldn't understand why Margaret didn't seem keen on the idea. We got permission from our parents and Mum found me a little suitcase and bought me a new sponge bag for the trip. On the Thursday morning Margaret's mum took us to the baths to meet Mr. Morris and waved us off in his car.

Mr. Morris had told us the journey to Darlington would take an hour, but no sooner had we set off than he braked suddenly and tapped his head with his funny finger stump.

"I'm sorry, girls, but I've forgotten a document. I'll just have to drive around by my flat to get it." He pulled up outside Wellington Court and got out of the car, then put his head back inside.

"Look, it's going to take me a few minutes to find what I'm looking for. Why don't you come and wait inside?"

We followed him up the stairs and into his flat like lambs to the slaughter and he shut the door behind us.

He kept us imprisoned there for three days and nights. I never found out what he did to Margaret during that time—afterward she wouldn't talk about it—but fortunately all he did to me was fondle me. I didn't like it, but it didn't make me cry the way Margaret used to cry every night after he'd taken her into his bedroom. The way he treated us was bizarre. One minute he'd be sitting next to us on the settee, touching himself, and grunting and groaning, the next he'd be lecturing us on how short life was and how we should make the most of it. Then every so often he started trying to entertain us as if he'd just remembered how old we were. Each afternoon he got Yorkie, his Yorkshire terrier, to do tricks for us. He'd put down ten different-colored scarves and say "Fetch the red one," and the little dog would run over and pick up the red one. "Now fetch the green one," he'd say and the dog would pick up the green . . . In spite of our situation I was fascinated. I thought it was really clever, but Margaret wasn't interested. She wouldn't even watch.

On Friday there was no food left in the flat and Mr. Morris gave Margaret some money and sent her out for fish-and-chips.

"But don't go getting any stupid ideas. If you don't come back I'll kill her." He nodded toward me. That was when I realized this wasn't just some weird adventure and became really frightened. Luckily for me Margaret was too scared to call his bluff but she still seemed to take forever to fetch the fish-and-chips. When she finally arrived back at the flat, out of breath from running, I was never so glad to see anyone in my life.

On Saturday Mr. Morris locked both of us in and went out by himself to get some bread and milk from the shops. As soon as the door shut behind him Margaret made for the window.

"I've had enough of this. I'm going to climb out and get help," she said.

But there was a twenty-foot drop from the window of Mr. Morris's flat. Although Margaret got herself half out and sat on the sill, she couldn't pluck up the nerve to jump. While she was sitting there, dithering, Mr. Morris came back in. Seeing her he dropped his shopping, launched himself across the room, and grabbed hold of her. As he dragged her back inside, she scraped her stomach on the window catch and fell onto the carpet crying. "Shut up or I'll give you something to really cry about," he growled.

Early on Sunday evening Mr. Morris sent Margaret out to the fish-and-chip shop again with the same warning about killing me if she tried any "funny stuff." But this time his blackmail didn't work. Half an hour later she still hadn't returned and, with a face like thunder, he locked me in and set out to look for her. I waited for ages, certain that when he came back he was going to murder me. Then suddenly there was a loud knocking on the door and Yorkie started yapping like mad. Frozen with fright I sat in the corner of the room as the knocking turned into a different noise. Now it sounded as if someone was hitting the door with a big hammer. Then, all at once, the door crashed open and six or seven policemen burst into the room. It was the most welcome sight I had ever seen in my life. I burst into tears. I was still crying five minutes later when they opened the door of the police car and led me back to Waterloo Court.

I was desperate to see Mum—for the last few hours I'd thought I'd never see her again in my life—but it was Dad who opened the door, wearing his favorite orange dressing gown that he liked to think was artistic. Even through my tears, I felt really embarrassed that the police should see him in that stupid dressing gown. I rushed past him and flung myself at Mum who was standing behind him looking pale and anxious.

"Oh, thank God, Heather," she said. "Are you all right?"

I started to explain where I'd been but someone had already told her.

"Hush, I know, I know," she said.

Shane and Fiona were sent upstairs out of the way while the police talked to Mum and Dad. Dad didn't say anything and it was left to Mum to explain to the police why they hadn't been worried about me even after three days.

"We thought she was still at the swimming gala," she kept saying. "We had no idea." One of the policemen made notes, then said to

Mum that they wanted to take me to Sunderland police station so I could be examined by a police doctor. Mum came with me in the back of a cold, blue police van. Margaret and her mother were already there. After more questions a lady police doctor took first Margaret, then me, into a side room and gave us internal examinations. For me at least that was a worse experience than what Mr. Morris had done to me. Afterward a policewoman gave us each a jelly baby.

For the next week a policeman and woman came to the flats every day interviewing both Margaret and me, asking exactly what had happened. One day, after the police had gone, Margaret and her mother came around for a cup of tea and Margaret suddenly announced that Mr. Morris had started to molest her in the manager's office at the baths. Mum was horrified.

"But why didn't you tell us about it, Margaret?" she asked. "None of this need have happened if you'd only told us then."

Margaret sat hunched up in her chair, tears running down her cheeks.

"I was too scared," she whispered.

Dad hid his head in the sand over the whole business, never mentioning it again. But it really shook Mum: For weeks afterward she hovered over me and kept asking me if I was all right, until it began to get on my nerves. I think maybe she felt guilty—after all she was a psychology student and she hadn't recognized a pervert when it mattered.

For several weeks she wouldn't let me play out on my own. Not that I wanted to go roaming. The police said Mr. Morris had never gone back to his flat and they still didn't know where he was, so I wasn't anxious to bump into him. Margaret and I had been warned by the police that when they did find him and arrest him we would have to appear in court to tell the judge what he'd done to us. I wasn't looking forward to that at all, but we were never called to appear and we didn't see or speak to our swimming instructor again. It was only years later that Mum told me that after we escaped Mr. Morris had driven to the coast and jumped off a cliff and killed himself.

I wish she'd told me then. It would have set my mind at rest. As it was, for years afterward, if ever I was walking down the street and passed a middle-aged man with a Yorkshire terrier on a lead, my heart would speed up and I'd find myself looking to check if he had a finger missing.

When we'd been living in Sulgrave for about a year our finances improved. New furniture appeared and one day Dad carried a new TV and record player in from the back of the car. He took up photography again and bought a brand-new Hasselblad camera. He never told us what he was doing to earn this money, but Mum said something about a new business venture. Then one evening he walked through the door in a really good mood, smoking a big cigar, and announced that he'd been made chairman of the Newcastle Theatre Royal.

Since we'd moved from Cockshott Farm, Dad had kept up his contact with the Newcastle Theatre and even when money was really short he'd still go and see new productions there, especially the operas, though he didn't often take Mum with him anymore. On opera evenings he'd dress up in a purple velvet jacket with a black bow tie, white dress shirt, and black trousers with a satin stripe down the side. Then he'd stride out in his shiny patent leather shoes through all the dog dirt and broken bottles of Waterloo Court. God knows what the neighbors made of him, but he'd obviously impressed the people who counted. I had no idea what being chairman meant, but I supposed he got paid for it because not long after his appointment we moved out of our run-down flat into a much more upmarket house, a lovely detached bungalow a mile or so away in Donwell, another satellite village of Washington.

Our new bungalow lay at the end of a cul-de-sac among landscaped slopes with trees and neatly mown grass. It was a real contrast to the shoddy council estate we'd come from. But I doubt whether anyone in Farm Close guessed our humble origins. Dad had always made a point of keeping up appearances, dressing smartly to go to work, as well as to the theater, and he made sure we fit the middle-class image too. Within weeks of moving to Donwell we all had new school uniforms, and Mum had several smart new outfits. That was one thing I have to admit: When Dad felt flush, he was generous.

He didn't leave himself off the gift list. An expensive quadraphonic stereo system was soon installed in the lounge at Number Twelve. Dad had always loved music and we'd grown up accustomed to the sound of opera, but at Farm Close speakers blasted out in every room. Wagner was his favorite. I used to quite like it myself, played on his old record player, but it was a different matter having to listen to *Die Walküre* or *Lohengrin* playing at top volume in every room in the house. Even the neighbors started to complain.

Dad had always been keen on mountain climbing but he'd hardly done any since we left Alnwick. Now he bought new tents and sleeping bags for all of us and started taking us with him on camping trips to the Lake District where he'd disappear up rock faces while we strolled around Windermere or Ullswater looking at the shops. I enjoyed those trips, but they were nightmare weekends for Mum, who was never much good with camping stoves and was always getting into trouble with Dad for some cooking disaster or other. The worst time was when the gas went out without her knowing it and she served us up some baked beans that had been "warming" for ten minutes over an unlit jet. Dad took one mouthful and threw the whole panful at her. It hit her in the face, and she stared at him with beans dripping everywhere, then she just got up and walked into the tent to clean herself up. I remember thinking, *Why doesn't she say something? Why doesn't she shout at him and tell him what a pig he is?* But I knew why. She was too frightened. I understood that because I was frightened too. Even though I sometimes stood up to him, as soon as he started to get angry I always toed the line just like Mum.

A good example was when he replaced the battered old Capri he'd bought when we were in Sulgrave with a brand-new Volvo. It must have been the most expensive car in Washington at that time, but I didn't appreciate it. I was really upset when Dad drove it up the drive because he hadn't told us what he was doing but had simply taken the Capri in that morning and part-exchanged it. I'd loved the Capri, which was young and sporty and fast. The Volvo didn't have the same image at all. As far as I was concerned it was a car for old bods with flat caps; I felt almost as upset as when he'd got rid of Ben. When Dad wanted to take us all out for a drive in his new toy I dug my toes in.

"I don't *want* to get in," I sulked.

Dad's nostrils flared. "You'll do as I say, Heather, or take the consequences," he said quietly.

Mum took my arm. "Just get in, Heather," she murmured. "Don't cause any trouble." Afraid, like her, of stepping over the line, I climbed in and allowed myself to be driven around the village.

The Volvo had only just been run in when it had to make the long journey down to Brighton. Grandad had suffered a stroke that year, and in the autumn he died quietly in his sleep. We all traveled down for the funeral. Over the years we'd been to Brighton a few times, though usually we'd gone by bus. The other times had been happy occasions when we'd played the slot machines with Grandad on the pier. This was different. I'd never been to a funeral before; although Mum went to the Anglican church in Sulgrave most Sunday evenings, Fiona, Shane, and I had hardly ever been inside a church. It was a Catholic service and the smell of incense made me feel sick. The priest said lots of nice things about Grandad and then we had to stand up and sing "All Things Bright and Beautiful," which proved to be our undoing. Grandma's best friend, Aunty Wynn, a large lady who never stopped talking, was standing behind us and sang so loudly and out of tune that it was the final straw. Everything was so bizarre: There was Grandad lying in his coffin at the front of the church; the priest swinging the incense as though he was getting ready to throw a lasso; Aunty Wynn warbling away. It was all too much and we three kids collapsed giggling under the pew.

"Stop it," Mum hissed, but we couldn't. The more Aunty Wynn trilled the more we gasped for breath, and tears rolled down our cheeks.

After we'd sobered up, we went around to Grandma's flat for food and drinks. There I didn't feel like giggling anymore, but strangely enough everyone else cheered up. I sat in Grandad's favorite armchair thinking, *Why are all these people still smiling when he's dead? Why are they looking so happy?* I didn't understand. All I understood was that I was going to miss him. It was hard to accept that I wouldn't watch any more wrestling with him, that he wouldn't ever again bounce me on his knee and serenade me with "Truly Scrumptious." It was my first contact with death.

Since he'd been made chairman of Newcastle Theatre Royal, Dad was hardly ever at home. Most evenings he'd be out until way past eleven. Usually, he'd go out on his own, but when visiting performers came to the theater he'd make Mum go down and help him entertain them. I don't think she enjoyed playing the role of chairman's wife—she'd always been quite shy. Anyway, socializing interfered with her university studies. But, as usual, when Dad said jump she jumped, even if it did mean staying up till past midnight to write her essays.

One evening, though, when they were supposed to be going to the theater, Mum didn't come home from the university. I was nine years old. For the first time I can remember, there was no tea waiting for us when we got back from school, and no message either. It was strange—Mum usually left a note if she was going to be late—but we weren't really worried. Fiona and I were always ravenous when we came in from school and we were more concerned about our stomachs than anything else. Shane had homework to do, and went up to his bedroom while we two stayed in the kitchen, making big doorstep "stottie" sandwiches.

Suddenly we heard the front door open and Dad's voice bellowed, "Shane! Fiona! Heather! Come in here! I've got something to tell you." Obediently we trotted into the lounge. Dad was standing in front of the telly looking very cross. I racked my brains to think what we might have done to annoy him. Had he somehow found out about Fiona and me setting fire to the waste bin when we tried to smoke one of his cigars?

"I want you all to sit down and listen to what I've got to say." Dad sounded husky, as if he had a sore throat.

We sat in a silent row on the settee and he settled in the chair facing us and looked from one to the other with a strange expression on his face.

"Your mother's left us," he said quietly. "She's gone off with a gambling man and she won't be coming back."

If he'd told us our mother had been run over by a bus his words couldn't have had a more devastating effect. Fiona burst out crying. Automatically I put my arm around her while I gazed at Dad in horror. Shane's eyes too were big and round. But through the shock and the hurt, I also remember feeling something else: relief. Relief that at last Mum had escaped from all the violence and shouting, that we wouldn't ever have to watch Dad break dishes over her head again or see her with that unhappy look in her eyes whenever she thought we weren't watching.

I had no idea who this man was that Mum had run off with. He might be a gambling man. He might even be a drunkard. But whatever he was, I knew he couldn't be any worse than Dad, not in a million years.

# Chapter 4

Over the next few weeks, by eavesdropping on Dad's phone calls to Grandma and on our neighbors' gossip, we pieced together the explanation for our mother's sudden disappearance. It seemed that the person our father called "the gambling man," who had lured Mum away, was in fact an actor called Charles Stapley, a star in the TV soap opera *Crossroads,* who'd been appearing in a play at the Newcastle Theatre Royal. Mum had met him at one of those theater social evenings when Dad had ordered her down to "entertain" the actors and she'd apparently fallen head over heels in love with him. She'd been quite discreet about the affair, but Shane was sure that we three kids had actually met him. "Do you remember that man Mum brought back to the house when Dad was away? The one she said was a lecturer at the university?" he asked.

I did remember. He'd been a tall man, with distinguished-looking gray hair. Mum had introduced him to us as Dr. Stapley.

"I bet that was him," said Shane.

If it was, even at the age of nine I could understand why my mother had fallen for him. I'd thought the day we met him how handsome he was and what a lovely posh voice he had. I didn't blame her for running off with him. I didn't even question why she didn't take us with her. I was sure she would explain everything when she wrote to let us know how she was getting on. But I was to be disappointed. Day followed day and no letter came.

In the months after Mum left, our lives changed dramatically. Dad had an old-fashioned attitude to domestic life and as he saw it, running a house was not a man's job. Since I was now the oldest woman in the house, most of the housekeeping became my responsibility. Overnight, I was expected to cook, do the shopping, and wash and iron my father's shirts. Shane and Fiona were roped in to do the hoovering, dust the venetian blinds, and clean the bathrooms. After school each day they also had to wash and polish the Volvo. Dad pinned a rota on the wall listing whose turn it was to do which job on a particular day. He soon had us so regimented he hardly had to lift a finger, and after dinner while we cleared the table and washed the dishes he would go into the lounge and listen to opera on the stereo or watch TV. Once he'd got over the first shock, Mum's leaving didn't particularly depress him; in fact if anything he seemed happier—often as we worked in the kitchen we'd hear him laughing out loud at the antics of The Two Ronnies or Russ Abbot. I suppose it wasn't surprising if he was happier since for years nearly everything Mum had done had aggravated him.

But we weren't happier. Shane didn't talk about his feelings but became very quiet and threw himself into his schoolwork, spending his evenings in his bedroom rather than stay in the same room as Dad. Fiona, who was only seven, missed Mum terribly. What made matters worse was that she wasn't too good at housework so Dad was always criticizing her. Every evening he'd inspect the venetian blinds and if he found a speck of dust he'd go crazy and make her do them all over again. She was terrified of him and I used to hear her crying into her pillow every night and I often climbed into her bed to comfort her.

My reaction was more like Shane's. I withdrew into my shell and refused to talk about how I felt. It was the way Mum had coped when things went wrong and it worked for me too, at least on the surface. But though I didn't show it the way Fiona did, I missed Mum too.

I hated all the housework we now had to do, but I especially detested ironing. It took forever because Dad wore two shirts a day and they had to be just *perfect.* But my new responsibilities did teach me one lesson that proved useful to me later on: how to organize my time.

Every morning I used to get up at seven, wake Shane to do his paper round, get washed and dressed, lay the table for breakfast, put the kettle on to boil, and then get out the ironing board so that by the time Dad came downstairs at eight his shirts would be airing on coat hangers and his favorite Earl Grey tea would be brewing in the brown teapot next to the stove. Then, while he was eating scrambled eggs and toast, I'd make three packed lunches for us to take to school and finally clear up the kitchen. In the beginning every morning was a mad panic, but after six months' practice my routine was running like clockwork.

A few months after Mum left, Dad's income took a sudden dive. The first clue came when we asked him for pocket money and he was always "a bit short of change." Then, one by one, the smart new pieces of furniture and our new Raleigh bikes disappeared as they were claimed back by credit companies. Soon afterward we moved from our beautiful big bungalow in Donwell to a much smaller rented house on a Barratt estate in Biddick, a mile or so away. But however hard up he was Dad always kept up the payments on two things, his Volvo and his music system. He needed his car for work but his music system was, quite simply, sacred. Since he'd bought his first stereo Dad had kept up with all the new developments in technology and every time a new sound system or model came on the market he'd be first in the queue to get it. I think he'd have starved before he gave up listening to quadraphonic sound.

We never actually did go without food but at times we came pretty close. Buying the groceries was my job now and Dad would hand me a pound note as he left the house in the morning saying, "Get something for tonight, Heather." It was quite a challenge—even in the late 1970s a pound didn't buy you much in the way of dinner for four—so shopping became an initiative test. My great invention was bean pie, which I made by tipping two tins of baked beans into a casserole dish and spreading mashed potato on top. Egg and chips was another standby. But my big breakthrough came when I discovered that Dewhurst, the butchers in the Washington Galleries shopping center, not only sold the cheapest pork sausages around but also stocked rabbit that was dirt cheap and, with a white sauce to disguise it, could easily be passed off as chicken.

If it had only been dinner I could have just about managed the budget but somehow, out of Dad's measly pound note I was also supposed to buy food to make packed lunches for Shane, Fiona, and me. It meant that day after day our pack-ups consisted of jam sandwiches. I don't know how Shane explained it to the other kids at his school—he'd started at the comprehensive now—but Fiona and I were so ashamed that we used to hide in a corner of the PE changing rooms to eat our sandwiches instead of going to the dining room like we were supposed to. If other children wandered in I'd squash my sandwich up in my hand and suck on it like an ice lolly so they couldn't see. "Oh, I've got turkey and lettuce and mayonnaise," I'd brag if anyone asked.

The stupid thing was that while we were living from hand to mouth during the week, often on Sunday Dad would take us out for lunch at the George Washington Hotel, which was *the* place to be seen in Washington. We'd have to get dressed up in our best clothes, sit in the restaurant smiling and saying hello to all the people he knew, acting like the perfect happy family. No one seeing us on Sundays stuffing ourselves with roast beef and Yorkshire pudding would have guessed that at home we were living on jam sandwiches and bean pie.

I suppose it was predictable that we'd end up shoplifting. By the time I was ten I was an old hand. Pinching food was really quite easy, I discovered. All you did was walk around Sainsbury's with a Woolco shopping bag in your trolley putting a few things in the trolley and then something in the Woolco carrier bag. When you got to the checkout you left the Woolco bag in the trolley while you unloaded it, then pushed it around to the other end of the checkout. The trick was not to be too greedy, and just to put two or three things in the bag so it wasn't too obvious. I only got caught twice. The first time I got away with just a warning, but the second time it was put on record. It didn't stop me. I knew there was nothing the police could do to me at my age except put me into care and that didn't frighten me at all.

Fiona started to shoplift too, but her target was clothes. We were both growing fast but if Dad couldn't spare money for food he certainly wasn't going to cough up for things like new dresses or trainers. When we followed Shane to Usworth Comprehensive we needed new school uniforms and Dad bought us just one school shirt and skirt each, which I used to wash and hang up to dry every night and iron the next morning. I wasn't too bothered about fashion and clothes at that time, but Fiona had always been very conscious of her appearance. She got sick of always looking like the poor relation and being teased when she played with her friends. She hated wearing skirts because her legs were really thin and bony. But jeans cost a lot of money, especially the sort of jeans Fiona's friends wore. She got in league with another girl and between them they stole hundreds of pounds' worth of clothes from the Savacentre in the Washington Galleries. Unluckily for Fiona her friend didn't have the sense to hide her haul: When her mother found this pile of brand-new clothes she rang the police and shopped her. She also shopped Fiona "for leading my daughter astray." However, because of her age Fiona got away with just a warning, though she had to return all the clothes.

Dad, who reacted to dust on a venetian blind as if it was a crime against humanity, treated our shoplifting as a bit of a joke. "Why didn't you get some trousers for me while you were at it?" he asked Fiona. As long as he saw benefit in it for him, he turned a blind eye to our thieving. Later, when Fiona had a friend whose parents owned a pub, Dad used to excuse her from his strict bedtime rules and let her stay out playing until closing time because this friend always used to pinch a packet of cigars for Fiona to bring home for him.

Up until the time Mum left, Dad hadn't hit us too often because most of the time when he lost his temper he'd taken it out on her. But now we found ourselves in the firing line. Shane came off worst, usually for the same "sins" that Mum had been punished for, like not washing the dishes properly. Now it was Shane who had crockery broken over his head. Shane's worst mistake happened one Bonfire night, before our money started getting tight. Dad had bought a brand-new washing machine from Rumbelows and Shane decided to try it out by putting all his dirty clothes in. Unfortunately, he hadn't a clue how to use it and he put nearly the whole box of soap powder in, so after half an hour the kitchen was full of bubbles. The next thing we knew the machine just gurgled and died and nothing we could do would make it work again. Dad went absolutely nuts and belted all three of us that time, grabbing us by the hair and punching us in the chest until we begged for mercy.

Although she was the youngest, Fiona didn't escape the violence. With Dad, the weaker you were the more he bullied you. The worst incident happened one Saturday soon after we'd moved to Biddick. I wasn't there at the time because I'd gone off early to Gateshead Baths where I was doing a sponsored swim for the Girl Guides. Dad had made me join the Girl Guides. He'd started giving lectures on climbing and camping to the Biddick Guides and he'd decided it was "character forming." I hated it, but obediently once a week I used to trudge along to take badges in things like lighting campfires and bird-watching.

On this particular day Dad had gone out for his daily jog and when he came in he asked Fiona what time I was doing my sponsored swim. He specially wanted to come and watch me as David Wilkie was making a guest appearance. Unhappily for Fiona, she couldn't remember what time I'd told her. At the thought of missing seeing one of his sporting heroes Dad had flown off the handle and chucked her against the glass panel of our front door.

It was Shane's "accident" in Wales all over again. All the glass broke and Fiona fell through it and landed in a heap on the pavement outside. By some miracle she escaped without a scratch and when he saw she was all right Dad had stormed off.

He arrived at the gala all smiles, too late to see me do my swim, but in time to shake hands with David Wilkie.

"Oh, well done, darling," he said to me, as if nothing was wrong. The first I knew about it was when I got home and found the front door with a great hole in it and Fiona lying in a bed upstairs staring at the ceiling with tears running down her cheeks. I couldn't get a word out of her so it was Shane who had to tell me what had happened.

Fiona still used to cry herself to sleep most nights, and she was always asking me when Mum was going to come back and see us. I used to comfort her by saying that one day, when Mum and Charles had bought a house together, they would come and fetch us to live with them, but I didn't really believe it. As time went by and there was still no letter or phone call I resigned myself to the fact that Mum had forgotten all about us.

Then, one Easter, a year and a half after my mother left home, I went on a school trip to Wales. Somehow Dad had managed to get hold of some money and he'd bought me some nice new clothes for the holiday—a khaki shirt and trousers and some of the new black shiny satin hot pants. I was over the moon because I was the first girl in the school to get a pair. We stayed in Llandrindod Wells, at a children's activity center where we slept in bunks, and spent the days walking and climbing and pony trekking and having swimming races in the center's pool. I really enjoyed sport so I loved every minute of it.

Behind the center there was a garden where someone had tethered a pet goat. It reminded me of the white nanny goat we used to have when we were small, and I used to save it bread from breakfast. One morning I was standing by the fence feeding this goat a roll and feeling a bit sad because it made me remember our life in Brecon when I heard a crunch of feet on the gravel and I turned to see my mother walking up the drive toward me.

My feet were rooted to the spot. It was like seeing a vision. It couldn't be Mum, I thought. Her hair was shining in the sun and she looked happier and younger than I ever remembered. My paralysis disappeared and I charged toward her and grabbed her around the waist. As I hugged her the armor I'd spent months building up fell away, and tears streamed down my cheeks and soaked into her shirt. When I looked up Mum's chin was trembling.

"Oh, Heather," she said. As she unwrapped me from around her waist I noticed behind her the tall handsome man who had once been introduced to us as "Dr. Stapley."

"This is Charles." Mum smiled. He held out his hand to me and I shook it shyly. He reminded me of Rex Harrison whom I'd just seen in *My Fair Lady.* I felt terribly in awe of him.

"Come on, Heather"—even his voice sounded like Rex Harrison's—"we're taking you out for the day. Our car's up the road."

I panicked. "I can't. I'm supposed to be going out for a picnic."

Mum shook her head. "Don't worry about it. We've asked your teacher. She said it'll be all right."

I don't remember where we went on our drive. I just remember sitting in the back of the hired car, leaning forward between the seats to be closer to Mum, feeling happier than I'd ever felt in my life. We stopped for lunch at a little pub and sat outside in the sun while I bombarded Mum with questions.

"Why didn't you write to us?" I asked. "We didn't know where you'd gone."

Mum frowned. "But I did write. I sent you lots of letters."

"We didn't get them."

She sighed. "All I can think is that your father didn't want you to see them."

So that was it. Dad had destroyed them. I vowed never to forgive him.

"Where are you living?"

"In London. We have a bedsit in Clapham."

"Did you finish your degree?"

She nodded. "And I have a job now too."

"What sort of job?"

She smiled. "It's called counseling. I work in a hospice, talking to people who are very ill, or dying, and trying to help them with their problems."

It wasn't what I'd imagined psychologists doing. I thought they worked with mad people. But it sounded like a worthwhile job and I felt a glow of pride.

Too soon, our lunch was over and Charles looked at his watch.

"We promised Heather's teacher we'd get her back by four," he reminded Mum.

Back at the center I clung to her, soaking her blouse a second time.

"Never mind," she consoled me. "Now we're back in touch, we'll stay in touch. You can all come and visit me in London. I'll take you into the hospice with me and show you where I work."

"Promise?" I sniffed.

"I promise." She pecked me on the cheek and gave me a sad little smile. "I'm very sorry I had to leave, Heather," she said. Then she turned quickly away and got back into the car with Charles.

For the rest of the week I was walking on air. I couldn't wait for the holiday in Wales to end so I could share the news with Shane and Fiona. When I finally arrived home and told them about my visitors, they were so excited that I plucked up the nerve to confront Dad.

"I think you should let us go and visit our mum," I announced, as Shane and Fiona held their breath. I was surprised by my own bravery. I was even more surprised when he said yes.

Two months later, during the school summer holidays, I caught the National Express coach down to London. I went on my own that first time because Mum said their flat was too small for us to all go at once—Shane and Fiona were to have their turn later in the holidays. It took the coach seven hours to reach London and it seemed to stop in every town on the way. I couldn't even buy a sandwich to keep me going because Dad hadn't given me any pocket money, so by the time I finally arrived at Victoria Coach Station I was ravenous. Mum was waiting for me and bought me a hamburger before taking me on the tube to Clapham South. From there we walked the last half a mile to her flat.

Up till that moment it had all been an adventure. Even the endless coach journey had been made bearable by anticipation. But the moment we turned off Abbeville Road and Mum pointed to a drab Victorian house on the other side of the street, I felt a stab of disappointment. When she put her key into the door and let me inside the flat, all my enthusiasm melted away. Mum lived in a dark and poky one-room bedsit with a double bed covered by a dowdy burgundy bedcover in one corner and a stainless-steel sink and ancient cooking hob in another. Apart from the bed the only seating was a sagging couch with a faded flowery cover. It was so *small.* There was hardly room to turn around. It wasn't at all what I'd imagined when I'd thought about Mum's new life in London.

Mum must have seen the disappointment on my face because she started to explain that she and Charles were quite hard up. Charles had finished acting in *Crossroads* and was appearing in *The Mousetrap* in the West End. It wasn't as well paid as television work Mum said, and her job at the hospice was only voluntary, so for the moment they couldn't afford a better flat. Actually, I didn't mind that Charles was working at the theater because it meant I had Mum to myself for the first night.

She seemed really happy that I was there, as if looking after me was an adventure.

"What would you like to eat tonight?" she asked. Before I could answer she said, "I tell you what. We'll go to Sainsbury's and you can choose whatever you want. All right?"

For me, after months of shopping for baked beans and potatoes it was better than giving me the keys to a sweetshop. When we came home an hour later the plastic shopping bags were cutting into our wrists they were so heavy. We had a feast that night. It was like a giant birthday party. I'd forgotten what it was like to eat such wonderful food. There were salads, flans, a fresh warm loaf of bread, strawberries and cream, a plateful of my favorite Mr Kipling Apple Pies, and to crown it all a wonderful cream-filled sponge that had sunk in the middle like a cushion someone had sat on. I hadn't seen a cake like that for nearly two years and it tasted just as good as I remembered.

When I couldn't eat any more, Mum said she'd take me to the room next door where she'd arranged for me to sleep. She said her landlord had agreed I could use the room because he didn't have a tenant for it at the moment. It wasn't hard to see why. It was a cold damp cupboard, with paper peeling off the walls and a horrid musty smell. When I saw it all my new happiness shriveled up. After being away from Mum for so long I wanted to stay as close as possible to her. I hadn't imagined I'd be farmed out like this.

Next morning I was out of bed and back next door at the crack of dawn. Mum was already up and preparing something near the sink and she put her finger to her lips as I opened the door. The room was in darkness apart from a table lamp on the work surface next to the cooker. I could just make out a big hump under the counterpane, which I guessed was Charles. Mum had warned me that because Charles worked late at the theater he slept during the morning. It meant we had to talk in whispers but I had some compensation for my awful night because Mum and I were able to enjoy breakfast on our own—more wholemeal bread (toasted this time), fried tomatoes, and mushrooms in Worcester sauce. I wolfed it down.

At eleven o'clock Charles stirred and, after disappearing to the bathroom, came back looking elegant and well groomed. He sat down on the sofa while Mum made him a coffee.

"Would you care to come for a walk, Heather?" he asked.

"Yes, why don't you, Heather?" Mum said. "Charles is really into walking."

That was an understatement. We marched from Clapham South past Wimbledon and halfway around Richmond Park until I thought my legs were going to drop off. I'm sure Mum planned the walk hoping Charles and I would get to know each other, but her plans went astray. We were both so wary of each other that we hardly said a word until we reached Roehampton when I complained I was tired.

Charles looked irritated. "Don't be so lazy," he said.

We walked on in silence. I wasn't particularly bothered. I couldn't understand half of what Charles said anyway, his voice was so posh. I was shuffling along, lost in thought, trying to avoid the cracks on the pavement because it was unlucky, when his voice boomed out again.

"Heather, Heather, the world is beautiful. You must look up at the sky not down at the pavement."

I gawped at him.

He smiled, then said, more gently, "You have to look *up*. The sky is blue. The sun is shining. Enjoy it. Walk tall. Then people will notice you."

But I didn't want to be noticed and I felt so intimidated by Charles's voice that I hunched my shoulders and put my head down even farther.

Before we got home he made one final attempt to break the ice, when he called in at the Nightingale pub in Clapham South. He bought himself a pint and me a glass of lemon and lime and we sat down opposite each other at a table. But it was no good. He seemed at a total loss as to what to say, which was hardly surprising. How could he converse with a ten-year-old girl who sat huddled over her glass and wouldn't even look at him? We finished our drinks in total silence and it must have been obvious to Mum when we returned that our walk had not been a success. Even more so when for the rest of my stay we avoided each other.

It wasn't Charles's fault that we didn't get on. I hadn't expected to be bowled over by the man who'd lured my mother away from us, while he for his part was obviously uncomfortable with children. He treated me a bit like a wild animal who might suddenly make an unexpected move. It wasn't exactly a recipe for a successful relationship.

But at least Charles seemed to be making Mum happy. She told me he often took her out dancing and that once a week they played tennis together, both things the doctors had told us she'd never do again. She hardly limped at all now, though one night as we sat in front of the electric fire she lifted up her dressing gown to toast her legs and I saw the scars on her left calf. I was shocked to see that where the skin grafts had been done it was still red and angry and the skin looked paper thin. I hadn't realized how bad it was because during the day she always wore brightly colored tights. She had two drawers full of tights. Striped ones, spotted ones, red, black, and purple ones. Her style of dressing had been transformed. When Mum was living with us in Washington she wouldn't have dreamed of wearing things like purple striped tights. But everything about her expressed her individuality now. She wore great big mad earrings and bright slides and combs in her hair. I decided I liked my new artistic mum.

She'd taken a week off work so she could take me sight-seeing and one day, as she'd promised, she took me to the hospice where she worked. The idea of a hospice was new to me.

"Why do people want to come here to die?" I asked her.

"Because we can make it less painful. It's hard for families to care for people at home when they're dying, so it takes the stress off the families as well." I noticed that Mum always talked to me like a grown-up, unlike Dad.

She told me she'd become involved with the local church and helped them with their jumble sales. "It keeps me busy until I find a full-time job," she said. It was the only hint that she wasn't completely happy with her new life.

Those five days in London were a mixed experience for me. When I'd set off from home I'd nursed the hope that Mum might ask us to come and live with her, but by the end of my visit my dream was in ashes. Not only was her flat too small to house us all, but the idea of living there didn't appeal to me at all. For one thing I sensed Charles didn't much like having me around and for another I didn't like London, with its noise and exhaust fumes and bustle, nearly as much as I liked it up north where my friends lived and I knew my way around. If I could carry on coming down to see Mum in the holidays then I would have two homes and the best of both worlds.

I'd half expected that while I was with her, Mum might explain why she'd left us, but after that brief apology during our reunion in Llandrindod Wells she never brought the subject up. It didn't matter. It was enough that we'd found each other again. At night as we sat around the electric fire watching telly I'd catch myself staring at her. Dad had got rid of all the photos of Mum and my image of her had become blurred since she left. I'd forgotten how beautiful she was. It was like suddenly discovering I had a lovely fairy godmother. A godmother who washed her hair in chamomile and kept mysterious creams and potions on her dressing table. I was captivated by this sudden exposure to femininity after nearly two years of living in a masculine environment. The sight of my mother carefully applying lipstick in front of the tiny wall mirror mesmerized me. At ten and a half I was going through the frumpy dumpy stage and I wanted to look like her so much.

Mum must have read my mind because the day before I was due to go home she gave me my first manicure. Afterward she took me to Superdrug and bought me a big bagful of face creams and shampoos and hand cream.

"These are for you to take home with you, Heather," she said. "You'll have to start looking after yourself, now you're growing up."

I packed them carefully in my suitcase and set off back to Washington, County Durham, with her words echoing in my ears. I was growing up! I could hardly wait.

# Chapter 5

As it happened I didn't have to wait very long. Soon after my trip to London my body began to change dramatically. I'd always been tall for my age but now I just started to shoot up. That September I started at Usworth Comprehensive School and before long I was towering over most of the girls in my class. Growing so fast meant I was always ravenous but because we were still on an economy drive there was never anything in the fridge at home, so I never put much weight on, just grew up like a beanstalk. The other kids in my class nicknamed me "the locust" but it didn't bother me. My height and long legs gave me an advantage in basketball and that was what mattered to me—it was my favorite sport.

But when my breasts started to grow I found it harder to cope. Suddenly, while most of my friends still had nice inconspicuous little buds, I had full-blown boobs. I did my best to hide them by wearing lots of layers of clothes but all my old clothes were too tight for me so it was only a matter of time before my secret came out. David Murphy was the first boy to notice it. He was walking through the park with Jackie Fairlamb and me after school. I was wearing jeans and a striped blue-and-white sweatshirt that was ready to be passed on to Fiona. As we walked past the fountain where we used to stop for a paddle, I bent down to test the temperature of the water and he suddenly looked at me with new eyes.

"Bloody hell, Heather, your tits are like *watermelons!*" He gave me a wicked grin. "Giss a look."

"Get lost." I was outraged.

"Oh, you bloody bore," he said and stalked off.

To me, boys' reactions weren't as important as the way my breasts handicapped me in games. Since starting at Usworth Comprehensive I'd become really keen on sport. Not just basketball but track events too. The school had its own games field and running track; every lunch hour, rain or shine, I'd be out there training. Now these strange growths on my chest got in the way when I was running and bounced around uncomfortably when I played basketball or ran over hurdles. I didn't know what to do about it. I really needed a bra but I was too embarrassed to mention it to Dad. Instead I used to sneak a roll of masking tape from Dad's toolbox and hand it to my friend Karen Atkinson in the changing room before games. She'd wind it around and around my chest as tight as she could, then, trussed up like a chicken, I'd go out on the field and run and jump to my heart's content.

It was six months before Fiona came to my rescue by nicking a bra from the Savacentre, which I wore until it fell apart at the seams. Until I was thirteen I only had one bra so I used to scrub the straps clean every night and dry it over my bedroom radiator.

During my first year at Usworth, Dad seemed to bounce back from his financial crisis and he decided that Fiona and I should have music lessons. Dad had always wanted us to play an instrument. He'd played the banjo himself once, and he'd also played the drums in a band. Shane was already having free trombone lessons from the music teacher at Usworth Comprehensive, but Dad had been nursing the dream that his girls would play the oboe and flute. That meant we had to have private lessons.

I enjoyed music but I wasn't happy at having to play the oboe. Usworth didn't have a school orchestra, only a brass band, so I had to go to Washington Comprehensive to play with their orchestra every Saturday. It meant I saw less of my friends. I would have much preferred to learn something like the saxophone or trumpet so I could play with Shane in the brass band, but Dad wouldn't hear of it.

"It's more feminine to play the oboe," he ruled. So the oboe it was, and every night after supper we had to practice for an hour. Fiona hated the discipline and never even got as far as taking exams. But for me being forced to practice paid off and I got a distinction in my first exam. Even so, my heart was never in it and I always breathed a sigh of relief when the hands of my bedside clock crept around to half past seven and I could shut the lid on it for another day.

Since we'd started visiting her, Dad had stopped confiscating Mum's letters. On my twelfth birthday she sent me a card and some prettily wrapped Superdrug creams together with a note to say that she and Charles were moving to a new flat. It belonged to someone she'd met at the local church. His house was too big for him to look after properly and he'd offered to rent her a couple of rooms cheaply in return for help with his cooking and cleaning. Mum had jumped at the idea. "It means that from now on you and Fiona will be able to come down to London together instead of one at a time," she wrote.

I was pleased: I wouldn't have to take the National Express bus on my own again. It would be much nicer having Fiona to chat to. Although there were two years between us, Fiona and I had become really close since Mum left. In many ways we were more like twins than ordinary sisters. We called each other by secret nicknames. I was Bugs Bunny while she was Hartley Hare—a private joke, based on the problems we were both having with our teeth.

That Easter, Fiona and I took Mum up on her promise. She now lived just off the main street in Clapham South. It was much nicer than the bedsit—a rambling Victorian house with a green gate and a path leading through a pretty garden to the front door. The door had a glass fanlight over it that let light flood into the passageway. It was a house full of character, quite unlike our tiny box in Biddick, and I loved it at first sight.

Mum's flat on the ground floor had just one bedroom and a sitting room, so Norman, Mum's new landlord, had agreed to let Fiona and me use two spare bedrooms in his part of the house for our week's stay. I would sooner have slept with Mum but there was no chance of that. During that visit and all the others that followed we were never allowed into my mother's bedroom—it was like a sacred place.

Every evening Mum used to go up to Norman's rooms and cook a meal for him and we were allowed to go with her. Norman was nearly eighty, the sweetest man I'd ever met, with wonderful tales to tell of travels in India and other exotic places. When, tactlessly, we asked him what had happened to his wife, he told us he'd never been married because he hadn't had the time. His mother had been an invalid and he'd taken care of her until the day she died. He was a religious man but not in a heavy way. He gave you the feeling that he was a really good person. I was sad he hadn't been able to get married and have a family of his own because I knew he would have made a wonderful father.

Charles was still appearing in *The Mousetrap,* but in the few hours that he spent in the flat he found little to say to us. Fiona and I sensed he didn't much like having us around, so from midday, when he got up, until six, when he left for the theater, we spent our time with Norman. He seemed to enjoy our company and never hinted he'd had enough of us. When we'd run out of things to talk about he'd let us watch the afternoon movie on his television.

By the end of the week we had assumed the run of Norman's house. It was full of elegant antique furniture and lovely old oil paintings. To me, the most wonderful thing he owned was a pianola, which stood in the corner of my bedroom. I'd never seen one before—I thought it was an ordinary piano—and one day I plucked up the courage to ask if we could play it. I was amazed when Norman produced a music roll and slotted it into place, then showed us how to pedal to make the music play. He chuckled to himself as we pedaled away madly and the *William Tell* Overture thundered out. We were playing it for the fifth time when Mum came upstairs to see what was going on. She came over and took the roll off, then she sat down on the stool and started to play. We listened openmouthed as her hands flew over the keys. Even though the piano wasn't in tune and a couple of keys didn't play, it sounded wonderful.

I was awestruck. "I never knew you could play."

She smiled. "There's a lot you don't know about me," she said.

By now I was having a lot of adolescent problems: spots, greasy hair, but nature waited till Sunday, my last day in London, to play her trump card. I'd got up before Fiona, and Mum asked me to go along to church with her, not to a service, but to help prepare food. Once a month, after the morning service, the local pensioners and out-of-work parishioners were given a sit-down Sunday lunch in the church hall for £1.50. That day it was Mum's turn to cook it. We spent all morning peeling potatoes and making Yorkshire pudding batter and then while Mum carved the roast, I served it.

I enjoyed myself. The smell of the food made my mouth water and all the old ladies went on about what a wonderful cook Mum was and what a lucky girl I was. I was looking forward to sitting down and stuffing myself full of roast potatoes and cauliflower in white sauce. Then, as I was handing out second helpings, something strange happened. There was a sudden warm feeling between my legs as though I'd wet myself. I rushed off to the loo and discovered there was blood on my pants.

I scurried back to the kitchen where Mum was taking a tray of apple crumble out of the oven.

"Mum, I'm bleeding." I grabbed her sleeve.

She set the hot tray down on the work surface, frowning. "What?"

"On my pants," I said. "There's blood."

Mum's face cleared. "Oh, my goodness." She smiled. "Don't worry. It's quite normal, Heather. It's called your period. It's a sign you're growing up. Haven't they taught you about it at school?"

I shook my head.

"Never mind. Come with me and I'll get you something to wear." She picked up her handbag and led me back into the loo where she gave me a sanitary pad and a condensed version of the facts of life. She seemed embarrassed.

"You mean it happens to you too?" I asked amazed.

"Yes, of course. It happens to all women."

I suppose I was lucky my periods started in London. How I'd have coped in Washington I can't imagine. I certainly wouldn't have said anything to Dad. I'd probably have convinced myself I had a fatal illness. Next time I wasn't so lucky. My second period began when I was at school—getting changed for a swimming match.

Fortunately Clare Jackson, an old friend from Farm Close, was swimming in the match. She was a year older than me so I guessed she must know about periods. Embarrassed but desperate I turned to her.

"Clare, I'm having this period. What should I do?"

"Oh, you just use a tampon. You wear them internally," Clare said airily. "Here. I've got one you can have." She burrowed in her school bag and produced a long cylinder wrapped in paper. I took it from her and disappeared into the toilet cubicle where I unwrapped it. I stared at the contents baffled. Deciding that the two cardboard tubes must be packaging, I ripped them off and found a soft squishy cylinder of cotton wool. I pulled off my pants and pushed the tampon experimentally between my legs. It wobbled and went sideways. The more frantic I got the more it seemed to have a mind of its own. It wanted to go anywhere but in the right place and since I wasn't too sure where the right place was anyway I was fighting a losing battle.

With five minutes to go before my race I managed to wedge the tampon halfway in. I went out for my breaststroke heat horribly aware that if I kicked too hard it would shoot out. You never saw anyone pull their legs back together as I did during that heat. It was a hundred-meter race, which meant I had to do four lengths of the pool and three turns. Amazingly, in spite of my handicap, I won it.

Afterward I dashed into the loo, pulled the tampon out, and put a pad on instead. As I came out of the cubicle Clare came up to me giggling.

"Heather, the string was wiggling out of your swimsuit behind you!"

I turned scarlet. "Did anyone see?"

"Only half the school. You can't have put it in properly."

"Well, I don't see how anyone can use those blooming things," I said crossly.

When she found out I'd thrown the applicator away Clare burst out laughing. She explained what I should have done and I tried again.

This time the Tampax went in perfectly. I was converted and from then on used nothing else. But how I wished Mum had told me.

Gradually, as the other girls in my class caught up with my physical development, we dropped our skipping ropes and Barbie dolls while clothes and makeup became the focus of our lives. I let my hair grow out of the Purdey cut I'd had since I was nine into a longer softer style and I started to use all the cleansers and creams that Mum had bought me from Superdrug. My spots were a constant worry but, rather than change my diet, I started to put more and more creams on my face. Of course it didn't work. Then someone told me that sunbeds helped your skin. After that, whenever I had any pocket money, I'd spend it on a half-hour sun treatment in the local beauty salon. I discovered makeup too. I never dared wear it when Dad was around but if I was going out I'd call in at a friend's house and put on lipstick and mascara, then stop off again on the way back to take it off. I discovered makeup could make me look four or five years older than I was.

Once a week there was a disco at the Biddick community center. If I'd finished the housework and oboe practice Dad used to let me go and disco-dancing soon became my favorite pastime. On the dance floor with the strobe lights and the crystal orb flashing away I would shut out everything else. I couldn't wait for Thursdays to come. Fiona was too young to be allowed in so I went with Lisa Tyson, a friend from school. I wasn't interested in boys at that age, just in dancing. Who needed boys? Most of the ones my age were six inches shorter than me anyway.

Then one day a seventeen-year-old boy walked into the disco and everything changed. The newcomer was called Stephen Leyton. He was tall, dark, and handsome; by the end of the disco I'd fallen head over heels in love with him. For months afterward I fantasized about him asking me to dance and falling in love with me, but it remained a fantasy. He didn't seem to notice my existence. At his age he was more interested in fifth-form girls than in second years. There were plenty of those drooling over him too.

Being in love meant that deciding what to wear to the disco became a nightmare. I had few dressy clothes and even fewer that would catch the eye of a boy like Stephen, but Lisa was a good friend and used to help me out. Once she even loaned me her best red silk blouse. It touched me deeply. I couldn't believe she would trust me with something so lovely. When I was rich I vowed I'd lend my clothes to my friends too. But even Lisa's silk shirt made no difference. Stephen carried on his way unaware of my devotion.

When she started at Usworth Comprehensive, Fiona was allowed to come with me to the disco. Dad used to tease us about our evenings out. He'd wait till we were all dressed up; then, just as we were going out of the door, he'd say, "What are you wearing? You look terrible! You look like the two ugly sisters." He was always putting us down. It was a joke to him. But it did nothing for our confidence, what with our buck teeth and Fiona's worries about her bony ankles.

"It's no good spending so much time in front of the mirror," Dad would scoff. "You two'll never be beautiful. You might as well give up."

At other times though, like when he wanted us to do something for him, our looks would miraculously improve. "You're my pretty girls," he'd say, cuddling us.

I was Dad's "pretty girl" whenever I went to the opera with him, which was quite often. Now Mum had gone, I had replaced her as his escort. He even bought me a posh dress to wear, but I wouldn't play ball. If he called me ugly then that's what he'd get. So while Dad used to dress up to kill in his purple tux and bow tie, I stubbornly wore jeans and sweatshirt, no makeup, and hardly bothered to brush my hair. In spite of myself I did enjoy the opera. Puccini was my favorite: *La Bohème* and *Tosca* both reduced me to tears.

We'd been at Biddick for nearly a year when Dad got itchy feet again and we did another moonlight flit—this time to a modern mews house in Lambton, two miles away. I hated it, chiefly because it was four miles to the nearest launderette. Dad had never replaced the washing machine that Shane blew up, so once a week I had to walk to Columbia carrying the laundry in a black bin liner.

For me the saving grace about Lambton was that I made a new friend there, a pretty girl called Julia Quinn who lived a few houses away. She was a couple of years older than me but we hit it off straightaway.

The Quinns were a really happy family and I used to sneak away to spend time with them. Her mother was sweet, a real storybook mother, and her father was a chef in the local handicapped school. On weekends when my dad was away "on business" I used to help them cook the Sunday lunch and Mr. Quinn would give me tips on how to make Yorkshire puddings. The atmosphere was wonderful. It was such a change to be with happy people.

Julia introduced me to the local disco, the Ox Close, and we soon had a regular date every week. We used to get ready together and help each other with our makeup. Like me, Julia had a bad skin problem, but her way of coping with it was different. Instead of lying on sunbeds she'd plaster very pale Miss Selfridge foundation over her face—she used to go through a whole tube every week. What with my deep tan and her chalky white face we must have looked like The Black and White Minstrels.

To avoid Dad commenting on what I wore, I used to get changed for the disco at Julia's. Her untidiness amazed me. At my house everything had to be kept in apple-pie order and Dad used to inspect our bedrooms every day to make sure it was. Julia just used to throw her stuff in the corner and her mother would run around picking things up after her.

"Julia, I'd give gold to have a mother like yours. You're so lucky," I'd say. She'd laugh, but I meant it.

I'd have paid even more to have a father like Julia's. Partly because I never heard him raise his voice, but mostly because he brought home the most wonderful leftovers from his canteen. It made my mouth water when someone opened the Quinns' fridge. They were such kind people I'm sure they'd have let me have some if I'd asked, but I was too embarrassed to admit our fridge was empty and I was starving. Julia knew though, and she'd sneak bags of food out of her house for me before the disco.

Dad had always been strict, but when we moved to Lambton some of his rules, especially the times he laid down for bedtimes and playtimes, became really eccentric. Unless it was disco night, Shane,

Fiona, and I were forbidden to play outside after school. Instead we had to come straight home, cook dinner, do our music practice, and afterward help with the paperwork for any projects he was working on. Only at nine or ten o'clock, when other kids our age were being sent off to bed, would Dad pack everything away and say, "Right, you can go out and play hopscotch now."

The most memorable thing about Lambton as far as we were concerned was that it was where the Wagner project was born. Dad usually had moneymaking schemes in progress, but most of his schemes were short-lived. The Wagner project was different: It obsessed him. Dad had always been a nut about that composer; in fact I sometimes think he saw himself as a reincarnation of Richard Wagner. The scheme he dreamed up in Lambton was an audiovisual presentation based on the *Ring* cycle, illustrating Wagner's music with pictures and images the way Walt Disney did with *Fantasia.* Eventually, if he could get sponsorship, he planned to make an animated film along the lines of *Fantasia,* but initially he'd decided to use thousands of slides instead.

Night after night we'd sit around the kitchen table, cutting out pictures of dragons and dwarfs from books by Tolkien. He'd photograph these pictures with his Hasselblad camera and, when the negatives came back from the processors, it was our job to cut them up and put them into mounts. Unfortunately, no sooner had we completed the project than Hasselblad brought out a bigger format, which meant we had to start all over again and reframe the slides to fit on the new carousels. Sometimes we'd be up till four or five in the morning, cleaning the slides with a little puffy blower and putting them in the correct order. Then, with Wagner's music playing at top volume, Dad would project them onto the wall—clunk, clunk, click—clunk, clunk, click—for hours on end.

"What do you think of this picture?" he'd ask. "Do you think I should follow that one with this? How about this for a sequence?" On and on he'd go until we were all falling asleep at the table.

Fiona and I acted as Dad's secretaries on the Wagner project. Fiona was very good at drawing and had once won a prize for handwriting, so Dad got her to do his posters and artwork. He'd lose all track of time when he was engrossed: Often, if he got an exciting idea, he'd wake her up at midnight and make her come downstairs to sketch for him. Not being artistic, my role was simply to type letters to the organizers of arts festivals asking if Dad could put on his presentation there. Soon homework took second place to Wagner.

"That's not important at the moment, girls," he'd say, when we moaned that we had essays to write. "Come and do this first." Helping Dad did give me some skills that were to come in useful later on, such as typing and setting out letters properly. I also became very knowledgeable about opera, and about Wagner in particular. To this day I only have to hear a few bars to recognize every chorus from the *Ring* cycle.

I'd been good at my lessons when I started at Usworth and had come top in most subjects, as had Fiona and Shane, but now that we were always exhausted we started to fall behind. It didn't seem to occur to our teachers to ask why three children from the same family should be falling asleep in class. All they did was put us on report. They knew Mum had left home but none of them put two and two together. Just as they'd never asked questions when we came to school with bruises, so they weren't interested now. All it would have taken was for one teacher to ask, "Is everything all right at home?" But they never did.

As I fell behind, I lost interest in lessons and my dreams of being a plastic surgeon faded away. By the time I was thirteen I couldn't wait to leave school. The one thing I did stay keen on was sport: I *adored* sport. If I was swimming or running I felt completely free. The running track at Usworth was my whole world. When I was selected to represent the North-East in school athletics events, it gave my confidence a big boost. I loved to win. The feeling when I beat everyone else was the greatest feeling in the world. I spent most of my time feeling pretty insignificant, but winning a hurdles or cross-country race did wonders for my ego.

Funnily enough, the only time I couldn't ever win was when Dad came to watch me. Perhaps it was because I wanted to win *so* much then—to get into his good books, to make him proud of me for once—that every time he turned up I used to freeze. When he started coaching me, telling me to breathe deeply and use the adrenaline, it was all over. My legs would turn to jelly and even before I took a step I *knew* that I was going to hit every hurdle or trail last in the fifteen hundred meters.

Every time it happened Dad would shake his head despairingly. “You’re useless, Heather,” he’d say. “Absolutely useless.”

My face would go red then; I’d stare at the ground and fight back the tears. *You’re wrong,* I thought. *One day I’ll show you. You wait.*

# Chapter 6

I wasn't the only victim of Dad's put-downs. He treated Shane and Fiona in just the same way. Dad's compulsion to criticize was so strong that nothing we did was ever good enough. As well as the mental abuse, the physical violence continued. If we thwarted or crossed him in any way, Dad was just unable to control himself. Whatever the sin—treading dirt into the carpet, forgetting a phone message, botching a tape recording—the result was the same. The wrongdoer would be grabbed by the hair, punched in the ribs, and hit around the head. For nearly five years after Mum left we all lived on red alert, the need to keep the peace ruling our actions. Stealing, lying, anything was in order to stop us getting hit.

We never rebelled openly against the way Dad treated us. It would have been more than our lives were worth. But that didn't mean he'd broken our spirits. Fiona and I soon found it was possible to outwit Dad, and deceiving him made our mischief all the more enjoyable. It was a bit like playing Russian roulette—the terror of what might go wrong added to the thrill when we got away with it. We were attracted like a magnet to anything Dad disapproved of. Fiona used to smoke his cigars and play pop music on his stereo system, while I played truant from school, pinched things from shops, and cadged lifts home from discos on the back of boys' motorbikes. I also started drinking.

I first got drunk when I was thirteen. Alcohol wasn't allowed in the Ox Close disco but an hour or so before the doors opened Julia Quinn and I used to pinch a bottle of cider from Woolco and take it to one of the unfinished shops in the Washington Galleries. There we'd crawl into one of the big gray pipes that the builders had left behind and pass the bottle between us until it was empty. Cider was great for giving you Dutch courage and with half a liter of Strongbow inside me I could really let rip on the dance floor. Sometimes we'd take along a pint glass and mix the cider with Ribena to make cider and black, or steal a can of lager and mix that with the cider. It was called snakebite, and if you drank it really fast you'd be walking on air for the rest of the night.

All the way home after the disco we'd suck mints to take the smell of cider off our breath, which must have worked because Dad never said anything. Dad didn't drink at all himself. Funnily enough his only vice (apart from belting his kids) was smoking the odd cigar.

Julia was still sneaking food out of her house. One unforgettable Thursday night she brought out a bag full of oven chips and a carton of peas and we both stuffed ourselves silly before we set off to pinch some booze. That night though, Woolco had run out of cider so we stole half a bottle of whisky instead. Unfortunately, I had no idea how strong whisky was and swigged it down like I did the cider. Julia was more used to drinking than me and took her time. When the bottle was empty we left it in the pipe and set off for the disco. I felt really great—but not for long. As soon as I walked on to the pedestrian bridge that leads out of the Washington Galleries and hit the fresh air, my head started to spin. I threw up, and once I'd started I couldn't stop. I was so sick I thought I was going to die, and all the way across the bridge behind me there were these little piles of oven chips with a pea on the top. I never made it to the disco that night. Afterward I vowed I'd never drink alcohol again. To this day if someone comes near me after drinking whisky I want to be sick.

I was only allowed out on two evenings a week, Thursday for the Ox Close disco and Tuesday for Girl Guides. But whenever Dad told us he wouldn't be home till late I used to plan a forbidden night out. Friday was a big night at the Newcastle Theatre and Dad never got back before half past eleven. By coincidence there was a disco at Springwell on Friday night that was really good. You were supposed to be fifteen to get in this disco and I was only thirteen, so as soon as Dad drove off to Newcastle I'd tong my hair, change into high heels and tight skirt, and catch the Springwell bus. I had the whole thing timed to perfection. I'd leave the disco at half past ten, catch the last bus back to Lambton, which would get me home by eleven, and by the time Dad's car pulled up outside the house I'd be undressed and tucked up in bed with my eyes tight shut.

But I played this particular game of Russian roulette once too often. One night I forgot to keep an eye on my watch and missed the last bus home. It was eight miles from Springwell to Lambton and I had no money for a taxi so there was nothing for it but to hitch up my skirt and run. I was very fit from all my athletics so the distance was no problem but my high heels were. By the time I reached the church halfway down the hill into Lambton, my feet felt like lumps of meat and I had pains shooting up and down my calves. Then, behind me in the dark, I heard a car changing gear and when I looked around I recognized the rectangular divided lights of a Volvo. I just knew it was Dad's car. My stomach turned over and I took off my shoes and belted down the footpath that was a shortcut to the back of our house. I had never been so frightened in my life. I knew I had to get to the house before he came in. If I didn't the world would end. I reached the back of our house and banged on the door until Shane opened it.

"Dad's at the front," I gasped. "Quick, quick. Let me in, Shane." I pushed past him and ran up the stairs, my insides exploding with fear.

"Oh, my God. What have you done, Heather?" Shane called after me. "Look."

I turned and saw a little trail of brown marks all the way behind me on the stair carpet. Oh, the shame. In my terror I'd shat myself!

"Never mind." Shane waved me toward my bedroom. "You get yourself into bed. I'll see to it." He grabbed a towel from the airing cupboard and started to scrub away at the carpet. I dived into my room, flung myself into bed, and pulled the sheets up over me.

A minute later Dad's key turned in the door and I heard him ask, "Is everybody in bed?"

"Yes, all quiet," Shane's innocent voice replied.

Dad's footsteps clumped up the stairs and then my door opened and the light from the landing spilled in. I kept my eyes tight shut and the door closed again. Half an hour later I sneaked into the bathroom and, as quietly as I could, washed all my clothes and sluiced myself down. My appetite for the Springwell disco was destroyed that night. I never went again.

I could usually rely on Shane to cover up for me; he was good that way, even though he didn't get up to much mischief himself. Shane's reaction to trouble was to put his head down and get on with his schoolwork. But Shane wasn't around the next time I needed him to clean the carpet.

Since we'd been at Lambton, Dad had started going off on expeditions—he didn't call them holidays—without us. His longest "expedition" was when he went on the Charles Darwin boat with David Bellamy to the Galápagos Islands. Dad had been introduced to him when David Bellamy had been narrating at a performance of *Peter and the Wolf* in Durham. A few months after the concert, Dad told us Mr. Bellamy had invited him to go on this boat as the navigator—though I suspect that was one of Dad's fantasies: He was probably a fare-paying passenger. He was away for a whole month. Shane, the eldest, was only fourteen, but we didn't mind being left on our own. It was great to walk back from school each day without being scared what mood we'd find him in. I celebrated by asking one of my school friends, Jackie Fairlamb, over to stay. Jackie brought Patch, her little Jack Russell. She also brought her boyfriend who in turn brought two of *his* friends, real punk rockers with jet-black hair and safety-pinned jeans and leather jackets. It felt great having rebels like Moonie and Echo in Dad's precious house. I said they could stay for a week.

On the last day of Dad's holiday I went off to school telling the boys to clear up and get themselves out of the house by the time I got back. Dad was due home in the early hours of the next morning. But when I arrived home Moonie and Echo were still there, taking turns to have baths. There was water everywhere and the house was an absolute mess. I threw them out. Shane wouldn't help me out this time. "It's your own bloody fault," he said. "You clean it up."

Fiona, who'd spent the past month staying with two school friends, took the same attitude. I had to work like a navvy to clean the place up by bedtime, but somehow I did it. By the time Dad came back at two o'clock the next morning the house was immaculate again. Or so I thought.

I was fast asleep in bed and I don't remember hearing him come in. All I remember is waking up suddenly and screaming in pain as he pulled me out of bed by my hair. He dragged me behind him up the stairs to his bedroom on the top floor; his face was bright red.

"What is *that?*" He pointed to a little brown thing like a walnut whip on the carpet. My heart sank. I knew at once what it was. A Jack Russell poo. I'd cleared up quite a few of them while Patch had been staying with us. I had no idea how I'd missed this one.

Dad knew what it was too. "That Jackie's bloody dog has been in the house, hasn't it?" he demanded. I couldn't deny it.

"Right," he said. "Get it cleaned up. Now!"

I knew better than to argue. I fetched the scrubbing brush and carpet shampoo, put on a pair of rubber gloves, and picked up the walnut whip. It was rock hard—it must have been there at least a week—and there wasn't a mark on the carpet underneath it.

"But Dad, there's nothing there!" I showed him. "Look!"

"It doesn't matter." He glared. "You clean that whole carpet."

So I did. Inch by inch in the middle of the night, I sat and scrubbed the entire bedroom carpet while Dad went off and slept in the spare room. Typical. It had been a whole month since he'd last seen me, but there'd been no "Hello, darling"; no "How've you been while I've been away?" Why had I imagined there might have been?

Dad went away a lot that year. He'd taken up climbing again and in the summer he'd often spend his weekends up in Scotland. He'd carried on helping teach the Girl Guides too. One day he came home and announced that he'd volunteered to help a deaf and dumb Girl Guide to climb a mountain in the Pyrenees. He went off for a week that time. They showed him climbing with this deaf and dumb girl on the television news. He was only a dot in the distance, but we could tell it was him because of his old blue climbing jumper. It was weird to think that this kindhearted hero was the same man who regularly beat the living daylights out of his kids. I wondered what the Girl Guide captain would say if she knew . . .

Dad could afford to go away a lot now. His fortunes had picked up again. Until recently he'd never talked about how he earned his living. But one night he'd come home full of himself and told us he was setting up a Youth Training Scheme. He said he had formed something called the Wagner Arts Society and he'd been given a big grant from the government to train YTS kids in audiovisual techniques. It seemed to be good news all around. From now on not only would these kids be mounting the slides and doing all the things we used to do, but there'd be more money to spare at home.

Soon after Dad made his announcement, pictures reappeared on the walls, followed by new furniture, a new stereo, and new cars. At one time we actually had three cars in our drive—a 3 series BMW, a Range Rover, and the trusty old Volvo. Our neighbors must have thought we'd won the pools.

That year all the effort we'd put into the Wagner presentation paid off and Dad started to get bookings. Not just little local bookings either. We were asked to put Dad's show on at the Brighton Festival, the Edinburgh Festival, and the Barbican in London. Dad had programs and tickets printed and rehearsed all three of us night after night in the lounge, getting us to sync the slides in with the music until we could have done it in our sleep.

The first presentation was a trial one at the local library. The room was packed. I couldn't believe it. All these people had actually paid £5 a ticket to see the slides we'd stuck together on our kitchen table. The responsibility was nerve-racking. More so because we were in sole charge of the projection while Dad saw to the music. Dad reveled in the role of impresario, swanning around and greeting people while we acted as program and ticket sellers. It was a bit like a family circus with Dad as ringmaster. Fiona and I had to wear dresses, which we hated, and Shane wore a suit that, being strictly a blue jeans person, he hated even more. Unlike us, Dad loved dressing up and playing a part. His image had always been very important to him: Even when he was really hard up he'd always gone to work dressed in a smart striped shirt and blazer. On that first night in his new blue suit, bought for the occasion, he looked like a film star. Even his hair had new blond streaks—could it be something to do with the box of Nice 'n Easy I'd discovered in the bathroom cabinet?

*Das Rheingold,* the first opera of the cycle, went well with no hiccups. To my surprise I enjoyed it. It was wonderful to see the dragons and dwarfs leaping out at us from a full-size screen instead of from our lounge wall at home. The audience seemed to enjoy it too and gave us a standing ovation at the end. We went on to present *Die Walküre* on the second night with much more confidence.

We staged each presentation over four days, with *Siegfried* on the third night and finally *Götterdämmerung.* Dad was in charge of the music—he'd hired commercial speakers and stereo tape decks—while our job was to slide in the screens and sync them in with the music. It was a complicated process. The idea was to overlap the slides from each projector so that as the music developed they blended into each other smoothly rather than changing abruptly. If you got it right you had a sensation of movement so it was almost like a film. Later on Dad got hold of a fire machine, which projected flames onto the wall all around the slides. It was a stroke of genius and really added to the feeling of animation.

We had ten projectors and spent each performance running up and down between them focusing, refocusing, and clicking on to the next slide at precisely the right note in the music. Our months of training paid off and in four hectic nights we barely made a mistake. The slide changes were all manual, though, which meant Shane, Fiona, and I had to press a slide button every few seconds. Since even *Das Rheingold,* the shortest opera, lasted an hour and a half, we found that by the end of the evening our fingers had seized up.

After our tryout in the local library, we went straight to London to perform in The Pit at the Barbican, which had only just been opened. It was a very prestigious booking, but we were still on a tight budget.

A lot of the ticket revenue was going on the hire of halls and Dad had earmarked any profits for his fund to make the animated version of the *Ring,* so our expenses had to be kept to a minimum. We traveled down to London by the new Clipper bus, which took five hours but was half the price of the train. On Dad's instructions, Shane, Fiona, and I had arranged to stay with Mum and Charles in Clapham, while Dad was booked into a cheap bed-and-breakfast near Victoria. The one luxury Dad did allow himself was to travel by taxi around London because he couldn't carry all the projection equipment on the tube.

In the end it was projection equipment that was to be Dad's downfall, but on this occasion everything went well. The Barbican presentation received rave reviews and we played to full houses every night. It was this that encouraged Dad to think about ways of polishing the production even more. He decided to use some of his profits to hire a computerized projector to automate the slide changes and reduce his dependence on us. (Our teachers had been making disapproving noises about the time we were taking off school.) He booked the equipment for his next production—the most prestigious one yet—at the Queen Elizabeth Hall on the South Bank.

It was tempting fate. For twelve performances Fiona, Shane, and I had changed the slides on ten projectors manually without a single hitch, but on the second night that we used the computerized slide changer the projector lamp blew just as the first notes of *Die Walküre* sounded, and the picture went out. For several minutes the music carried on in the dark while Dad hunted about for the spare bulb, but when he found it he discovered the hire company had given him a dud one.

That was it. The Queen Elizabeth Hall officials put the house lights back on and announced that the ticket money would be refunded, and when everyone had gone they told Dad they were canceling his other two shows because his management was unprofessional and not up to the standard they expected in their productions. Dad was devastated. He just stared at them shaking his head in disbelief. It was the only time I remember feeling sorry for my father.

But by the time we'd packed everything up, Dad had pulled himself back together. The company that had rented us the computer equipment was due to come to the hall and pick it up, but Dad had other plans.

"Right, you lot. Grab all the stuff," he told us. "They're not getting that back."

Five minutes later the four of us were out of the doors of the Queen Elizabeth Hall carrying all the computer equipment and running up and down Waterloo Bridge looking for a taxi.

"Dad, you can't just take it home," Shane protested as we piled into the back of a cab. "They'll set the police on us."

But Dad was beyond reason. "I'm keeping their blooming stuff—they're not getting any of it," he said. "Not after they've ruined my production."

I don't know if he ever did return it. He certainly never paid the company for hiring it.

It wasn't the end of the Wagner project but it did mark the end of the big time. When word of the fiasco spread, several of our bookings were canceled and inquiries for our presentation dried up. We did go to the Edinburgh Festival where we were already booked to appear in a small fringe venue and to the Brighton Festival, but after that interest petered out.

It was probably no coincidence that soon afterward the bailiffs started to call around at the house again. Bailiffs were nothing new to us. Over the years they'd become a fact of life. We never kept anything in our house for years the way other people did. Things used to come in the door and go out of the door before we'd had time to get attached to them. Dad bought most things on HP and used to regularly fall behind on the payments. We only ever had our bikes for a month or two—the tires would hardly be worn when they were taken back. So it was no real surprise when the latest spell of prosperity came to an end.

The BMW and the Range Rover were the first things to be repossessed. It put Dad on his guard. After that he warned us to look out of the bay window whenever someone knocked on the door.

"If it's men you don't know, then don't answer," he said. One day when Dad was out, a van pulled up outside and two men got out and walked up the path. Forgetting Dad's instructions, Fiona opened the door and the two men pushed past her and started to carry furniture out of the house into their van.

"How could you let them in? What on earth did you open the door for?" Dad kept asking her when he came home that night. He was so cross you'd have thought it was all Fiona's fault. Dad never actually admitted he was in debt. According to him it was always a mistake.

"Oh, there's been a mix-up," he'd say when Shane asked him where his trombone had gone. But the night it went he hid all his good stereo equipment upstairs, so he couldn't really have believed it was a mistake. Sometimes I think Dad lived in a fantasy world. He was a real Walter Mitty. He never believed and never wanted to believe the truth about himself. Years later when I tried to talk to him about his violence he denied it. "What are you talking about? That didn't happen. You're imagining it."

But we weren't imagining the bailiffs. They came again. And again. After they'd taken the furniture they came for our television and all the shiny new electrical gadgets. If Dad was in the house when the knock came he used to make us tell them he was out but it didn't stop them. They'd push past us until eventually they had virtually stripped the house.

Then one morning when I was about thirteen and a half, Dad came down for breakfast earlier than usual dressed in his best dark gray suit and a smart blue-and-white-striped shirt with gold cuff links. Most days he wore his blazer and slacks to work, so I knew he must be going somewhere especially important.

"I'm going away for two days on business," he said. "I'll be back at the weekend. Shane'll look after you two. Just make sure you lock the house up while you're out." With that he went out to his car. We didn't think much of it. Dad had been making a lot of overnight "business" trips recently.

That afternoon I was sitting in an English lesson reading out loud from *A Midsummer Night's Dream.* I loved reading. Whenever Miss

Askey, our English teacher, asked if anyone would like to read I was always the first to stick my hand up. I especially liked Shakespeare. High up in the corner of the classroom there was a loudspeaker and, suddenly, just as I was getting into the swing of the play, the voice of the headmaster's secretary blared out. "Would Shane Mills please come to the headmaster's office." I almost lost my place—what had Shane been up to now? But I managed to keep going. The next minute the voice on the loudspeaker spoke again. "Will *Heather* Mills please come to the headmaster's office."

Miss Askey raised her eyebrows. "Well, it looks as if Oberon will have to wait. You'd better go, Heather."

I walked down the long corridor to the headmaster's office with my mind reeling. *Help, what have we done?* I thought. Then the loudspeaker went a third time. "Will *Fiona* Mills come to the headmaster's office."

Oh, my God. All three of us! Perhaps someone had died.

I'd never been called to the headmaster's office before. When you were put on report for not doing homework or for playing truant you saw the deputy head. The head only dealt with major problems so I knew something really serious must have happened.

Nervously I tapped on the door of his study and when a voice said "Come in" pushed the door open.

The room was full of people, but in those first few seconds my eyes saw only one, a uniformed policewoman sitting in the corner of the room.

"Come in, Heather, have a seat." Mr. Yates, the headmaster, a big imposing man with gray hair, stood up behind his desk and waved me toward an empty chair. Two men I'd never seen before were standing next to his desk and they turned around as I came in. Sitting near them, almost on the edge of his chair, was Shane, who gave me a quick lift of his eyebrows. As I was struggling to make sense of it all there was another tap at the door and Fiona crept in. Mr. Yates pulled up another chair for her, then stepped back and stood next to the policewoman.

One of the two men spoke. "Shane? Heather? Fiona?"

We stared at him.

"I have to give you some rather bad news. It appears that your father has got himself into serious debt."

He paused and cleared his throat, then went on. "I'm afraid that as a result of that debt he has been sent to prison."

# Chapter 7

There was a long pause when nobody said anything. Then Fiona let out a high piercing wail and started sobbing. I put my arm around her. Typical Fiona, I thought. I didn't feel at all like crying myself. In fact I didn't feel anything. I was so shocked I couldn't really take it in. I looked at Shane. His mouth was hanging open. So that's what it meant when you read about people's jaws dropping, I thought coolly. It was true. Then my brain clicked back into gear and I thought, *What's going to happen to us?* and my heart started pounding. Maybe we'd be taken into care. But no, Shane was nearly sixteen. He could look after us. I didn't feel worried anymore then, just angry at Dad for doing this to us, and in a guilty sort of way, relieved.

Fiona was really crying now, her shoulders heaving up and down and going, "Oh, God! Oh, God!" over and over again. She was in a worse state than the day Mum left us.

The policewoman came over and put a hand on her arm. "Fiona, we've been in touch with your mother. She'll be arriving from London tonight. She's arranged for your grandmother to come up from Brighton too so you mustn't worry, there'll be plenty of people to look after you." Her words only sent Fiona into more floods of tears. "Look, we're going to take you home now," the policewoman said gently. "One of your neighbors has agreed to look after you until your mum gets here."

As we stood up, Mr. Yates, our headmaster, stepped forward. "I do hope everything turns out all right," he said to us. "I'm so sorry this has happened." He looked sorry too, not as if he was just saying it.

It wasn't until ten minutes later, when I was sitting with Shane and Fiona in the back of the police car, that it dawned on me why Dad had been all dressed up this morning. He'd been going to *court!* And he hadn't told us. Why? Hadn't he guessed he might be sent to prison? What did he think was going to happen to us? What he'd been doing, I realize now, was denying reality again. In Dad's fantasy world, as long as he kept pretending everything was all right, nothing could go wrong.

At the back of his mind, though, he must have known what it might come to, because he'd dropped a hint to Shane. I didn't learn about that until we arrived back at our next-door neighbor's house. Once we were safely inside Audrey's front door, the police drove off and the minute they disappeared Shane shot next door into our house. Half an hour later, he returned, out of breath and covered in cobwebs.

"What *have* you been doing, Shane?" I asked.

He put his fingers to his lips. "Shh," he said. "Tell you later."

Audrey was watching us like a hawk—maybe she thought we were going to start pinching her stuff—and it wasn't until she went into the kitchen to make a pot of tea that Shane was able to enlighten me.

"Dad told me this morning if he didn't come back tonight I was to hide his stereo equipment and cameras under the floorboards in the attic," he whispered.

At ten o'clock that night a big blue hire van pulled up outside Audrey's house and Grandma, Mum, and Charles stepped out. It wasn't exactly a joyful reunion. All of them looked tired and worried and after thanking Audrey for looking after us (which, come to think of it, was a joke, considering how many weeks we'd spent on our own in our house) we all trooped back next door. There, while Grandma put the kettle on, we sat around the kitchen table and talked about what had happened. Grandma shook her head as we told her what we knew, which wasn't much. She didn't defend Dad.

Neither did Mum, though I noticed she didn't say anything against him either. She never had done, I remembered, even when he'd been beating her up. Now, instead of joining in the conversation, she concentrated on making sandwiches with a stale loaf and a tin of corned beef she'd found in the cupboard.

I didn't really understand what Dad had done. I had no idea people could be sent to prison just because they were "in serious debt." But Grandma just said the police had told her it was more than just debt. What Dad had done was called fraud and had something to do with the government Youth Training Scheme. They said Dad had pretended to be training more people than he really was and as punishment the judge had sent him to prison for two years. I was still confused, but I was too tired to think about it anymore. Besides, I was more concerned about what was going to happen to us.

We were all yawning by now and Grandma took charge and sent us to bed. Charles was tired too after driving nearly three hundred miles and he followed us upstairs carrying his case into Dad's bedroom. (I couldn't help picturing Dad's face when he found out the "gambling man" had been sleeping in his bed!) But when I climbed into my bed I couldn't sleep and downstairs in the lounge I could hear Grandma and Mum talking for ages.

By the time we got up in the morning our future had been decided. "We think it will be best if Shane goes to live with Grandma in Brighton and you and Fiona come back to London with Charles and me," Mum announced.

It was a bombshell. It hadn't occurred to me that Mum would want to look after us and I didn't like the idea at all. It had been too long. Taking holidays in London was one thing. Living full time with Mum and Charles was another—and Charles didn't look overjoyed at the prospect either. I didn't want to be uprooted. Washington was my home, the only security I knew. I couldn't imagine life without Julia and the running track and the Ox Close disco.

I didn't want Shane to live somewhere else. I knew there wasn't room at Cavendish Road for all three of us, but somehow we had to stay together. One glance at Fiona's face told me she felt exactly the same.

"Why can't Shane look after us in our house here?" I demanded.

Mum shook her head. "Because he isn't old enough, Heather, that's why."

"But he'll be sixteen soon. Anyway he's done it before."

Mum let out an impatient sigh. "For heaven's sake," she snapped. "You have two choices. Either you all come down south to live with us or you go into care."

Fiona looked horror-struck.

Grandma tried to calm the situation. "Try and see it from Shane's point of view, Heather," she said gently. "He'll be leaving school soon but he won't be able to get a job if he has to look after you two, will he?"

Grumpily I said, "He won't be able to get a job anyway in Washington. There's no work here."

"Ah," said Grandma. "But that's one good reason for him to come to Brighton. There's plenty of work there because of all the hotels, so he'd have no trouble finding a job. *And* he'd have time to practice his music." She smiled. "Maybe you could even join a band, Shane. There are lots of bands in Brighton." Shane's eyes lit up when she said that, and I knew Grandma had won. For the last year he'd been telling everyone he wanted to be a professional musician. I knew there wasn't much chance of him joining a band in a place like Washington.

Although I still wasn't happy about it, I had to accept that what Grandma was saying made sense. Since neither Fiona nor I really wanted to go into care, we gave in. Once it was settled we started packing. I'd imagined we'd just walk out of the house that day—it only took me an hour to pack my clothes and face creams. But it took almost a week to sort everything else out. Mum had to arrange for things like the telephone and electricity to be disconnected and the milk and paper orders had to be stopped. While we were waiting to go I half thought about going back to school. I really wanted to say good-bye to all my friends, but in the end I decided I couldn't face them. What would they say about Dad going to prison? Maybe, after all, it was a good idea to make a fresh start. At a new school people wouldn't know anything about Dad. I did go over to Julia's house to say good-bye, but I didn't even manage that. Julia had left school and started a job in the local VG store now, and was working late the night I called.

Six days after Dad was sent to prison, Charles drove us down the A1 to London in the blue Transit van. With us, we took all our worldly possessions, which amounted to several black bin liners full of clothes; a briefcase containing our medical cards, birth certificates, and school reports; and our musical instruments.

Mum and Grandma sat up in the front of the van with Charles while Shane, Fiona, and I traveled in the back. There were no backseats but, before we set off, Charles took three deck chairs out of the garden shed and set them up for us to sit on. On them he put three of Dad's sleeping bags—the duck-down ones he used for mountaineering.

"Snuggle down inside them. It'll be cold in the back of the van," he warned.

I remember thinking Dad was going to be pretty upset that we'd taken his best sleeping bags but I didn't argue. After all, it would be at least two years before we saw him again, which seemed too far away to worry about. At the last minute I decided to take a leaf out of Charles's book and ran back in the house and pocketed Dad's treasured personal stereo.

Before we were half an hour into the journey south we were extremely pleased that Charles had thought of the sleeping bags, because he'd been right, it *was* freezing cold in the back. The trip took forever. A few hours after we set off it grew dark outside and we settled down in our bags and tried to sleep, but it wasn't easy because every time Charles braked, all the bin liners fell down on top of us.

Charles dropped us off at Clapham before continuing on down to Brighton with Grandma and Shane. We were too tired for emotional farewells and once we'd waved the van away all I wanted to do was collapse into bed. Norman came down the stairs to greet us, his face creased with smiles.

"Heather! Fiona! How lovely to see you again. Come upstairs, I've made your rooms nice and warm for you."

Norman had agreed to let Fiona and me have the adjoining bedrooms on his top floor permanently and we followed him upstairs dragging our bin bags behind us. Mum had loaned me a tape to play on Dad's personal stereo and I drifted off to sleep that night to the strains of James Galway playing *The Magic Flute.* Maybe, I thought, things weren't going to be so bad after all.

I did everything I could to make a fresh start in London. As a first step I got rid of everything that reminded me of Dad. I hadn't brought a single photograph of him with me, but there were still things that, when I looked at them, conjured up his memory. Things like my oboe. The day after we arrived I told Mum to sell it.

She didn't want to. "You'll regret it later, I promise you, Heather. Look what happened with me. I'd give anything now to have kept up my piano lessons."

But I was deaf to her arguments. Now that Dad wasn't around to force me to practice I was sure I wasn't ever going to play the oboe again.

Since Fiona followed my lead in most things, she decided she didn't want to keep her flute either. Eventually Mum gave in and took them both to a music shop in the West End where she got cash for them, which came in handy to feed and clothe us. The expense of looking after two growing girls must have come as a big shock. Mum had a paid job now at the Royal Marsden Hospital, counseling cancer patients, so she wasn't as hard up as before, but Charles was temporarily out of work. For the past year or two he'd been appearing as Professor Higgins in *My Fair Lady,* but that had now closed and he was faced with doing touring theater productions, which not only paid badly but required him to spend money on digs. It meant that between them they didn't have a lot of cash to spare. In any case Charles had already paid to bring up four of his own children so the prospect of feeding another two mouths can hardly have gladdened his heart.

Not long after we arrived Fiona and I were enrolled at Hydeburn School, a big comprehensive one stop down the Northern Line. I hadn't been blissfully happy at Usworth school but I absolutely loathed Hydeburn. There was no indoor swimming pool like there was at Usworth, no running track, and no grass tennis courts. On top of that the other pupils were streetwise and tough. Kids always pick on newcomers who don't fit in, and I didn't fit in at all. Most of the girls in my class were skinny and black with strong South London accents. I was white, with long blond hair, big boobs, and spoke in broad Geordie. On top of that I was better at basketball than them. They hated me. Soon I couldn't walk through the corridor without someone jabbing me in the ribs with their elbow or sticking out a foot to trip me up.

One girl in particular had it in for me. Lizzie was on the basketball team, and my big mistake was to knock the ball out of her hand during a game. It was a legal move as long as you didn't make contact with the body—which I didn't—but Lizzie threw an absolute fit. After the game the rest of her team came up to me in the changing rooms and said, "You'd better watch out. Lizzie's going to beat you up at Balham station." I couldn't chicken out and walk home so I decided to brazen it out. The trouble was I wasn't dressed for a fight. The uniform rules were lax at Hydeburn and, although I had my black school trousers on, I was wearing them with high heels. As I walked onto the platform I saw Lizzie waiting for me with a big grin on her face. A bunch of her friends stood behind her.

*Oh, my God, I can't fight in these,* I thought. *I've got to put my trainers on.* I reached into my kitbag and started to change my shoes. I had one trainer on and one trainer off when Lizzie came at me. She had really long nails and she just marched up to me and stuck them in my face.

It was the worst thing she could have done. If she'd tried to kick me or punch me I might have backed off, but at the thought of my face being scratched I went absolutely nuts. I was so vain because of all the trouble I'd had with my acne. Now that I'd finally got my complexion looking good with creams and vitamins, Lizzie was threatening to undo it all.

I don't remember how it happened but suddenly I found myself on top of her. Her nose was bleeding and she was crying and I was smashing into her with my fists. A moment later, all her friends were laying into me, kicking and pulling my hair. But my blood was up.

"Get off me!" I yelled and they all stepped back.

I got up slowly; then, as I stood on the platform enjoying my moment of glory, my trousers fell down. Everyone, apart from Lizzie, who was still clutching her nose, fell about laughing. I only had a little pair of black knickers on underneath.

"Oh, my God, has anyone got a safety pin?" I asked. One of the girls smiled and handed me a safety pin; I knew I was in.

After that, because I'd beaten up the hardest girl in the year, things were different at school. Now instead of being given the elbow, I was greeted with, "Yo, Heather! How're you doing?"

I decided to change my image. If the girls at school thought I was hard then I'd better look hard. I had my long hair cut really short, then I got Fiona to bleach it chalk white and dye a burgundy border all around the sides. I held two plastic rulers against my head while she painted the line with a paintbrush. When it was finished Fiona got me to do hers to match. When he saw it Charles went off the deep end.

"They look like a pair of skunks," he said to Mum. "For God's sake don't let any of my friends see them."

Mum's only reaction was to suggest that perhaps we might tone down the color a bit. But Charles's attitude made us determined to stick with it and every few weeks we'd touch up each other's roots. When we went to get it trimmed the hairdresser couldn't believe we'd done it ourselves—we'd made such a straight line between the burgundy and the white. It was very important to me that it *was* straight. One quality of Dad's that had rubbed off on me was his perfectionism. I hated things to look amateurish.

On the surface I must have seemed to be adapting well to life in London, but underneath I wasn't happy at all. Things weren't working out at home. Charles and Mum were having lots of rows. I'd never heard them argue when we'd come down on holiday visits, but now they seemed to quarrel all the time. I knew I was the cause of most of the rows. I'd been looking forward to some freedom when Dad wasn't around, but to my annoyance I found Charles wanted to know all my movements. When I went off roaming the streets in the evenings, it didn't go down well at all.

I felt Charles treated me like a kid. Although I was only thirteen, I didn't feel like a kid. For the past five years I'd been cooking, washing, and keeping house for four people. Now I found myself being spoken to as if I couldn't make a decision for myself. I resented it and I let it show. When Charles told me to be in by seven o'clock at night I'd get in at seven-thirty just to make a point. It drove him mad.

It didn't bother me too much that Charles disliked us being there, but I worried that secretly Mum might hate it too. After all, she'd made a new life for herself and when we descended on her it had changed dramatically. All in all it wasn't a happy time. I was terribly homesick. I missed the North and the Geordie accent, I missed Shane, and most of all I missed my friends. Every day I dreamed of going back to Washington. Ironically it was Charles who caused my dreams to come true.

Charles hadn't been feeling well for some time. When he went to hospital for tests the doctors discovered stomach cancer. For my mother it was all too similar to what had happened with her mother. I'm sure she felt somehow responsible for his illness. Charles had been going on about the stress we'd caused him.

But every cloud has a silver lining: For Fiona and me the good news was that we were being sent back to Washington for the school holidays to stay with an old school friend while Charles received hospital treatment. We had a wonderful time, but sending me to the Richardsons proved to be the worst thing Mum could have done because it gave me a tempting taste of independence.

When Charles was discharged from hospital we were recalled to London. But now when Charles started to lay down rules again I totally rebelled. If he was in the house I just wanted to be out. There was a fair on Clapham Common and I started to hang around there in the evenings and on weekends. The rides were expensive and I could go through the pocket money Mum gave me in one night; but the fairground people were friendly and didn't mind me being there, even when I had nothing to spend. I got to know a bloke called Peter who worked on the twister, a gentle quiet man in his twenties with long brown hair and lovely blue eyes. Peter would always give me a hot dog or a candy floss if I was hungry and I used to stop by to see him three or four times a week.

Charles didn't like me spending so much time at the fair, but he was still recuperating and seemed to have decided it wasn't worth the hassle of arguing with me, so he mostly left me to my own devices. It was what I'd thought I wanted but still I wasn't happy. I felt left out. Mum was at work most of the day and when she came home her attention was focused on Charles. There was no denying it: I was jealous. For five years I'd been deprived of Mum's attention and I wanted it. Why should he get it?

I wanted so much to feel close to her but there was a barrier between us. Neither of us was even able to put our arms around each other. The only time the barrier ever came down was one night when Charles was away and I asked Mum if I could spend the night in her bed. To my surprise, when I got into bed with her and lay on my side she put her arm around me and cuddled me. A lump came up in my throat. This was how I wanted to feel—warm and loved. Why couldn't Mum and I stay like this? Why did *he* have to come back and spoil things?

When Charles did return the atmosphere in the house became even worse. Charles and Mum argued continually, mostly about Fiona, whom Charles said I was leading astray. Unlike Dad, Charles didn't get violent when he was annoyed. Being an actor, however, meant he could use words to great effect and Mum often ended up in tears. But the trouble with Mum was that she wouldn't defend herself. She was just as passive when Charles lost his temper with her as she'd been with Dad; for the first time I realized how irritating that could be. In my opinion Mum was just too Christian. Turning the other cheek was all very well in theory, but in practice it just made people get even crosser. I knew one thing. If any man said horrible things to me when I grew up I wouldn't behave like her: I'd give as good as I got.

Mum was still working full time. Some days when she came home tired from work and had to face a new problem at home, she looked so exhausted and unhappy it reminded me of the bad old days in Washington. But in London Mum had found a new way of coping with life's stresses. When she'd been living with Dad I'd hardly ever seen Mum have a drink, but now she always kept a bottle of Glenmorangie handy in the kitchen and most evenings she'd get through several generous measures.

One off-license, on Cavendish Parade, became like a second home to us. It was owned by Sam and his partner Gill. They were lovely, happy people who reminded me of Julia's family back in Lambton. I made friends with Gill's daughter Toni, who was a few years older than me, and soon Fiona and I were being invited back to their flat. Mum often used to join us there and would gossip with Gill over a glass of whisky. I think she felt the same attraction as us. Gill's flat had the sort of calm relaxed atmosphere we'd all have liked to have at our home. By now, though, I'd accepted it was an impossibility.

What made it harder to bear was the fact that Shane was really enjoying himself. I used to catch the train down to Brighton sometimes to see him on weekends. All Shane's wishes had come true. He'd left school, taken a job as a waiter in the Old Ship Hotel in Brighton, and was playing in a local brass band. That Christmas his band played on the promenade outside the Brighton Centre so Fiona and I went down to watch and stood in the freezing cold for two hours. I really wished I could go and live in Brighton with him and Grandma. I loved it there. I still had fond memories of walking along the beach with Grandad. But I knew there wasn't room for two kids in Grandma's little flat and anyway pride wouldn't let me ask Grandma to rescue me. I didn't like begging other people for help. I'd always preferred to deal with my own problems rather than talking about them to other people. I had a need to be self-reliant, to cope by myself with what life presented.

But by now there was so much simmering under the surface at home that it was like living on top of a volcano. And just like a volcano, when it finally exploded it took me by surprise. One night I took Fiona with me to the fair. Our curfew was seven-thirty and Fiona went home on the dot, but I stayed on chatting to Peter and lost track of time. It was very dark and I was standing near the twister still chatting when suddenly I looked up and saw Mum and Charles coming toward me across the grass. I hardly recognized

Mum. She looked like a ghost figure. Her hair was down as if she was ready for bed and she had her big blue coat on, which was swinging open. Underneath, I could see her dressing gown.

"Oh, Heather. We've been really worried about you," she said. "Why on earth didn't you come home with Fiona?"

Charles didn't wait for me to answer. "Where on earth have you been?" he demanded. "What sort of time do you call this?" He sounded just like Dad.

Something snapped. "You're not my father!" I yelled at him. "You can't tell me what to do."

His face was livid. "This is the icing on the cake, young lady." He turned to Mum. "That's it. I've had enough of your flaming kids. Either she goes or I go."

I went cold inside when he said that. I didn't say another word but as soon as we got home I went up to my room and took all my clothes off their hangers. Then I packed them into a bin liner. I wasn't going to wait for Mum to choose between Charles and me. I knew she was bound to choose Charles. So I would make the decision for her. I was seething with rebellion: against school, against life, against everything. I was fed up with being treated like a kid; of having other people trying to run my life. I wanted freedom.

The solution lay on my doorstep.

# Chapter 8

*I* ran away from home just a few weeks before my fourteenth birthday, though in the end I didn't so much run as walk out. When I told Mum what I was doing she gave me her blessing. I felt a bit put out that she didn't try to stop me, but I knew she had no option if she wanted to keep Charles. Fiona wasn't happy. When I told her what I was doing she went very quiet, but I was too wrapped up in my own feelings to realize she felt I was deserting her.

My new home was a tiny caravan at Freddie Gray's fair on Clapham Common. I'd managed to talk Dorothy, the lady who ran the candy-floss stall, into finding me a job making tea and cleaning the carousel horses and spinning the waltzers. My age wasn't a problem. The fair had a big turnover of staff and no one asked too many questions. In return for working seven days a week, I got my keep, my caravan, and £30 pocket money.

The work was hard, with long hours. The fair didn't shut till midnight and, after a night spinning the waltzers, I had to get up the next morning at dawn to make the tea and take it to all the people who worked in our area. Afterward, I'd help Peter oil the cars and make sure they were all working properly. Sometimes I had to clean them up because people had been sick on them. "Your fault," Peter would say. "Don't spin the cars so hard." When the waltzers were prepared to Peter's satisfaction, I'd open tins of hot dogs ready for the evening, set up the sugar in the candy-floss machines, and get apples out of the crates and coat them with toffee. I was a gofer, at everybody's beck and call, but I didn't mind. I'd never been work-shy. As far as I was concerned my new independence made it well worth being a dogsbody.

I loved my little caravan, even though there was hardly room to turn around once I got out of bed. The important thing was that it was mine. It was the first place I'd lived where I felt that. Each week I spent my wages on bits and pieces to brighten it up and turn it into my own private den. I'd taken Dad's duck-down sleeping bag with me, but with my first pay-packet I went out and bought a duvet and a pretty blue-and-white-striped cover. The second week I bought some scented candles and joss sticks to make it smell nice. On my third payday I bought myself a cheap personal stereo—I'd left Dad's behind—so I could listen to music in bed at night.

The food at the fair wasn't up to Mum's standard. Most of the time I ate leftover hot dogs and hamburgers. I'd always had a sweet tooth and I couldn't resist the candy floss and sweets on sale in the booths, but to compensate I swallowed every vitamin under the sun. They became like a religion to me and I spent every spare penny at the health food shop. It was as if I thought with the right vitamins everything in my life would get better—my skin would be clear, I'd be happy and healthy and in charge of my destiny.

I was a real lad while I was on the fair, always dressed in jeans and denim jacket with my hair stuffed away inside a baseball cap. I did everything I could to disguise my femininity. My big boobs were the only giveaway. They were the bane of my life and if I could have chopped them off I would have. Although I'd had a few snogging sessions in the Washington discos, I was really an innocent as far as boys were concerned and I had no wish to grow up in that way yet. I had enough on my plate as it was. I really loved Peter, my kindly friend on the waltzers, but only as a brother. Luckily, Peter seemed to sense the way I felt, because although we spent a lot of time together he never made sexual advances to me.

To me, living on the fair was like being born again. I'd broken all connections with home—I never went to see Mum and she didn't try to make contact with me. I bumped into Fiona just once, when I called in at Gill and Toni's off-license to buy some Mr Kipling French Fancies for my tea one Saturday afternoon. I hardly recognized her. She was a complete punk. She'd dyed her hair black, wore chalk-white makeup and all-black clothes. She also told me she'd become a vegetarian. She behaved quite coolly toward me and informed me she was going around with a new friend, Martha, now. *So I don't need* you *anymore* is what she meant, I knew. I hardened my heart. If I was going to be independent, I couldn't afford to feel guilty about Fiona. I allowed myself only one worry these days—that the truant officer might catch up with me. I was supposed to stay at school for at least two more years so I was sure they'd be out looking for me. In fact my fears were needless. Mum had told Hydeburn School that I was carrying on with my education privately.

The fair traveled on a circuit around the commons of South London: Tooting Bec, Morden, Mitcham, Cheam, and several others, moving on every two or three weeks. As the weather got warmer I used to wander across the commons in the afternoon before the fair opened listening to my personal stereo. I enjoyed that time to myself. I liked being with my mates at the fair but it was nice to have space and time to think. It didn't occur to me it was dangerous to go around on my own until the day two black guys jumped on me, slashed my face with a broken bottle, and stole my personal stereo. I ran back to my caravan in shock, with blood all down my T-shirt. Peter wanted to take me to casualty to be stitched but I was terrified of any contact with the authorities. At the fair I was anonymous and safe. A hospital might pass my details on to the police. Other people from the fair crowded into my van and were as angry as if I'd been one of their own family. I was so touched by their concern, I almost forgot the pain. To me the fair and Peter were my family now.

Standing on my own two feet did me good. After six months as part of that small community, my whole personality had changed. I wasn't rebellious or moody anymore but self-confident and contented. I really believed I'd taken control of my life.

But the sad truth is you can't ever control life. The unexpected will always come along to knock you sideways. The debacle happened one Saturday morning when the fair was pitched in Barnet.

Every day without fail, Peter used to wake me up to oil up the waltzers. But that morning I woke and realized it was already light. I went around to his van and hammered on his door but there was no answer. When I asked the two men from the van next to his they said they hadn't seen him that morning but he'd been there the night before because his light had been on till the early hours. As time wore on everyone on the fair started to get worried and in the end they hammered his door down.

We found him lying on his bed with a hypodermic needle stuck in his arm. His face was white as a sheet and he was very still. I knew straightaway he was dead.

"Heroin," the ambulancemen informed us when they came to take him away. "Overdose."

All my illusions were shattered. Peter had been my best friend. We'd shared our deepest secrets. I thought I'd known him better than anyone in the world. But I'd been kidding myself. I hadn't known him at all. I hadn't even known he took drugs.

"Heather, you'd better go back to your caravan," said one of the blokes who'd broken down the door. "The police'll be here in a minute. It's better if you don't get involved." Numbly I went back to my van and sat there while Peter's body was loaded into the ambulance. Then, when the police had finished interviewing everybody, I stuffed all my things into a black bin liner and took off.

I had no idea where I was heading, but every instinct in my body was telling me to run. I went into High Barnet tube station and got on a train. I couldn't think straight. I wanted my mum. I felt somehow she would make everything all right but as the train got closer to Clapham I came to my senses. I couldn't go back to Cavendish Road. No way could I run back to Charles and Mum with my tail between my legs. Devastated as I was, I had too much pride for that.

As the tube train pulled into Waterloo Station I suddenly remembered a young Liverpool kid who worked at the fair talking about the arches at Waterloo. He'd told me he spent three weeks there once and that loads of people slept under them. That was my answer. I got out, asked a porter where to go, and five minutes later arrived at my destination. As lodgings the arches weren't exactly inviting. They were dark and damp and the ground underneath them was littered with broken glass. But the stories Keith had told me were true. Every archway was sheltering people, some huddling around small makeshift fires, some sitting and staring into space, some still sleeping in the cardboard boxes they used as beds. I stared in dismay. *I need a cardboard box,* I thought. *I don't have one.* I was so naive. I thought they wouldn't let me in without a cardboard box.

Then inspiration hit me. I caught the tube back to Clapham South and walked to Gill and Toni's off-license.

"Have you got one of those big Pampers nappy boxes?" I asked.

Gill grinned. "What on earth do you want one of those for?"

"Oh, just to store some stuff on the fair."

Unsuspectingly, she went out to the storeroom and came back with a huge flattened box. I took it back on the tube to Waterloo, found a vacant patch of ground under an arch, unrolled Dad's sleeping bag inside my box, and settled down.

It was easier than I expected. No one challenged me or asked what I was doing there. The only entrance requirement seemed to be that you were desperate enough to want to sleep on the street. A scruffy-looking man with wonderful blue eyes offered me an apple. I hadn't eaten since the night before and I took it gratefully. Someone else held out a cigarette and although I rarely smoked I took that too. I was surprised by the community spirit. I had the same feeling that people were looking out for each other as I'd had at the fair.

Over the next few weeks I made loads of friends. My neighbors under the arches came from all sorts of backgrounds. Some, like the man with blue eyes, were businessmen who'd gone bankrupt, others were men whose wives and kids had left them and they hadn't been able to cope. Some had had nervous breakdowns, and some had just given up on life. There were alcoholics and meths drinkers; there were young kids from up north; there were youngsters who'd come from good families but had just rebelled against their background. On the fringes, drifting in and out, a night here, a night there, there were rent boys and prostitutes.

It was a rowdy place to live and most nights there'd be a fight somewhere down the line. I wasn't frightened—I'd never been physically frightened of anyone in my life except Dad—but I kept myself to myself and didn't talk to the others about why I was there. Even though most people were nice to me I didn't really feel I fitted in. From the first morning when I woke, cold and stiff inside my Pampers box, I knew this wasn't going to be a permanent solution to my problems.

Even so I lived under the arches for nearly four months. It took that long for the gloom about Peter to lift—for ages I couldn't bring myself to mention his name—and for me to see a way forward. I had a phobia about drugs now and I avoided the Waterloo druggies like the plague. The mere sight of a syringe on the ground was enough to make me pick up my box and bin liner and send me scuttling into the next archway.

I avoided the beggars too. It really pissed me off to see people holding their hands out and hassling passersby in the street as if the world owed them a living. Up till now I'd muddled through life without much of a philosophy. Under the arches, I thought about things like independence and self-reliance for the first time. These people are wrong, I thought. However poor you are the world doesn't owe you a living. You have to *earn* your living, even if that means cleaning people's windscreens at traffic lights or playing the violin in subways. Unless you were so disabled you couldn't work why should people give you money? You didn't see the real tramps of London begging. They had too much pride. If you went up to them and gave them a tenner they'd be insulted and tell you to go away. And that was how it should be.

My days started to fall into a routine. I'd wake between six and seven, wander around to one of the soup kitchens near the bridge for a cup of tea, then set off for the West End where I'd spend the day window-shopping in Oxford Street and looking for work. No one offered me a job. People knew I was homeless. It was hard to know what gave it away. It wasn't the black bin liner I trailed behind me everywhere because I soon saw that put people off and left it around the corner while I was being interviewed. And I wasn't dirty—I used to wash religiously in Victoria Station ladies' room every morning. But when you don't have a mirror and you sleep in the same clothes that you wear all day, it shows. It took me a while to realize that.

To start with, feeding myself wasn't a problem. I had some money saved from the fair and the other people under the arches were generous. Every day complete strangers would come up and offer me food and cigarettes and anyone who had anything would share it. It made a real impression. When people had plenty it was surprising how stingy they could be, but these people who had nothing would share their last tin of beans with you.

Shared tins of beans couldn't fill my stomach, though, nor could the soup kitchens—they only opened for limited hours—and after six weeks I started to get really hungry. My wages from the fair had run out and I couldn't claim the dole because I was only fourteen. Since begging was out of the question I revived my shoplifting skills. My personal morality didn't yet forbid shoplifting. I'd never thought much about the rights and wrongs involved and I couldn't afford to start now. If I'd been challenged, I'd have just shrugged and said, "They can afford it." To me, pinching things from supermarkets wasn't like stealing from real people.

I was an expert fare dodger too and whenever my cardboard box got damp or fell apart I'd pick up my black bin liner and take the tube back to Clapham to beg another box from Gill and Toni. In the end that was my undoing, or looked at in another way, my salvation. Gill and Toni still thought I was working on the fair and I hadn't disillusioned them. They used to tease me about my bin liner and call me the bin lady but they never guessed why I had to carry everything around with me. They were very good to me and used to give me something to eat whenever I called in.

"To make up for all the junk food you're eating at the fair," Gill would cluck.

One Sunday, I plucked up courage to ask if I could have a bath at their place. Up till then I'd been going to the ladies' at Victoria Station to have a shower, but it cost 10p and I was broke.

Gill looked at me suspiciously and I realized how dirty my clothes were. My hair needed a wash too.

"Heather, what's wrong?" she demanded. "Why can't you have a wash at the fair?" Four months of waking to the smell of rotting vegetables and other people's BO had weakened my resolve and I confessed my secret.

They were horrified. "That's ridiculous. You can't live there. You'll get murdered!" said Toni.

"Why don't you go back to your mum's?" Gill coaxed.

"No way!" I wouldn't even consider it.

"Well then, you'll just have to come around and stay at ours," Toni said. "Won't she, Mum?"

Gill nodded. "No arguing, Heather. I'd never forgive myself if anything happened to you in that place. Come on. Let's go."

They marched me around to their flat where Toni ran my first bath in months and poured in half a bottle of bath oil. While I lay back and let the Waterloo grime soak away, Gill peeled extra vegetables to go with the Sunday roast.

When I came out of the bathroom Toni handed me her dressing gown. "Here, put this on," she ordered. "I've put all that stuff in your bin liner in the washing machine. I'd half a mind to burn it."

An hour later, bursting with roast beef and Yorkshire pudding, I allowed Gill to make me up the spare bed in Toni's room. I didn't have the energy to argue. I didn't want to be dependent on anyone, but the nights were getting colder and I didn't know how much longer I could keep going. In any case I didn't want to stay under the arches forever. They'd been a stopgap for me to sort my head out and get over Peter, but I wanted more out of life than just to drift and pinch things. I wanted to earn my living, to get some money. But I was smart enough now to know I couldn't earn money with no fixed address. Gratefully, I accepted Gill's offer.

A week later I heard about a Saturday job at a jeweler's shop down the road from Sam and Gill's. I really wanted full-time work but as I was still supposed to be at school, I didn't dare apply for any. A Saturday job was better than nothing and would let me pay Gill something toward my keep. I went for an interview and the owner, a short fat man who drove a Rolls-Royce, said I could start the following weekend. My duties would be selling jewelry and helping to set up the window each morning—it was emptied at night to deter thieves.

I knew Gill was concerned about me, but I hadn't anticipated that she'd tell Mum I was living with her now. I was really upset when I found out—I desperately wanted Mum and Charles to think I was standing on my own two feet—but I couldn't be cross after all Gill had done for me.

Fiona was stacking shelves at the off-license in the evenings now and one evening she arrived with an invitation.

"Mum wants you to come around on Saturday for something to eat," she said.

I was dubious. "What about Charles?"

"He won't be there," Fiona assured me. "He's touring."

I still didn't want to go—I felt my independence was under threat—but Gill talked me around. On Saturday, I walked around the corner from Gill and Toni's and knocked nervously on the door of Norman's house.

Mum answered the door looking cool and collected. "Hello, Heather. How are you?" She smiled. "Come on in." For all her reaction I might have been away for a week's holiday. She'd cooked me my favorite supper of fish poached in milk with mashed potato and peas, and I devoured it. While I was eating, Norman came in and gave me a big hug. He seemed to think I'd been up north. When he'd gone I hesitantly told Mum what I'd been doing since I left. She listened politely, but I felt I was talking to some distant aunt rather than to my mother. With all that had happened it didn't surprise me. Actually, in many ways it suited me. I certainly didn't want Mum telling me what to do. It would have been nice if she'd been emotional about our reunion, but it was enough that we were talking to each other again. I hadn't admitted it to myself but our estrangement had been nagging at me like a toothache the whole time I'd been away. Perhaps, after all, I reflected, blood was thicker than water.

After the ice had been broken I started going back regularly to Cavendish Road and even spending nights there.

I never visited Mum if I knew Charles was going to be there. I'd grown out of my childish jealousy but to avoid opening up old wounds I'd decided it was better to stay out of his life. While Charles was touring the provinces in *Arms and the Man* he rarely came home and I was soon splitting my time equally between Gill's flat and Mum's. Fortunately Gill and Toni were tolerant and put up with my toing and froing without complaint.

It was while I was spending a night at Cavendish Road that I learned that Dad had been released from prison. Mum told me he'd been let out six months early for "good behavior."

"He says he wants to see you all again," she said.

Fiona and Shane had refused to go up and see him, but I was really torn. I was desperate to see Washington and Newcastle again and I was also curious to see if Dad had changed. I had the naive idea that prison might have transformed him. I decided to go up for a week to test the waters. If things worked out I thought I might even stay.

It wasn't a good idea. Dad hadn't changed at all. Instead he spent the whole time ordering me around. It was a recipe for disaster because I *had* changed.

"What was it like in prison, Dad?" I asked one night.

"I haven't been to *prison,* Heather," he said. "I've been on an open farm *and* I had the best job there. I ran the library. I was in charge of everything, so I could study all the time."

"Well, that's funny. The police told us you were sent to *prison,*" I said.

I'd never cheeked him before. In a flash he'd grabbed my hair and slammed me against the wall. "Don't try and get clever with me, Heather. You're still only fifteen. Don't you forget it."

My head was spinning but I wasn't afraid. I'd seen a lot of life since Dad had been sent to prison. *I don't need to take this,* I thought. I rang Mum to tell her I was coming back and that afternoon I caught the Clipper to Victoria.

Back in Clapham I spent the weekdays cooling my heels. I was bored, but there was never any question of me returning to school. I'd missed too much now to catch up even if I'd wanted to. The trouble was I couldn't work full time because I still wasn't old enough, so until I was sixteen and could get my P45 I had to be content with my Saturday job. It was all right, but the money wasn't great. I was desperate to earn more so I could stand on my own two feet. Gill and Toni were wonderful to me but I hated being in their debt. I hated being in Charles's and Mum's debt even more.

The solution was presented to me on a plate. For the past few months watches and rings had been going missing in the jeweler's shop. It happened often enough for the owner, Mr. Penrose, to start making accusations. There were three other assistants working there, all male. I never saw any of them take anything, but since it wasn't me it had to be one of them. But Mr. Penrose saw it differently. In his eyes, because I was the Saturday girl, I was the prime suspect, and he dropped heavy hints every time something disappeared.

One Saturday he discovered a Rolex watch had vanished and all morning he kept insinuating that I knew something about it, until I was really fed up.

"Exactly *when* do you last remember seeing the watch, Heather?" he grilled me. "How are you so sure of the time? You seem to have a very good memory for someone who doesn't go to school."

Something inside me snapped when he said that. Mr. Penrose only paid me £2 an hour and I was really broke that day. Well, I thought, if he thinks I'm doing it I might as well *do* it. When the other assistants went for lunch I said I wasn't hungry and would work through my lunch hour. I waited till Mr. Penrose nipped out to go to the loo, then I reached into the drawer where the gold chains were kept, grabbed a black velvet roll, and stuffed it in my shoulder bag. I had to wait until I went home that evening to find out what I'd won in my lucky dip.

When I locked the door of my room and opened the roll out on the bed my heart nearly stopped. Glittering up at me from the black velvet were literally hundreds of gold chains. I suppose I'd expected about ten. Oh, my God, I thought. But what could I do? I could hardly take them back and say there'd been a mistake.

On Monday morning I caught a bus up to Streatham, wandered up the main street, and walked into the first jeweler's I saw.

"Do you want to buy these?" I asked the man behind the counter. He undid the roll, took a quick look, and peered suspiciously at me over his glasses.

"Where did you get these from, young lady?"

"They're not mine. I'm selling them for someone else," I said.

He grunted and I knew he didn't believe me. For a moment I thought he was going to call the police. What if he had a panic button under his counter? But his hands stayed on the chains, fingering them expertly as he examined the hallmarks. Suddenly he wound the roll back up and walked to the till.

"I'll give you a grand, no more. All right?"

I'd expected a hundred pounds, maybe two. Struck dumb, I nodded and he counted out the money in £50 notes. I reached out for it, but he lifted his hand.

"Not so fast." He scribbled something on a notepad. "I need a receipt to show where I got them from. You'll have to sign it." He pushed the pad toward me and, drunk with the sight of all the money, I scribbled *Heather Mills.* Too late, I realized my mistake. How could I have been so thick?

"Where do you live?" he asked.

I wasn't going to be caught twice. I said the first address that came into my head. "Number Seven, Davies Mews, W1." It was the address of a hairdresser's where I'd had a really disgusting haircut the week before. He raised his eyebrows skeptically but he wrote it down.

He pushed the money over and I grabbed it, shoved it into my handbag, and shot out of the shop like a frightened rabbit before he could change his mind.

A thousand pounds! I felt drunk with the very thought of it. It was like winning the pools. What on earth could I spend it on? On the way back to the bus stop I passed a motorbike shop and something clicked. That was it! I would buy myself a moped. I'd always dreamed of having my own transport instead of having to rely on tubes or buses.

There was another bike shop next door to Toni and Gill's on Cavendish Parade and there, two days later, I found the moped of my dreams, a bright yellow creation. It cost me £350, and the red crash helmet I bought to go with it cost almost as much again. When the shop assistants saw my wad of £50 notes they didn't even stop to ask how old I was. One of the mechanics showed me how to use the controls, sold me some L-plates, and I wobbled off down the road and parked it in the driveway outside Gill and Toni's house. I kept it there for the next month. By now I was living a pretty independent life on the top floor in Norman's house, going in and out as I pleased, and I don't think Mum even realized that I had a scooter. If she did she decided it was safer not to ask where it had come from.

The rest of the money was burning a hole in my pocket and over the next few weeks I went through all of it, down to the last penny. What I didn't spend on clothes, makeup, and beauty treatments, I spent on taking Fiona and her new friend Martha to Freddie Gray's fair, which had just reappeared on Tooting Bec. I knew I was living on borrowed time but I bluffed it out. I even carried on working at Mr. Penrose's shop on Saturdays since I was smart enough to realize that not turning up would have been as good as admitting my guilt. Of course, Mr. Penrose asked me about the missing chains and, of course, I looked innocent and denied all knowledge. He shrugged. "Well, it doesn't matter. We'll find out sooner or later. This time I've called the police in."

*God, what have I done?* I thought.

To make matters worse Mr. Penrose started to be really nice to me. I told myself it was a ploy, that he was only trying to get me to confess, but it made me feel even more guilty.

To compensate for the guilt, though, there were new pleasures in my life. Riding my moped liberated me. I used it to tour all around London seeing the sights. Soon, I knew the city as well as any black-cab driver. The trouble with the moped was it was always breaking down. Fortunately, it was still under guarantee, so wherever it packed up on me I could ring the bike shop to come and pick it up in their van. The shop was next door to Sam and Gill's off-license and they used to poke fun at me when I got out of the garage van with this big red helmet on my head. I refused to take it off because I didn't want anyone to see the terrible haircut I'd had, especially not the nice-looking garage mechanic . . .

My days of wanting to be one of the lads were over. I was getting really conscious of men now. Unfortunately, my skin was still causing me a lot of heartache. To help clear it up I started having sunbed sessions again. The sun parlor also did beauty treatments and I soon discovered the joys of facials, leg waxes, massages, and eyelash tints. It ate away at the remains of my gold-chain money but it was worth it. When it was time to apply for a real job I knew my appearance would be important.

The acne I'd suffered from in Washington had left me with some bad scars and one day I read in the *Evening Standard* about an expensive deep-peel treatment called a chemopeel. I blew the last of my money on it. The treatment involved being smeared with a gel that dried into a transparent film and had to be left on for three days—I came home looking like a shrink-wrapped prune. At seven o'clock the next morning, Saturday, I was lying in bed wondering how I was going to explain my appearance to Mr. Penrose when there was a loud knocking on the front door. I heard Mum open it, then there were heavy footsteps on the stairs, and the next moment the door burst open and three men crowded into my room. One of them was wearing a police uniform, but it was another man who flashed an ID card at me.

"Heather Mills? You're under arrest. Get dressed and come with us."

They waited outside while I dressed. I kept hoping Mum would appear, but she stayed downstairs. I could hear her moving about in the kitchen. As they led me down the stairs, my face still all screwed up under this gel, she was waiting by the front door in her dressing gown. She opened it for us.

"I'll see you later," she said. There was no expression on her face.

I was taken down to Kennington police station near the Oval cricket ground. When I got there they let me ring Mum. "Are you coming down?" I asked.

Her voice was icy cold. "No, I'll come down tomorrow. I've got to cook Charles's dinner now."

I felt nervous then and very alone. I knew I'd done wrong and I knew too that this wasn't like pinching a pork chop or a bar of chocolate from Sainsbury's. It was serious. There were five policemen in the interrogation room and they were looking at me as if

I was a *criminal!* Unconsciously, my fingers went to my face and I started to pick at my expensive chemopeel treatment.

When they accused me of doing the jewelry theft I admitted it at once. There didn't seem much point in denying it when I'd signed for £1,000 at the jeweler's in Streatham. After I'd given my statement I thought they'd let me go, but instead they kept me overnight in a small cell with a tiny window and a couple of blankets. I hardly slept at all because they'd arrested some gypsies and one of them had been put in the cell next to me and was moaning all night. "I want me mam, get me mam." He sounded about thirteen and I felt really sorry for him. I couldn't believe my eyes the next morning when they led us out of our cells and the little boy turned out to be a big burly man of about thirty.

It was eleven o'clock before Mum came to fetch me and by that time there wasn't a trace of chemopeel treatment left on my face—I'd scraped it off with my fingernails. I spent the six weeks before the case came to court in a state of absolute terror. I was still only fifteen, so I knew they wouldn't send me to prison, but I could be put in care and the thought terrified me.

Fortunately, one of Charles's friends was a barrister. He agreed to represent me and in court he used the excuse that I'd had a bad childhood. It worked and they let me off on probation, which meant I had to report to a probation officer once a week.

I'd had a narrow escape and it brought me up short. Not only had I nearly lost my freedom, but I was tormented by guilt for betraying Mr. Penrose, who had been so nice to me. I'd behaved like an idiot. Pinching things, I realized, was going to bring me nothing but trouble. I resolved never to do it again.

# Chapter 9

There can't be many people who had their first orgasm in the Vauxhall South Bank Squash Club. It happened quite by accident when I was nearly sixteen. Indirectly, I suppose it was one of the rewards of my new lifestyle because one of the first things I did after deciding to "go straight" was to take up sport again. Since leaving Washington I'd hardly taken any exercise, but now, encouraged by Mum and by my probation officer, I started to run on Clapham Common and took up squash and tennis. Squash was a new game to me, but Anna, one of my mother's friends, offered to coach me and I soon became quite competent. The third time I went to the club I actually managed to win. Afterward Anna went for a shower but I didn't want to have one because I'd just washed my hair.

"Why don't you sit in the Jacuzzi instead?" Anna suggested, pointing to a bubbling tub in the corner of the changing area. In my innocence I didn't even know what a Jacuzzi was. But obediently I stepped in and settled down to wait for Anna. These days they don't have hot tubs where the bubbles go upward but they did then and the effect on my body was instantaneous. *Ooooooh! What* is *this?* I thought. People were strolling by at the other end of the changing rooms, but I was oblivious to them. I was oblivious to everything except this wonderful new sensation. I sat there completely hypnotized and moments later the earth under the South Bank Squash

Club moved. After that I went to the club every day for eight weeks. My mother thought I'd become a squash fanatic.

Hot tubs were one thing. Real sex was another and I was wary about "doing it." It wasn't that I didn't want to, but I knew that my first time had to be special. So far, I'd had a few casual boyfriends but hadn't yet met anyone nearly special enough.

Once I'd turned sixteen I didn't have much opportunity to go out with boys anyway, because I was working six days a week. Not long after my court case I saw a job advertised in the *Evening Standard* for an assistant in a croissant shop and the owner agreed to take me on. The shop was right outside Holborn tube station so did a very good trade. The pay wasn't good though and the uniform was worse—a horrible pink overall and a straw hat with a pink-and-blue ribbon around it. But the job carried one major perk. "You can eat as many croissants as you like," the owner promised the day I started. "Just help yourself."

The poor man didn't know what he was saying. After months of going hungry at the fair and under the arches, I could eat like a horse. Soon I was getting through fifteen croissants a day.

I really wasn't the ideal employee. Apart from scoffing the profits I rebelled against wearing the straw hat. I'd taken a liking to the guy who sold flowers on the stall next door and because the hat made me look about eight years old I was always taking it off. The boss never used to say "Good morning" to me, just, "Heather, get your hat on."

The hat can't have put the flower guy off too much because he invited me out to a disco. It was the first time I'd gone dancing since I'd been in London and it made me feel really nostalgic for the Ox Close disco. Dave and I had a good laugh and I let him kiss me but I knew he wasn't the special one either. He didn't take offense when I said no, and we went to a couple more discos and stayed friends.

My job lasted for four months until one morning my boss called me over and said, "You're eating too many croissants," and that was that. I wasn't too bothered. At sixteen I hadn't much ambition beyond keeping out of trouble. Makeup, clothes, and boys occupied most of my thoughts.

I also thought a lot about Washington. It was pulling on me like a magnet and while I was between jobs I decided to go back up to see Julia and my other school friends. The only problem was where to stay. I certainly didn't want to stay with Dad—I hadn't spoken to him since he'd hit me on my last visit—and I knew Julia didn't have room for me in her house. In the end I rang Andrea, another old school friend who lived near Julia, and her mother agreed to let me use their spare room for £10 a week. Intending to stay for about a month, I caught the Newcastle Clipper the next morning. As soon as I'd settled in at Andrea's house and unpacked my customary bin liner, I rang Julia.

"Hi. Guess who?"

"Heather!" she screamed. "Where are you?"

"About four doors away. Do you fancy going to a disco this weekend?"

"Great!" Julia had always been game to go dancing. "There's a new place in Washington called Miss Sirroco. Why don't you come around to mine to get ready?"

It was just like the old days, putting our makeup on in front of the mirror—Julia still used half a tube of foundation, I noticed—and fixing each other's hair.

"Brilliant." Julia admired the result. "Will we pass for eighteen d'you think?"

Tarted up in my black leather miniskirt and red silk shirt I'd have passed for twenty-one that night, never mind eighteen.

The disco was great and we danced nonstop all evening. Except for the couple of discos I'd been to with Dave, the lad from the flower shop, I hadn't had an evening like this for two years. Most of the time Julia and I danced with each other; I noticed that all the couples dancing around us were women too. Then I remembered that this was the way up here. When I was thirteen I'd never been much bothered about dancing with boys, but after all the trouble Julia and I had taken to doll ourselves up I felt a bit put out. It wasn't that there was a shortage of men in the club. There were plenty, but they stayed at the bar all night, drinking. Now and then one of them would stare across at the dance floor and give one of the women the eye but most of them seemed more interested in knocking back their Newcastle Brown.

"You wait," Julia said. "The disco closes at two. At ten to they'll think, *Bloody hell, I haven't got a woman to take home, man.* Watch what happens then."

Sure enough, ten minutes before closing time there was a mad scramble and half the blokes fell off their bar stools and lurched across the floor to try and "chat up a bird." I watched in disbelief as women smiled and flirted back. They just seemed to accept this way of behaving.

"I tell you what, if anyone comes up to me I'll bloody well tell them to get lost," I said to Julia. "Who do they think they are?"

She nudged me. "Looks like you're going to get your chance now."

I turned and saw a tall dark-haired man weaving his way across the dance floor.

"Hello, darling, aren't you smashing." He rocked backward and forward breathing beer fumes into my face. I drew myself up to my full height, all set to send him packing, then took a second look. There was something familiar about this guy. With a shock I realized that I was looking at Stephen Leyton. *The* Stephen Leyton whom I'd had the hots for when I was a spotty-faced eleven-year-old at the community disco. Stephen Leyton whom half the girls in my class at Usworth Comprehensive would have died for. He clearly didn't recognize me. Apart from the fact that he was drunk as a skunk he'd been seventeen when I'd had a crush on him and he'd obviously never noticed my existence.

He'd been skinnier in those days—the Newcastle Brown was giving him the beginnings of a potbelly—but in spite of that he was still absolutely gorgeous.

"Can I walk you home?" His smile made my knees go weak.

"I think I'd better walk *you* home," I told him.

I tucked my arm through his and guided him the two miles back to Andrea's house. Andrea's mum had given me a key and I slipped it into the lock. Then with my fingers to my lips, I guided him up the stairs and along the landing to my tiny box-room.

I'd never believed in fate till then, but I couldn't help feeling it was more than coincidence that led the man I'd always dreamed of sleeping with to be in the right place at the right time. By the time I smuggled him out of the house at dawn, I was in love. Hook, line, and sinker.

Over the next few days Steve and I began spending nearly all our time together. He was not just my first lover. He was a really nice guy. All I wanted was to be near him, and for the next two months I kept putting off my return to London.

It caused some problems. Because I was still on probation, social workers chased me up at Andrea's house, which was embarrassing. Then, as soon as I'd changed the arrangements so I could report to the probation office in Washington every week, my money ran out. I tried to look for a job locally, but it wasn't as easy as I expected. I applied for dozens of hairdressing, shop assistant, and office jobs but there were always about fifty other people queuing up with me to be interviewed. Unemployment was a way of life in Washington. In the end in desperation I registered on the dole. I hated the idea but I had to eat and pay the rent to Andrea's mother. I told myself it was just until I found a job. Four weeks later, as I was queuing up at the post office in the Washington Galleries to cash my unemployment benefit check, a hand suddenly clasped my shoulder. I turned and found my face inches from a bright yellow oilskin jacket. I gasped in absolute terror. I didn't need to look up to know who it was.

"Hi, Heather!" Dad's smile was friendly. "How are you? I thought you'd gone back to London." He spoke as if nothing had happened between us.

Instinct took over. I didn't stop to think. I felt like a small kid again and, like any kid caught where she shouldn't be, I ran. There was a rope barrier keeping the queue in line. I hopped over it and bolted.

"I think I'm going back to London," I told Stephen the next day.

He looked stunned. "Why? I thought we were okay together."

"We are." I hugged him. "We really are, but I've got to find a job, Steve. I can't stand being on the dole."

It was true, but I couldn't bring myself to tell him the other reason. That seeing Dad had unsettled me so much I hadn't been able to sleep the night before.

Stephen wasn't happy. "You're trying to say we're finished then. Is that it?"

"No, of course not. Don't be daft. We can still see each other. If I'm earning decent money I'll be able to come up here on weekends. You can come down and see me too." I was serious. Steve meant a lot to me.

But he wasn't convinced. "What sort of job are you looking for?"

I shrugged. "Anything. I don't mind." Except when I was eight and planning to be a plastic surgeon I'd never thought in terms of a career. I had no burning interest in any particular job. My only ambition was to earn money, because money—as I'd learned when I stole the gold chains, as I'd seen with Dad—gave you power. To me, money seemed the answer to all my problems. It always had. Years ago when we were living in Biddick and I was trying to feed four of us for a pound, I'd often lain in bed at night, dreaming what it would be like to be rich. I'd fly away, I promised myself. I'd go on holiday, buy clothes instead of borrowing them, eat whatever I liked. Above all, I'd be *happy.* Now, six years later, I still saw money as the cure-all.

Back in London and lodging again with Gill and Toni, I rang Sharie, a girl I'd met at the fair. She was out of work too and we went around looking for jobs together.

"There's a place in Old Compton Street that's advertising for hostesses." She winked. "Are you game?"

I didn't know what a hostess was but I didn't want to show myself up by admitting it.

"Does it pay well?" I asked.

"Brilliant," Sharie said. "I had a friend who used to do it and she came home loaded with cash every night. She said it was money for old rope."

That was all I needed to hear. I went along with her to Soho for an interview. Sharie was ten years older than me so was wise to what was required.

"They won't take you on if they think you're under eighteen," she warned before we set out. "Put a lot of makeup on and wear something sexy."

I slapped on some heavy red lipstick, black eyeliner, and dark gray eyeshadow and picked out the shortest skirt and lowest-cut top I had.

At the club a dark-haired foreign-looking man and a pretty blond girl invited us into the office.

"Right," the man said. "The hours are from eight till three. Your duties are to sit and talk to the customers."

I frowned. "Is that all?"

"Anything else is up to you," he said. "All *we* ask is that you talk to them."

I didn't have a clue what he was talking about. I was so naive. "Can't Sharie and I talk to each other?" I asked.

I saw a look pass between the man and woman, then the woman smiled.

"Would you like to work behind the bar?" she asked. "Perhaps that might suit you better."

I took her word for it and for the next month I worked in the wine bar situated below the club. The hours were long—often I'd do a whole day and a night without a break—but I enjoyed the job and worked hard at it. I was so keen to be a good employee that I'd do any odd jobs that were going. If the boss needed stationery for the office the other girls would all disappear into the woodwork but not me.

"I'll get it, I'll get it," I'd say and race down the street to Ryman.

But, good little girl that I was, I still didn't earn as much as Sharie. By the end of the month my eyes were well and truly opened as to what a hostess did. Sharie got £25 for every bottle of champagne she talked a customer into buying. In spite of what we'd been told at the interview, she'd expected pressure to go off and sleep with the men as well, but she said there wasn't any, though some of the girls did occasionally. But the police must have thought differently, because four weeks after we started work, the club was raided and closed down and I was out of work again. I'd earned enough money to go back to Newcastle though, so I enjoyed a snatched week with Steve before coming back to London to look for more work.

I'd quite enjoyed serving drinks. Chatting up customers from behind the safety of the bar was fun. I knew though that a job like Sharie's where you got commission or tips from the customers would bring better money, so I replied to an ad for a waitress at a nightclub near Oxford Circus. I changed my mind when I found that the waitresses at Bootleggers had to wear horrid little tutus that made me look even worse than the croissant shop's straw hat had.

"Can't I work behind the bar?" I begged. "I know what to do behind the bar."

The manager wasn't keen because they'd never had a woman behind the bar before. "Still, there has to be a first time for everything," he said. "We'll give you a trial."

Stupidly, I hadn't realized that a cocktail bar wasn't the same thing as a wine bar. I didn't know the first thing about cocktails, but somehow I bluffed my way through my first night. The next day I dashed to the library, found a cocktail recipe book, and put in three hours of intensive study. Within a week I was mixing Singapore Slings and Manhattans like an old hand. The pay was much better than in the wine bar, but I wasn't as rich as I'd hoped because I was still living at Gill and Toni's and the tube and taxi fares were taking up half my wages. I had a moan about it one day to the club's cloakroom attendant, a short Joan Collins look-alike called Gloria. She was sympathetic.

"Look here, darling, if you want somewhere to stay you can come and live at my place," she offered.

Gloria lived in a two-bedroom flat off the Roman Road in the East End. It was only a few minutes from the club and very convenient so I took her up on her offer and moved in the next day. I was really set up now and everything was looking rosy. Although I had to pay Gloria a tenner a week I would still be better off than when I was traveling to Clapham every day plus I had my independence again. I thought I might even be able to see Stephen every week instead of once a month. But the rug was about to be pulled out from under my feet. I'd conveniently forgotten to tell the club manager I was only sixteen. I thought I'd get away with it because I was expecting to be paid cash in hand like I'd been at the wine bar. But

Bootleggers liked everything to be aboveboard and my secret came out when they got hold of my P45 form.

"Sorry, Heather." The manager shook his head. "You made a good bartender. Come back when you're eighteen."

Yet again I had to start job hunting. Fortunately, Gloria had heard that her local sunbed salon was looking for an assistant and I spent the next three months putting out towels and wiping down the beds after use. It wasn't exactly riveting work, but it paid well and after two weeks I was able to buy a return train ticket for Stephen to come down and see me.

I didn't save any money apart from what I put aside each month for Stephen's train tickets. It was such a novelty to have a big wad of cash each week that I couldn't wait to spend it. I bought lots of leather gear—I was really into leather—and what was left I spent on beauty treatments. One of the perks of the job was that I got free sunbed sessions and I used to spend half an hour each day stripped off under the tubes. I felt better with a tan. It gave me a healthy glow and made my extra pounds less noticeable. I wasn't doing any sport now and I'd never really lost the weight I'd put on at the croissant shop. With my sweet tooth it wasn't surprising. I was going through a Cherry Bakewell Tart phase. Gloria used to nag me about it all the time.

"Mr Kipling'll be able to retire on what you spend. You eat far too much—*and* it's all the wrong sort of food."

She was like an old mother hen, but she was right. I never ate sensible things like fruit or vegetables; it was cakes and chocolates, cakes and chocolates all day long. Gloria's diet was much healthier—her fridge was full of salads and low-calorie drinks.

"When you're a model you have to watch what you eat," she confided one day.

I pricked up my ears. "I didn't know you were a model. What sort of model?"

She gave me a coy grin. "Glamour."

I was none the wiser. "What's that?"

She tutted despairingly. "Topless, darling." She laughed at my amazed look. "I've got a shoot on Saturday. You can come along if you like."

The shoot was in the East End in a big cold studio. When the photographer was ready Gloria took off her top, clipped on some earrings, and draped a string of horrible plastic beads around her neck. Then she twisted and turned in simpering schoolgirly poses while the photographer snapped away. I had to try hard not to laugh; they both seemed to be taking it very seriously.

When he'd finished, Gloria said to the photographer, "Do me a favor. Take a picture of Heather for me?" She found a tuxedo, swimsuit, and a top hat in a prop basket and got me to pose in front of a white sheet.

"You ought to be a model too, darling, with knockers like yours," she said. "Get them out! Don't hide them away. Let the world see them!"

"No thanks," I said. How could anyone want to be a model? It couldn't even pay that well or Gloria surely wouldn't have to work as a cloakroom attendant.

Over the next few months I went up to Newcastle every three to four weeks but it was difficult when I was working. I hardly got up there before I had to turn around and come back. It wasn't much better if Stephen came down to see me. He was working as a jig borer at a factory in Sunderland and had to be at work by seven on Monday morning. I not only missed cuddling up with Stephen, I missed having someone to talk to. However, Gloria was good company and during the time I shared her flat we became very close. She was generous toward me, seemed interested in my problems, and was happy to let Fiona come up to the flat to visit me. Fiona was still at school but unhappy because she wasn't getting on with Charles. As my friendship with Gloria grew I found myself telling her all about my past, not just about Mum and Dad's separation and Dad's prison sentence but even about stealing the gold chains and being put on probation.

"That's all behind me now," I told her. I really thought it was. But your past has a way of catching up on you.

About three months after I moved in with Gloria, she went on holiday. While she was away, one of her friends, a boy from across the road, invited Fiona and me to a party. Lance's parents were away and he'd decided to take advantage of it. About a hundred people turned up and during the course of the evening £400 belonging to his parents went missing from a cupboard. When his parents came home and discovered the theft they went spare. Lance was afraid to tell them he'd had a party so he said, "Well, the only people who've been here are Heather and Fiona."

His parents gave the police our names and of course when the police looked me up they found my record from the jewelry shop and arrested me. I was absolutely terrified. I knew that I wouldn't be given a second chance. If I was convicted I would be locked up and this time I hadn't even done anything wrong! When I rang her, Mum said she wanted nothing to do with it. She obviously believed I was guilty too. I suppose you could hardly blame her.

Fortunately, the case never went to court. When the police questioned him, Lance had to admit there'd been loads of people in the house and it could have been anybody. The police let me go without charging me but his parents still acted as if I'd done it and so did Lance. I was a dog with a bad name. I regretted taking those stupid chains more than ever. I realized now they could haunt me for the rest of my life.

The whole experience left me feeling very friendless and insecure. Afterward, sleeping alone in Gloria's flat, I desperately wanted to be with someone I could love and trust and who loved me. I wanted to be with Stephen: He was my one true friend. Admitting it to myself was all I needed and the next morning I started to pack my things. I should have started sooner. Gloria came back from holiday that day and walked through the door just as I was folding my leather gear into my trusty bin liner. Her face was like thunder.

"What the hell do you think you're doing, Heather?"

I tried to explain what had happened but she interrupted.

"How dare you?" she said. "How dare you? After all I did for you."

"I thought you'd told Lance about the chains," I said weakly.

"Damn the chains!" She flung my bin liner on the floor and came toward me, her eyes dark with anger. "I was in love with you. Didn't you know that?"

I sat down suddenly on the bed. Oh, God. What next? I'd had no idea. So that was why Gloria had always been so funny toward Stephen. Why hadn't I suspected? Nothing was ever what it seemed in London. I ached for the North. You knew where you were in Washington.

It was another day before I managed to leave. Gloria refused to let me pack my leather clothes, threatening to kill me if I tried. When, in desperation, I called the police she came out of the front door brandishing a knife.

"Get away from my door," she hissed at the young policeman who had come to reason with her. "Or else . . ."

He looked at me and shrugged. "I'm sorry, love, I can't do anything about this. It's a domestic matter."

In the end, all my labors in London had been for nothing—or very nearly nothing. When I got on the Clipper bus to Newcastle I had just £20 in my pocket and a bin liner full of old clothes. The only thing that consoled me as the bus sped up the A1 was the knowledge that I'd have the best suntan in the North of England.

# Chapter 10

I realized that in a way scarpering north was like running away to the fair. What I was doing was trying to escape from my problems. But perhaps running away wasn't always a bad thing to do. Good things could sometimes come out of it. Just as living on the fair and under the arches had helped me become more self-reliant and less dependent on Mum, so moving up to Washington might help me sort out my relationship with Dad.

Recently, I'd discovered that both Shane and Fiona had been back in contact with Dad and it had made me feel a bit left out. When I'd been arrested after Lance's party I'd felt a strong urge to get in touch with him. I'd never felt so isolated in my life as when I was locked in that police cell. I hadn't just wanted to be with Stephen—I'd desperately wanted to be part of a family again. When Mum had refused to come and see me at the police station it had hurt and I felt very alienated from her now. Dad was all I had left. Lately I'd begun to think of him more kindly; to make excuses for his behavior in the past. After all, I told myself, he'd brought all three of us up for four years on his own, which couldn't have been easy for him. He could have put us in a home, but he didn't, so we must have meant something to him.

I felt sorry now that I'd run away when he'd spotted me in the post office queue. Running away, refusing to face up to him, had been how Mum behaved and I'd criticized her for that. So why hadn't I stood my ground that day, spoken to him and tried to mend our relationship? Maybe it wasn't too late, even now.

To be honest I had a practical reason for getting back in touch with Dad too—I needed somewhere to stay in Washington. Steve lived in a small flat with his mum, so I couldn't stay there and I had no money to rent a room. When the Clipper bus stopped at a service station, I found a pay phone, plucked up all my courage, and dialed Dad's number.

He answered on the third ring, before I had time to bottle out. His telephone manner was as disarming as ever.

"Heather. Where've you been all this time? It's so good to hear from you."

Apprehensively, I explained where I was and told him I'd like to meet him again. Then I recited my prepared piece.

"But I'll only see you if you promise never to lay a finger on me, Dad. If it ever happens again I'm going to the police. Do you understand?"

"Heather, darling, I don't know what you're talking about. Your bed's made up. Come and stay for as long as you like." It wasn't the apology I'd been hoping for but it would do. Three hours later I arrived in Newcastle.

I'd rung Steve asking him to meet me at the coach station and he was waiting with a big smile on his face. It was so good to see him. Folded in his arms I felt I'd really come home.

He held me away from him. "Is it for good this time, Heather?"

"Steve, I'll never go away again," I promised. I meant it. I felt so safe, so happy, at that moment I was sure I'd never *want* to leave again. After the traumas I'd just been through I really believed my future lay here with Steve and Dad in the familiar surroundings of the town where I'd grown up.

After a quick kiss and cuddle Steve dropped me off in Lambton where Dad gave me a warm welcome. My warning must have got through to him because he handled me with kid gloves. When I washed my hair that night and realized I'd left my hair dryer behind, he even ran next door and borrowed one for me. I was touched by that. In the old days he'd never have done anything so thoughtful. Dad seemed different somehow. He'd mellowed.

It turned out that a civilizing influence had been at work on him. I found out about her at breakfast the next day.

"Heather, I've something to tell you," Dad said, pouring me a cup of Earl Grey. "I've got a girlfriend."

I stared at him. It was the first time I had ever seen Dad look embarrassed.

"I'd like you to meet her."

I was totally taken aback. I'd never thought of Dad in relation to other women and my heart didn't exactly jump for joy at the idea. But I had to admit I was curious. What sort of woman would be attracted to a man like Dad with his unpredictable temperament: a masochist?

But Helen was far from being a masochist. She turned out to be an intelligent well-balanced woman of thirty-nine. I met her when she came to pick him up that evening and liked her at once. She was a chief librarian and as different from Mum as chalk from cheese. Where Mum had never ventured an opinion of her own in front of Dad, Helen was confident and argumentative. Over the next few weeks I got to know her well and very soon decided that she was just the sort of woman Dad needed.

As I settled back into life in Washington there was just one cloud on my horizon—Dad didn't think that Stephen was the sort of man *I* needed. He hadn't met Steve before, but every time he came around to the house to pick me up Dad made snide remarks about his lack of a car, his clothes, and his appearance. Steve was tall and thin with very big shoulders and Dad thought it was hilarious to yell, "Hey, Heather, The Nail is here for you again," whenever he knocked on the door. I tried not to rise to the bait. In all other ways Dad had heeded my warning and was behaving himself. It was too much to expect perfection.

I wasted no time in job hunting. This time I bypassed Washington and went straight to Newcastle where all the top restaurants were. I'd seen enough of Julia's job at the VG store to know it wasn't for me. I liked working with people and I'd no intention of stacking shelves for a living. I hit the jackpot at the first attempt when Amigos, an Italian restaurant in the center of Newcastle, agreed to take me on. The hours were long—eight-thirty in the morning till one the next morning with a few hours off in the afternoon—but I didn't mind that. The pay was good, which was what counted.

After work the manager paid for a taxi to take me home to Lambton. If Dad was away I'd arrive home to find Stephen slumped in the doorway waiting for me. It didn't make for an ideal relationship, but I daren't give him a key or invite him home when Dad was there. Dad treated Stephen like a lecherous womanizer whom I had to be protected from. He can't really have imagined I was still a virgin, but sex was never mentioned in our house and I never quite had the courage to raise the subject myself.

However, it was soon to be brought up in a way I'd never dreamed of, and one that made Dad look rather two-faced. Dad's new girlfriend Helen lived at Wylam, near Newcastle. On weekends I'd sometimes go to her house and spend a few hours with her and Dad. One day they decided to go swimming.

"Would you like to come with us?" Helen invited. "I'll lend you a suit."

It was ages since I'd been in a pool and I really enjoyed it. Afterward we went for a cup of coffee in the baths restaurant and sat and chatted about sport and keeping fit. Helen was very sporty and a keen jogger.

"I must start taking exercise again," I said. "It'd help me lose a few pounds." I told her about the croissant shop and how I'd never managed to get rid of the weight I'd put on there.

Helen laughed and patted her tummy.

"Well, I'm afraid I'll be putting on a lot more than five or six pounds in the next few months, won't I, Mark?" She raised her eyebrows at Dad.

If I hadn't seen it with my own eyes I'd never have believed that Dad could blush.

"What Helen's trying to say is that we're going to have a baby," he said, avoiding my gaze.

I stared at him dumbstruck. All sorts of emotions battled inside me: I was afraid; I was excited. But most of all I realized I was relieved that Helen, who was such a stabilizing influence on Dad, looked like being a permanent part of his life.

"Don't worry. I've no plans to move in with your dad," said Helen, reading my thoughts. She said she intended to carry on working and maintain her independence. I was relieved about that too. If Helen turned into a housewife, I was sure Dad's attitude toward her would change.

Even so, Helen being pregnant gave her new status and I began to feel uncomfortable in Dad's house. For a while Stephen had been talking about us living together. Maybe it was time to think about moving out. But when I mentioned it to Dad he got really upset.

"That boy isn't good enough for you, Heather," he said. "What's the problem? Aren't you happy living with me? Have I done anything to upset you?" I felt guilty. I couldn't deny that since I'd been back Dad had been on his best behavior and it seemed ungrateful to throw it in his face. But then Steve wasn't happy with our relationship the way it stood—never being allowed to stay in the house when Dad was there, being forced to listen to Dad's thinly veiled insults all the time. I felt I was being forced to choose between them. It took a bizarre incident to help me decide.

Dad was still working on his Wagner presentation. I'd imagined his spell in prison would have finished it off for good, but apparently not. He was now planning to go ahead with the animated version. Because of the scandal when he'd been sent to prison for embezzlement, he'd changed his name. It was an exotic change. For business purposes, instead of calling himself Mark Mills, he was now known as Mark de Paul.

One weekend he told me he was off to London the following Monday. The actor Christopher Lee had agreed to do the voice-over for a thirty-second pilot film.

"Do you want to come with me? I've got a studio booked."

Monday was my day off and it would be a chance to see Fiona again, so I said yes.

Dad didn't have a car now—he'd had to sell it to pay off his debts—so the plan was for him to drive Helen's car to the Granada service station on the A1(M) where we would catch the seven o'clock Clipper bus. Unfortunately, it was a freezing-cold morning and when he tried to start the engine of Helen's old battered Mini nothing happened.

"We need to push-start it," Dad said. "Do you know how to drive?"

"No, of course I blooming well don't," I said.

"Never mind," Dad sighed. "Just get in. Look, press your left foot down on this pedal and let it off when I say. Then when the engine fires rev this other pedal with your right foot. Keep it revving and don't let it stop."

I followed his orders to the letter. Everything went brilliantly for the first stages of the operation. Dad pushed, the car rolled forward, he shouted go, I let out the clutch, the Mini jerked and roared into life, and I revved the engine. I kept revving it, just as Dad had told me. The trouble was he'd forgotten to say anything about taking it out of gear and the car carried on moving forward, steadily gathering speed, while I sat helplessly behind the wheel.

Terrified to disobey Dad's orders, I kept my foot down full blast on the accelerator as the car shot down the perimeter road that ran around Lambton. Behind me Dad was yelling, but I hadn't a clue what he was saying. All my attention was focused on the road ahead. A mini-roundabout appeared in front of me and I shut my eyes as I went straight across the middle of it. Fortunately, it was so early in the morning there was no traffic about. The car can only have been in second gear—its engine was screaming like a jet plane—but it seemed to be going as fast as any car I'd ever been in, and I had absolutely no idea how to stop it. It didn't occur to me to lift my foot off the pedal because Dad had told me that was the one thing I mustn't do. I had a vague notion of trying to pull it around in a skid turn the way people did in films, so I'd be pointing the right way and could drive back toward Dad, but the road didn't look wide enough for stunts like that. In the end, as I passed some newly built houses, I decided it was do or die. Taking a deep breath, I swung the wheel around, swerved into an unmade garden, and smashed into the larch-lap fence at the end. The impact made my foot slip off the pedal and the engine coughed and died.

A deathly silence followed, and I sat there with my heart pounding until I heard the sound of running footsteps. Terrified that Dad would rip me limb from limb, I got out, only to step into ankle-deep mud. The car's tires were already half buried in the mud and as I watched they sank even deeper.

"You bloody stupid girl," Dad panted. He grabbed my arm and dragged me around to the front of the car. "Here, help me push it out." I felt I'd escaped lightly, but Dad was too preoccupied with his appointment in London to waste time on me.

"We're going to miss the coach. We're going to miss the coach," he kept saying. After heaving and pushing for five minutes we managed to get the car back onto the road but it refused to restart so we had to run all the way back up to the house again. There, Dad picked up his briefcase and projection equipment, then ran out into the street waving like a madman and stopped the first car that passed.

When the driver wound down his window Dad put on his best public speaking voice.

"Would you mind terribly taking me to the Granada services on the A1? I'll make it worth your while."

The poor guy was on his way to work but obligingly he let Dad load all his equipment into the boot of his car. Unfortunately, just as we pulled into Granada services we saw the Clipper bus pulling out. Dad's civilized mask slipped completely.

"Follow that bus, follow that bus," he yelled as if the guy was a taxi driver.

"But I'm going to be late for work," the man protested.

"Never mind work!" Dad roared. "I've got a studio booked in London. Just follow the bus. We've got to stop it."

The man took one look at Dad's face and decided not to argue. We set off after the Clipper bus like a bat out of hell. As we started to overtake, Dad wound the window down and hung out, waving and shouting, "Stop, stop the bus." The bus driver looked down with his eyes popping and then he looked at me in the back as if to ask, *Who is this maniac?*

Crimson with shame, I mouthed, "He's supposed to be on the coach . . ."

The driver wound *his* window down then and started shouting back, "I can't stop on the motorway. It's illegal!"

"Pull off at the next exit then," ordered Dad.

Amazingly, the driver did and Dad unloaded everything out of the car and got on. I stayed where I was. There was no way I could face spending five hours sitting next to him after that performance. My eyes met the car driver's eyes in the mirror and I collapsed in embarrassed giggles. But I did a lot of thinking as we drove back to Washington.

Dad hadn't changed at all, I realized. It had all been a sham. He would never change. So far, true enough, he had kept his word about not hitting me, but under the surface he was as volatile as ever. He was a real Jekyll and Hyde. Maybe he was even a bit mad. I suddenly knew with absolute certainty that I didn't want to live with someone like that.

As soon as I got home I dialed Stephen's number, hoping to catch him before he left for work.

"Hi, it's me. Do you still want to look for somewhere to live?"

It was an impulse decision and perhaps impulse decisions aren't the best ones. But at the time I felt sure I was doing the right thing. Stephen jumped at the idea. Two weeks later we'd put a deposit on an ex-council flat in Sulgrave only fifty yards from where I'd lived with Mum and Dad.

I was determined to make a real effort to be a good partner to Stephen. When he complained he wasn't seeing enough of me because of the hours I worked at the restaurant, I gave up my job and found work as a valet in a casino in Newcastle. The job was a dream come true with massive tips. I opened my first savings account and started to put money away for the first time in my life.

It was while I was working at the casino that Dad phoned me to tell me that Helen had given birth to a little girl, Claire. I went to see her in Newcastle General Hospital. My half-sister was lovely, with blond hair and big blue eyes, but I didn't feel broody and maternal when I saw her. I admired Helen; I saw her as a role model. She had achieved so much and then she'd had a baby. Like her, I wanted to be financially secure and successful before I tied myself down with kids.

Sadly, Steve didn't share my vision of our future. He even wanted me to give up my casino job now because, although the hours were less strenuous than the restaurant, he still felt he didn't see enough of me. To keep the peace I handed in my notice. But I soon realized domesticity wasn't for me. I'd had enough of housework and cooking to last me a lifetime. Sitting at home I had too much time to think and all my thoughts were of how different Steve and I were and how we were going in opposite directions. Too late, I realized we had different expectations of life. For the next forty-odd years Steve's weekdays would follow the same pattern: nine to five at the factory followed by a night at the pub drinking with his mates. And he was totally happy at the prospect.

I, on the other hand, was ridiculously, stupidly ambitious. A year in Newcastle had helped me regain my confidence. I knew who I was and who I wanted to be and it wasn't a stay-at-home housewife. I dreamed not just of money now, but of success, of new experiences. I dreamed of being the next prime minister, of being a TV presenter. I wanted to try everything life had to offer. The only thing I didn't want to try, at least not yet, was the future of pram pushing and supermarket shopping and TV watching that was looming ahead of me like a dark tunnel.

The question was how to break it to Steve—dear kind Steve, who'd shown me love and helped save my sanity when it felt as if the whole world was against me. How could I possibly hurt him by telling him the truth? I don't know what would have happened if I hadn't decided to go down and visit Fiona and Mum in London one weekend. Maybe I'd still be living in Washington now with half a dozen kids trailing on my apron strings . . .

Mum hadn't gotten back from work when I arrived to visit. When she did come in she brought a copy of the London *Evening Standard* with her and after supper, as we sat chatting in front of the TV,

I flicked through it. The *Standard* was always good for giving you a feeling of what was happening in London. It had interviews with stars, and reviews of plays and concerts. I don't know what made me turn to the jobs page but when I did a little classified ad sprang out at me. *Showroom model required this Saturday. Apply Roadshow Fashions, Margaret Street, W1.*

I knew Margaret Street. It was the street Bootleggers Club was in just off Oxford Circus. I'd seen the name Roadshow before too. It had been engraved on the brass plate next to the stairs leading to the floor above Bootleggers. I stared at it with my heart pounding. It had to be more than a coincidence. Maybe I was meant to see this ad.

I said nothing to Fiona or Mum, but the next morning I caught the tube to Oxford Circus and knocked on the door of Roadshow Fashions. An Indian woman in a sari answered the door and looked me up and down. "Yes, can I help you?"

"I've come about the job," I said. "I'd like to be your showroom model."

"Oh." She seemed taken aback, which I thought was a good sign. Obviously they hadn't been overwhelmed by applicants.

The owner of Roadshow Fashions was a cheerful-looking Indian man called Raj who didn't seem bothered by my lack of experience. He explained that he needed someone to show a range of dresses to buyers from different stores. All the model had to do was walk up and down on the shop floor in front of them.

"We are looking for a size ten to twelve," he said. "What are your measurements please?" I saw him looking doubtfully at my bust.

"Ten," I lied, hunching my shoulders. It was half true. I did take a ten in skirts but I had to squash my boobs flat to get into a size twelve top. I vowed that if I got the job I would start a diet that day.

I did get the job. I think that what swayed Raj was the fact that when he asked what my rates were I said I'd take whatever he paid. I spent the day there on Saturday and thoroughly enjoyed myself. My job was exactly as Raj described: walking up and down, twirling around a couple of times, and going off to do a quick change into the next outfit. If this was all there was to modeling I thought I wouldn't mind doing more. After the show Raj called me into the office and paid me. "Heather," he said, "would you by any chance be free for a month at the end of January?" I nodded, pushing the complications of Stephen and housework from my mind.

"And would you mind traveling?"

"Where to?" I asked.

"Delhi," he said.

"You what?" said Stephen.

"I want to go to India for a month."

"You're kidding."

"No, I'm serious. They're going to pay for the flight, everything. All I have to do is try a few clothes on."

"What's the pay like?"

I swallowed. "They won't actually pay me, but I'll be able to see the country. It's the chance of a lifetime, Steve."

Stephen laughed. "I don't suppose there's much point me saying no then, is there?"

"Oh, thanks," I said, hugging him. "Thanks, darling."

It was a wonderful month. Roadshow Fashions was a family business that sold clothes manufactured in India to British chain stores. I traveled over to Delhi with Raj and his partner Stuart and was given lodgings with Raj's family over there. It was like being on another planet, never mind another country. Whenever I went out into the street I had to wear a sari and cover myself from head to foot. I'd only been abroad once before—on a cheap package holiday to Corfu the previous year—and Delhi was a real eye-opener. This wasn't tourist India. The streets were full of crippled beggars, many of them amputees. I saw people with no legs pushing themselves along on skateboards, and people with no arms putting food into their mouths with their feet. Seeing them I felt horribly rich and privileged. I wanted to give them all my money but Raj stopped me.

"No!" He grabbed my hand as I handed out rupees right left and center. "You mustn't, because they don't get to keep the money. They have to give it to their manager. It's a big racket. Sometimes children even get their hands cut off to make people feel sorry for them. If you give money you only help make more amputees . . ."

For a while it made me depressed, but there were too many wonderful things to see in India to stay depressed. On the days when I wasn't working I traveled. I went by car to Kashmir with some friends of the family. I visited Agra, saw the Taj Mahal, and toured the Pink Palace in New Delhi. My eyes were opened to another world.

Again the work was easy. My role was to go into local factories and try dress samples on so the manufacturers could get the sizes right before they went into mass production. I had to walk and stand around while the fitters adjusted them. They were European outfits but in Indian cotton and silk and the most fiddly adjustments were in getting the sleeves and necks right. It was quite boring but I didn't mind. It was worth it for the experiences I was getting once I finished work.

Raj's family seemed to be pleased with me. I'd kept my resolution to lose weight and could now model a size-twelve top comfortably.

"Next month we have to go to Hong Kong to fit jumpers. Would you like to come?" Raj asked.

I was dying to say yes, but I'd promised Stephen I'd be home by the end of the month. I knew I couldn't let him down when he'd been so understanding about me coming to India in the first place. Reluctantly, I declined.

But back in Washington, living with Stephen in Collingwood Court, I was even unhappier than I'd been two months earlier. I felt so restless. I'd always known there was a world beyond Newcastle. That had been part of the reason I couldn't settle. Now I knew there was a world beyond London too, and I wanted to sample more of it.

The trouble was I didn't know how to tell him. I just couldn't face it. Then one day, Steve came home from work and told me he'd been offered a promotion. "They want me to train to be a manager." He grinned.

"Oh, Steve, that's great!" I said and threw my arms around him. Maybe after all there were better things ahead. If Steve got ambitious too maybe we wouldn't be condemned to a humdrum run-of-the-mill existence.

"You will take it, won't you?" I asked.

He shook his head. "No, I don't see how I can really."

I stared at him in shock. "Why ever not?"

"Well, the other lads wouldn't like it, would they?"

I looked at him and something in my head went *Bing!*

I knew I couldn't spend the rest of my life with someone who was so anxious to keep in with his friends and to conform. If you always played safe, afraid to go out on a limb, how could you ever expect to rise above the crowd?

The next day, after Stephen left for work, I packed my things and rang for a taxi. Then I got out my writing pad. I looked at the calendar. It was April 1.

*Dear Steve,* I wrote. *This is not an April Fool. I have left you and you will not be seeing me again. I'm really sorry things didn't work out. Love, Heather.*

This time as I stepped onto the coach at the Granada services I knew it would be for the last time. My days of yo-yoing between London and Newcastle were over. I'd made an important discovery. Life could either be something you drifted through passively or it could be something you took in both hands and turned around. As a child I'd had no choice. But as a grown-up I did. My life, my happiness was my own responsibility now. I didn't have to be a victim any longer. For the first time in my life I knew exactly where I was heading. I was going to be a model.

# Chapter 11

*If* I'd thought I could walk into modeling the way I'd walked into club work I was in for a rude awakening.

"Sorry, we don't employ freelances," said the manager of the first clothes firm I applied to. "You need to apply through an agency."

Crestfallen, I went back to Clapham, where Toni and Gill had once more agreed to put me up, and looked up model agencies in the yellow pages. In the weeks that followed I applied to every model agency in London. One by one, they all found different excuses to turn me down.

"Your hair isn't right."

"Your boobs are too big."

"You're overweight."

"You're not editorial enough."

That last remark threw me. "What?"

The agency director shook her head. "It means you simply haven't got the look that magazine editors want."

I wasn't put off. "Well, it doesn't have to be magazines. Isn't there any other sort of modeling I can do?"

"I'm afraid five eight and a half just isn't tall enough for catwalk modeling. These days they want five ten, five eleven . . ."

I refused to give in. The attitude of the agencies just made me determined to prove them wrong. However, while I was thinking about my next move I still had to eat and pay rent, so to keep the wolf from the door I took a job as a waitress at a club in Wardour Street. The boss said I could choose my own uniform and I went back to Roadshow Fashions where I picked out a little black skirt and a brief tie top. The family seemed pleased to see me again and Raj was interested to hear I wanted to do more modeling.

"We're going to the Harrogate Fashion Fair next week," he said. "You can model there for us if you like."

It wasn't much but it was a start. It was the first time I'd worked with other models and I kept my eyes and ears open and tried to pick up tips.

"Keep trying, Heather," Raj encouraged as he handed me my pay after the fair. "If you are really determined I'm sure you will make it in the end."

I was only earning £15 a night at the club, which didn't go far in London, so it was a relief when I was offered a second job doing backing dancing for a band. It wasn't choreographed—I just had to do my own thing—which meant it wasn't like work at all. The band had a woman manager called Diane, who took me under her wing. When she heard I wanted to be a model, she gave me the phone numbers of several agents she knew.

One afternoon when I came in with news of yet another rejection, she suggested another approach.

"You know, maybe you've been barking up the wrong tree trying to do fashion modeling. Perhaps your best bet would be glamour."

I pulled a face. I remembered Gloria's "glamour" modeling all too well.

Diane laughed. "I don't think you can afford to be fussy if you want work. With your figure you'd probably stand a good chance in glamour. Go on," she urged. "Give it a try. It might not be as bad as you think, and at least it'll get your foot in the door. Lots of models start off doing glamour."

I hesitated. "How do you get into it?"

"There are glamour agencies. The makeup artist for our band works for one of them. I think their number's on her card." She rummaged about in her handbag. "Yes, here you are: Panache Model Agency. Why don't you give them a ring?"

I was torn. After accompanying Gloria to her topless session, I'd sworn I'd never do glamour photography. But if I wanted to get started maybe I hadn't much choice. Back at Gill's I swallowed my pride and rang the number on the card. A week later Panache, impressed by my 32E bust, had taken me onto their books.

I lasted for only a few shoots. On each occasion I went up to a studio in Old Street and stood about shivering while a photographer tried to talk me into looking saucy and provocative. I was terribly nervous. I didn't know where to look or how to place my hands and I felt about as saucy as a plank of wood. The photographer was sympathetic.

"I'll put a mirror behind me so you can look at your reflection," he said. "It'll give you something to focus on."

It seemed a good idea but he put the mirror too far away and in the first pictures my eyes were bulging like balloons as I strained to focus. By the third session I must have got it right and a week later I found myself smiling out cheesily from page three of the *News of the World.* Seeing that picture convinced me that my first instinct had been right and glamour photography wasn't my cup of tea. It wasn't that I was ashamed of my body (though I cringed a bit when I thought that certain people might see it) but posing topless just didn't satisfy me. I wanted to do something more artistic and challenging than just showing off my boobs. I wanted, more than anything else, to do fashion modeling. After a period of time doing "glamour," I realized that Diane's claim that it would help me get a foot in the door of fashion modeling was a myth. Not one of the photographers I'd worked with had offered to photograph me with my clothes on. In fact one of them had asked if I was interested in taking even more off! So how *did* I get into the other sort of modeling? It seemed to be a closed shop.

Again it was Diane, though indirectly this time, who provided the answer. Although her first introduction was a nonstarter, she arranged another meeting that was to prove much more successful—with her brother Alfie. Alfie Karmal was a dark-haired bearded man, seven years older than me, who had recently split up from his wife. He had exotic origins—a Greek mother and Arabic father—and was handsome, cultured, and charming. After months of living with northern bluntness, I was hungry for sophistication, and to me Alfie seemed everything I desired in a man.

It was Alfie and Diane who were jointly responsible for my big break.

"Look at this," said Diane one day, handing me a leaflet. "Cinzano is running a competition for Model of the Year. Why don't you enter?"

"Don't be silly," I said. "I couldn't stand there in a swimsuit in front of a crowd of people. I'd be too embarrassed."

But Alfie egged me on. "Go on, try for it," he said. "If you don't you'll never know what might have happened."

"But I'm too pale," I protested. "My legs would look ridiculous in a swimsuit." During the long months in Newcastle my glorious tan had faded away and I was as pale as a ghost.

Diane studied the rules. "It says here you don't have to wear a swimsuit. It can be a sports outfit if you prefer."

"But it'll still mean showing my legs," I grumbled.

"Go on a sunbed then," said Diane.

But there was no time. The first round of the competition was the following Saturday and I'd end up looking like a boiled lobster if I tried to cram six weeks of treatment into five days.

Alfie came up with the answer.

"You'll just have to get a bottle of fake tan," he said.

Every night that week Alfie devotedly rubbed fake tan all over my body. After his first attempt my skin looked like orange marble but several layers later he'd perfected his technique.

"Like a bronze goddess," he smiled, as he admired his handiwork.

I thought that was exaggerating just a *tiny* bit, but I wasn't going to quarrel over it.

The first heat was held in the Middlesex and Herts Country Club. To show off my fake tan I'd bought a little pair of pink shorts and a pink half-cut top. As I paraded around on the podium with twenty other girls, I had no idea what to do or what the judges were looking for. But neither, I suddenly realized, had the other girls. A lot of them were shuffling around with hunched shoulders, looking as if they'd rather be anywhere in the world but on stage with hundreds of people staring at them. Most of them kept their eyes fixed firmly on the floor. All at once I thought of Charles's instructions all those years ago: "Walk tall, Heather, don't look at the pavement. Walk tall, then people will notice you."

I threw my shoulders back, put my chin up, and stepped out. When the results were announced, I learned I'd won second prize.

My elation at being placed was soon replaced by ambition. Even on the running track at Usworth School second had never been good enough. For me, like Dad, winning was what counted. I was through to the regional finals now and next time I was determined to go one better. On the running track, success sometimes depended on assessing the opposition. Maybe it was the same in beauty contests. The girl who'd won my heat hadn't been the prettiest in the competition, but she'd looked relaxed, smiled a lot, and joked with the interviewer. I resolved to learn from that.

Three weeks later, at the regional finals in Watford, I felt much more nervous but managed to control it. This time it was Dad's words that came back to me. I remembered his instructions about running.

"Use the adrenaline, Heather. Control it, don't let it control you. Let it help your performance."

As I changed into evening dress before my interview I took several deep breaths. When the time came for me to be asked individual questions, I not only kept my head up, I smiled.

The questions were pretty banal, about hobbies and ambitions. Most of the girls before me answered them in different shades of southern accent but I'd never tried to put an accent on and I didn't start now. They could accept me for who I was or not at all, I thought. When the woman interviewer asked where I came from I answered in my best Geordie, "Newcastle," adding quickly, "though I don't suppose you'd guess to hear me speak."

There was a chuckle from the audience, which boosted my confidence.

"And what's it like up there in Newcastle, Heather?" She made it sound as if it was on another planet.

"Well, you can see our weather's a lot better than yours," I said, holding my arm up next to hers so the audience could get a good look at my tan. They roared and I realized my nerves had gone and I was actually enjoying myself. This time, when the announcements were made at the end of the evening, I was awarded first prize.

A month later it was time for the last stage of the contest. The London finals of the Cinzano Model of the Year competition were a much grander affair than the qualifying rounds and were held in the Thames TV Studios, while the finalists were put up in the White House Hotel off Great Portland Street. I invited Fiona and Mum to see my big moment and got them seats next to Alfie and Diane on the front row. Fiona, Mum, and I were getting on okay again now, though I didn't see much of them.

Cinzano had hired Wayne Sleep to provide the entertainment and as part of the evening's events the sixty finalists had to dress up in leotards, top hats, and tails and do a dance routine with him. We spent so long rehearsing that damned dance routine that there wasn't time to rehearse the competition. They wouldn't even let us go backstage to have our costumes fitted until Wayne was happy with the performance. It meant several people ended up in outfits that didn't fit, and I was one of them. This time, instead of wearing our own clothes we had to wear gear that Cinzano provided. My costume was a revolting blue-and-white-striped two-piece in a size twelve. It fit okay on top but as my hips were a size eight now the skirt hung off me like a tent. When I asked for a smaller one the fitter just shrugged and said there wasn't one, then ran off because Wayne Sleep was rehearsing his solo routine on stage and she didn't want to miss it.

I nearly blew a fuse. In the earlier events we'd been dealt with as people. This time I felt we were being treated like props, of secondary importance to Wayne Sleep. What the hell had we been doing prancing around like prats on stage when we should have been getting ready for the competition? By the time it was our turn to go on stage I was in a foul mood. Everything seemed to be conspiring against me. My hair, which I'd only just washed, had gone all lank and disgusting, I had a spot on my chin, and my skirt not only hid my best feature, my legs, but made my hips look about forty inches wide. All of Charles's and Dad's advice deserted me and I stomped on stage with a face like thunder. A TV company was there filming the event for Cinzano and I glared crossly at the camera, not even bothering to try since I obviously hadn't a cat in hell's chance of winning.

It was a self-fulfilling prophecy. I came nowhere, not even getting through to the interview stage, and for days afterward I skulked around like a bear with a sore head, furious with myself for having bothered to enter. Everything people said about beauty contests was true, I told myself. They were cattle markets pure and simple. My modeling career was no farther forward than before.

Then, a week after the competition, a girl I'd met in the semifinals rang up.

"Did you get the letter?" she asked.

"What letter?"

"The letter from Phillip Goodhand-Tait at Trillion Pictures. He's asking all the girls from the Cinzano finals to audition to present a video."

Trillion Pictures had been the name of the television company whose cameras I'd glared at.

"Well, he hasn't asked me," I said.

"Oh, dear. Well . . . maybe it'll be in the post tomorrow."

But it wasn't. Nor the following day.

Being rejected was a hard pill to swallow, though I knew I'd no one to blame but myself. By throwing in the towel that night I'd also thrown away the best chance that had yet come my way. The irony was I knew I could present a video. Doing that interview in the semifinal had shown me I could control my nerves and talk naturally into a microphone. Even in the finals few of the other girls had done that. Most of them had frozen and given giggly, one-word answers. I was positive I could do better. But I wouldn't be given the chance now. I'd blown it.

Or had I? I felt rebellion rise inside me. If I took this brush-off lying down I'd just be letting life happen to me again. When I left Washington I'd vowed that I'd stop being a victim, that I'd grab hold of life and swing it around in my direction. Somehow I had to make this Phillip Goodhand-Tait realize he needed me as much as I needed him. I looked up Trillion Pictures in the yellow pages and rang their number. A secretary answered.

"Could I speak to Mr. Goodhand-Tait please?" I asked sweetly.

"May I ask who's calling?"

"Heather Mills. I was a finalist in the Cinzano Model of the Year competition."

"Hold the line please." There was a long pause, then she spoke again. "I'm afraid Mr. Goodhand-Tait is busy just now."

He was "busy" the next time I rang too. And the next.

"Could you tell me how I *can* get to speak to him?" I asked his secretary in desperation. "I want to talk about the video he's making. I'd like to audition for it."

"He's a very busy man, Miss Mills. Why don't you send some pictures in? If he's interested I'm sure he'll contact you."

I didn't have any pictures, apart from my topless ones, and I didn't think they'd be quite the thing. I went to a photographer who'd taken pictures of Diane's band.

"It's for an audition," I told him. "I want to look like a television presenter."

He scratched his head. "You could do with a bit less hair then, I think." For my glamour pics I'd had my hair permed and it still hung in long blond curls halfway down my back, in the Sam Fox tradition. I tied it back hoping I'd look a bit more intellectual. The results were quite convincing, if I said so myself.

I posted the photographs to Trillion Pictures and a few days afterward, when I hadn't heard anything, I rang them again. This time the secretary put me through to the great man himself and my hopes rose.

"Mr. Goodhand-Tait? Did you get my pictures?"

"Yes, I did." His voice was very brisk. "Thank you for sending them. They're nice pictures, but we think we've already found the right person."

"Oh." The wind left my sails. "Are you sure? Wouldn't you just like to see me? The pictures were taken in a bit of a hurry."

"Heather, I'm *quite* sure," he said. "We'll return the pictures to you in the next day or two."

Slowly, I put the phone down, feeling not dejected, but indignant. This wasn't good enough. How could he possibly know I wasn't suitable for the job without seeing me? A new plan formed in my mind.

The next day, wearing a smart suit, I took a taxi to Trillion Pictures' West End offices. My intention was simply to barge in and present myself, but to my dismay the offices had a security entrance with a buzzer and intercom. I pressed the buzzer, thinking quickly. If I announced myself as Heather Mills I suspected I'd be left standing on the doorstep. The secretary's voice came through the speaker.

"Trillion Pictures. Who's calling?"

I made my voice low and gruff. "Courier service. Parcel for Mr. Goodhand-Tait."

The door opened and I stepped inside. Trillion Pictures' offices were on the third floor and as I stepped out of the lift the secretary eyed me suspiciously.

"Can I help you?"

"I'd like to see Mr. Goodhand-Tait," I said.

She pursed her lips. "I'm afraid he's busy at the moment."

At that moment the office door behind her swung open and two men came out. One of them had to be the boss.

I held out my hand. "Mr. Goodhand-Tait?"

The younger of the two men turned toward me, eyebrows raised.

I flashed what I hoped was a confident smile. "I'm Heather Mills. Could I have a word with you for a minute please?" Putting my arm through his I steered him back into his office.

I had the advantage of surprise, but his confusion would wear off in a few seconds so I had to get my message over quickly. I hadn't rehearsed my plea. It came straight from the heart.

"Look," I said. "I'm certain I'd be perfect for presenting your video. I know I looked awful in the Cinzano competition, and I understand completely why you didn't invite me to audition, but I promise you I can do it. Why don't you let me prove it? Give me a chance. I guarantee you won't regret it."

Phillip Goodhand-Tait looked completely flummoxed as he listened to this speech and I could see him thinking, *Who is this girl? Where did she escape from?*

But suddenly he smiled. "Okay, Heather, you win. We'll give you a screen test."

All my pushiness had paid off. Not only did I get the trial, I got the job. A month later Phillip decided that out of all the finalists they tested I was the most suitable. The video in question was a promotion for a heavy-metal band and Phillip was so pleased with my presentation that he asked me to do several more music videos. Some were about obscure rock stars, others about even more obscure country and western singers. My job was to sound enthusiastic and knowledgeable about albums and singles I'd never heard of. It was quite a challenge.

It marked a turning point in my modeling career. With a concrete achievement under my belt, people began to take me seriously when I applied for jobs. I didn't exactly wake up and find people hammering on my door, but slowly I started to get work, first lowly jobs like showroom modeling, then photographic shoots for catalogs. Alfie helped me make the next breakthrough when he sent a swimsuit photo of me to the *Daily Mirror* Dream Girl Competition. I got through the early rounds and was doing a photographic shoot for the finals when someone from the *Sunday People* saw me, liked the look of my legs, and asked to use me for a fashion spread on short skirts. That was my first photographic fashion shoot and as a result I finally persuaded a fashion model agency to take me on. Not a London agency—it was based in Berkhamstead—but still an agency. It was called Models Out of Town and it got me an Argos catalog shoot and several similar jobs.

I still couldn't talk any London agencies into putting me on their books, but I didn't let that daunt me. Pushiness had paid off once. I decided to use it again and I devised a plan to bypass the agencies. When they had commissions most photographers held casting sessions where they took sample pictures to decide the best girl for the job. By chatting with girls who were on agency books, I started to find out where these casting sessions were being held, and simply turned up. It didn't matter what the casting was for—fashion shoots, calendars, or commercials—I'd be there. There was immense competition. Often I'd arrive at a photographer's studio to find models queuing out of the door and down the street.

In a situation like that it was no good being a shrinking violet and I wasn't. Even if I didn't get the job at the casting I'd leave my card and telephone number with the photographer, offering to do direct work if he needed a blond model in the future. It was cheeky but it worked. Direct work was cheaper both for photographers and clients because they didn't have to pay agency fees.

Underneath I wasn't nearly as confident as I tried to appear: My first stand-up photo shoots were nightmares because I felt so self-conscious about my body position. It was a while before I grasped the secret of posing side-on and turning my shoulders toward the camera and learned that the most exaggerated poses could look normal through a camera lens.

The key to modeling, I discovered, was relaxation, especially for close-ups. To get your face looking right the trick was to forget the camera was there. At first, when I looked into the camera I'd imagine I was on a beach. Later, when I became more blasé, I'd make a mental shopping list for my next supermarket trip. *Now let me think. I need some carrots and some peas and . . .* "Oh, are we finished? Thank you."

Sometimes I'd do my own makeup, but I wasn't patient enough. Some of the girls took an hour to put on their makeup. Ten minutes was the limit for me. Fortunately, on most shoots there was a makeup artist in attendance. I loved being made up. I'd sit down, shut my eyes, and just go into a trance. It meant I never did learn about makeup technique because I was always too relaxed to concentrate on what was going on. To this day I'm not brilliant at doing my own makeup.

In that first year of modeling I had to work really hard to get each job. I learned to be realistic about my strengths and weaknesses so I didn't waste time going to casting sessions where I had no chance. There was no point, for instance, spending a morning queuing when the client wanted a redhead, or a Kate Moss look-alike. Nor was there any point in turning up for catwalk castings: I was too short. That didn't bother me too much. Run-of-the-mill catwalk bookings didn't pay good money anyway. The most lucrative jobs were for things like corporate brochures, where companies that made plastic widgets wanted pictures of smiling girls holding the widgets. Jobs like those sometimes paid a couple of grand a day.

There was one sort of catwalk job I could apply for and that was swimwear. Swimsuit models were allowed to be shorter than five foot ten, provided they had good legs and boobs. Fortunately I'd inherited both and I started getting lots of swimsuit bookings. The nice thing about modeling swimsuits was that the clients often wanted to see their suits in exotic locations. Setting them against a background of palm trees and shimmering sand sold more bikinis than photographing them in the local public swimming baths. My first swimwear brochure was shot in Jamaica. It was followed by several other Caribbean trips.

It was all terribly exciting. It was hard to believe that less than four years ago I'd been pinching food and living under the arches. Sometimes, when I opened the post and found a big check, I felt like pinching myself. But the big checks were few and far between. There were weeks, sometimes months, when I had no work at all. Very few of the models I met worked full time. Even fewer felt financially secure. I began to realize that modeling wasn't a profession a school career mistress would recommend. Life was a succession of traumas. You'd wake up on the morning of a shoot to find a huge spot on your chin, or your hair wouldn't behave. Even if you went on holiday you wouldn't relax and enjoy it because you were too afraid of putting weight on. It was a cutthroat business: If you didn't make the grade, you were out.

All you could do to help your prospects was to be as reliable and competent in your work as possible. Turning up late with a hangover or red eyes after a row with your boyfriend didn't endear you to photographers at all. They had long memories. I tried to make sure that all they'd remember about me was my professionalism.

At times the payoff seemed a long time coming. My eighteenth birthday passed, then my nineteenth, and I was still only scraping a living. I didn't let it get me down. Whenever I had days at home, instead of mooching about I used to dream up "get rich quick" schemes. Maybe it was Dad's entrepreneurial streak coming out in me. His Wagner venture might have come to grief but it had so nearly succeeded. This had taught me one important thing: to have a vision.

My first vision was called the Joli-Bust project. I came across Joli-Bust by chance. Since starting modeling I'd become very diet-conscious and used to spend hours in the local health food store. One day, while stocking up on vitamins, I bought an American health magazine. While I was browsing through it that evening I came across an advert for self-adhesive plastic breast supports to wear with backless dresses. The idea was that you stuck one Joli-Bust under each boob and they gave you an incredible cleavage.

I thought it was a great idea. When you had a big bust, wearing backless dresses could be a real problem. Either you wore a bra and worried about it showing or you went braless and bounced around all night giving people black eyes. Stick-on push-ups seemed the perfect answer. I looked for shops where I could buy the Joli-Bust but no English suppliers were listed. That was when things started ticking in my head. I was sure lots of women would buy these things if they could get hold of them. What if I brought a whole load over from America to sell here? I reached for my writing pad—I'd never been one to sleep on a good idea—and three weeks later I was appointed as the British distributor of the Joli-Bust.

Getting the business off the ground was fun. It satisfied something basic in me to pound around the shops chatting up buyers. Over the next four weeks I got nearly every big store in London onto my books. Then, just as the business started to bring in a good steady income, I lost interest. When all I had to do was sit at home filling in invoices and order forms, the fun went out of it. Recognizing it was time to call it a day, I sold the distributorship for a nice little profit. It had been a good experience. Next time money ran low, I thought, I might set up another business.

Modeling work was scarce that winter and it was barely six months before I tried my hand again. My next venture was similar to the Joli-Bust in that I imported an American idea. This time the product was frozen yogurt. I'd first tasted it on a trip to Florida with

Alfie. When I came home and discovered you couldn't buy it in England I wrote to the manufacturers and bought the British franchise. A few months later I sold it. It fetched enough money for me to buy my first car. Success boosted my confidence. Anyone could start a business, I realized. You didn't need to have studied at university or business college—in fact it didn't matter if you'd left school at thirteen. You just needed cheek and the hunger to succeed, and I had both.

For a while, I wouldn't need to call on them. Soon after my twentieth birthday the trickle of modeling work grew to a steady stream. My look still wasn't "in" with English clients but many firms and magazines in Europe and America weren't interested in ultrathin models anymore, so I had an advantage when I went to their castings. It was a European job that led to my next big break. I was on a fashion shoot in Paris when the photographer said he had another client, a subsidiary of a big French makeup company, that was holding a casting the next weekend.

"Why don't you stay on in Paris and go along," he said. "I've a feeling you could be the right person for them. They want a good body and a European face."

I booked an extra couple of nights at my hotel, turned up at the casting, and, in competition with several hundred other girls, got the job. It was a real coup, a huge contract that involved being "the face" for all the company's cosmetic promotions for the next year. I would have to live in Paris for twelve months with an option of another year if things went well. But the best thing about it was the money—I'd be paid £1,500 a day for every day I worked and I'd be working most days. It was the chance of a lifetime. There was just one complication: Alfie.

I'd been going out with Alfie now for eighteen months and for the past six months we'd been living together. For some time he'd been asking me to marry him but I'd shied away from that. I was very fond of Alfie and of his two small children, Matthew and Christopher, but having escaped being tied down with Stephen I'd no intention of risking it again.

Alfie took my decision to go to France very badly and issued an ultimatum. Either I turned the job down or our relationship was over. It was the worst thing he could have done. When I'd struggled so hard to get my career off the ground, I wasn't going to give it up for anyone, certainly not for someone who issued ultimatums. There was no big row. I hated rows. But two days after that "discussion" I flew to Paris.

# Chapter 12

It was the big time and I loved every minute of it, at least at first. For two months I lived in splendor, all expenses paid, at the Royal Monceau Hotel on the Avenue Hoche, until the company found me a luxurious apartment just around the corner from the hotel. As promised, I found myself modeling nearly every day, though it was a bit of a shock to find that a typical working day lasted twelve to thirteen hours. Still, I was young and fit enough to take it and the money helped sweeten the fact that I had no time for a life of my own.

Having so much money went to my head. It never occurred to me to salt my wages away for a rainy day. Instead I indulged in all the Paris shops had to offer. I bought my first-ever set of suitcases, a beautiful gold and diamond bracelet, and several outrageously expensive designer outfits. But after a few weeks, unable to think of anything else I needed, I started sending most of my pay home to Dad.

Dad was still paying off massive debts after his fraud conviction and I wanted to help him. Shane and Fiona didn't approve.

"I think you're barmy," Fiona said when she found out.

Even I didn't properly understand my motives. My feelings for Dad were as confused as ever. Recently I'd been feeling more and more guilty for falling out with him. After all, I told myself, whatever his faults he was still my father, and if it hadn't been for him, Fiona, Shane, and I would have had no home at all. He'd been the one who had stayed with us when Mum walked out. Surely I owed him something in return? But more than that I owed something to my little half-sister Claire. I didn't want her to grow up with Dad's debts hanging over her head the way they'd hung over ours.

After I'd been in France for four or five months I noticed something strange. Although I was leading a very healthy lifestyle, eating lots of salads and plenty of lean meat, I hadn't nearly as much energy as I used to have. Since my life had changed direction two years ago, I'd been bouncing out of bed every morning at the crack of dawn. Now dragging myself from under the sheets was hard work, and going to the gym for my twice-daily workout seemed more and more of a chore. It took me some time to realize what the trouble was. I was bored. Not only that: I was lonely. I'd picked up a bit of French but it was no use to me, because I had no friends to talk to. I was the only model working for the cosmetics company and because of my long hours I had no time for a social life. After three months the only people I'd got to know were the makeup artist and the girl who did the hairstyling. I never went sight-seeing or to discos and my only recreation, apart from the gym, was watching videos in my apartment. Or rather, watching *a* video. There was only one English video in my apartment—*The Scarlet Pimpernel*—and by the end of my fifth month in France I'd watched it over thirty times.

When the company told me they were taking me to Cannes for some beach shots, I breathed a sigh of relief. It was just what I needed: A few days of being pampered in the best hotels on the French Riviera worked wonders and by the end of the week I felt revitalized. But then, on the morning of the biggest shoot, disaster struck. At dinner the night before I'd gone mad on the delicious little cherry tomatoes you get in the South of France. When I woke up in my bed in the Majestic I could hardly open my eyes. Struggling to the mirror, I prized my eyelids apart, then wished I hadn't. My face was covered in huge oozing boils . . .

I was still staring in horror when there was a hammering on the door.

*"Allez-vous-en!"* I screamed. "*Vous ne pouvez pas entrer! Revenez plus tard!*"

Jean-Pierre's voice came back through the door. "Don't be ridiculous, Heather. We have to start the shoot in twenty minutes."

"No, no!" I shrieked. "You can't believe what's happened."

Eventually Jean-Pierre persuaded me to open the door.

*"Oh, mon Dieu!"* he said.

I thought he was going to faint.

The shoot was canceled and I was sent to an allergy clinic in Cannes where doctors stuck lots of needles into my arm and told me I would have to wait twenty-four hours to see which jabs swelled up. It turned out I was allergic not only to tomatoes, but to strawberries and air-conditioning as well. The doctor said it was the air-conditioning that could have been making me feel so tired in my apartment in Paris. He gave me antihistamines and a special soap and after three days my boils had almost disappeared. With the aid of clever makeup they managed to get their photos and I got a few more days on the Med, so in the end everyone was happy.

But for me it didn't last. Once I was back in Paris I got really lonely again. I missed Alfie badly and began to wonder if finishing with him had been a good idea after all. I'd achieved money and success but it didn't mean anything because I had no one to share it with.

One day, on the spur of the moment, I rang him and afterward we spoke on the phone regularly once a week. The trouble was, instead of consoling me, it made me even more homesick. One of the few things keeping me going was the knowledge that I was helping pay back all those people Dad had swindled. Then, one day, Fiona rang with some bitter news. She'd found out from Helen that Dad had been keeping the money I'd been sending him each month and had squandered it on a brand-new BMW. That did it. I'd had enough. As I put the receiver down I knew I didn't want to spend another day in Paris. Unfortunately I still had another six months of my contract to run.

I talked it over with the company's makeup artist and on her advice I decided to come clean and put myself at my employer's mercy. I made an urgent appointment with a director and asked to be released from my contract. My plea was not well received.

"I'll look into it," was all he'd say.

That night the buzzer to my flat rang. It was another of the directors.

"I'd like to come up and talk to you, Heather," he said on the intercom.

I pressed the release button to let him in. I'd met this man three or four times. Sometimes he used to turn up at shoots and stand in the background watching the proceedings, but I hadn't exchanged more than a couple of words with him. As I slid the catch of my apartment door he barged in, grabbed hold of me, and slapped me across the face.

"How can you let our company down like this?" he screamed and slapped me again. Then his face crumpled. "You can't leave me. I'm in love with you. You must know that."

My jaw dropped. *"What?"*

He began pacing up and down my apartment, begging me to stay, promising me anything if only I would change my mind. I was terrified. It was like having a madman in my flat. Then there was another buzz on the doorbell and his chauffeur came running up the stairs yelling in French.

"M'sieur, M'sieur! Your wife is leaving for Cannes. She is taking the children."

He stopped in his tracks. "To Cannes? Why?"

"Because she has found the pictures of Heather in your bedside cabinet, M'sieur."

I couldn't believe this. It was like a scene from a French farce. The chauffeur ran back down the stairs and the boss started to follow him but at the door he turned. "Don't think about going anywhere, Heather. I will return."

I freaked out. Now I *knew* I had to go. The man was a nutter. I'd heard about French crimes of passion and I had no intention of waiting for him to come back and commit one. Frantically I flung things into my new suitcases. Twenty minutes later I was standing outside my apartment calling, "Taxi! Taxi!"

A cab stopped but when the taxi driver asked where I wanted to go, I hesitated. My first thought was the airport but then I thought if the boss told the police I was breaking my contract they might be watching the airports. While I wavered, I looked into the driver's mirror and saw the boss's black limo pulling up behind the taxi and I went whump under the seat. *"Calais! Calais!"* I shrieked. *"Vite!"*

Slowly, the driver turned around. *"Comment?"*

"Just GO!" I was literally shaking with fright now, sure the boss was about to peer in the window and see me.

*"Ah, oui!"* The taxi driver seemed to get the message, but in fact he'd only understood half of it. Instead of taking me to the ferry port he drove me at top speed to Rue Calais, Paris. I tried to correct him. But I'd forgotten the French word for ferry. I'd forgotten the French word for channel. In fact, every French word I knew had gone right out of my head.

"Boat! Boat!" I made water noises. "Whoosh!"

He looked blank.

"The sea!" I mimed doing the breaststroke. "Swimming. The sea!" At last the penny dropped and the taxi driver set off toward the French coast two hundred miles away.

The trip cost me 3,000 francs or about £300. When we stopped at a service station to fill up with petrol I found a public call box and rang Alfie.

"Alfie, I can't explain now but please can you meet me in Dover tomorrow?"

He sounded baffled. "Dover? What time?"

"I don't know. The first ferry tomorrow morning."

"Are you all right?" Alfie's voice was concerned. "What on earth's happened?"

"I'll tell you all about it when I get there," I promised.

There aren't many tourists on early-morning ferries, and even fewer with long blond hair, short skirt, and high heels. As I struggled into the ferry restaurant with my six suitcases in tow I saw all these burly long-distance lorry drivers with huge tattooed biceps nudge each other and grin.

*Oh, God, what have I done with my life?* I thought. *I will never, ever do anything like this again.*

I expected a long wait on the other side because I thought Alfie would wait at home for me to phone him when I arrived. But as I walked through customs I saw him lying fast asleep on a bench in the arrivals lounge. Dropping my cases, I ran over and flung my arms around him. I'd never been so pleased to see anyone in my life.

Two days later I walked into his office carrying a small box from Hatton Garden. I walked past his secretary, past all the salesmen, and handed the box to him. He opened it and his eyes widened as he saw the gold wedding ring inside.

"Alfie, will you marry me?" I asked.

It was the beginning of December 1988 when I proposed. We planned the wedding for May. Before that, though, there was something I had to do. Although I'd kept in touch with Fiona and Shane, I hadn't seen much of Mum while I'd been concentrating on my career and we'd drifted apart over the years. If it wasn't too late I wanted to heal our differences so we could feel part of a family again.

Charles was touring and over the next few weeks I went to see her several times. Reconciliation is a slow process but gradually we grew closer. Over a drink to celebrate my twenty-first birthday in January we had our frankest and most revealing conversation ever. Maybe, because I was officially grown up, she felt free at last to talk to me as another adult. We talked of everything under the sun. Things we'd never discussed before: politics, religion, even sex. I was quite shocked when Mum confessed that as a student she'd once smoked a joint. Since Peter's death I'd been staunchly antidrug.

"Oh, come on, Heather," she said. "Don't be so puritanical. I wish my cancer patients were allowed to smoke grass. It would take away a lot of the pain. Honestly, it's no worse for you than this." She took a sip of her Glenmorangie.

She was in such a mellow mood that I decided to risk opening up another can of worms.

"Mum?" I hesitated. "There's something I've always wanted to ask you. Why didn't you stop me running away to the fair?"

She sighed. For a minute I thought she wasn't going to answer but then she took hold of my hand.

"Heather," she said softly. "Don't you see? I felt I'd no right to tell you what to do with your life. You'd brought my family up for five years, so how could I? When you were living with us you never behaved like a child. You were so sure of yourself, even at thirteen . . ."

I interrupted. "I wasn't really sure of myself though, Mum. It was only a show, I wanted you to stop me going. When you didn't I thought it meant you'd rather lose me than lose Charles."

She nodded. "Yes, I can see that. I suppose in a way I felt I'd already lost you. Charles was all I had left."

"How do you mean you'd lost us?"

"I mean that after I left you all I gave up any rights as your mother." Mum gave a crooked smile. "I'm sorry, Heather."

It was the only time since our reunion in Wales that I'd heard Mum express any regret for leaving us.

As I got up to go she gave me a hug, the first for years. I felt we'd never been so close.

"By the way, Heather," she said. "Did Fiona tell you I'm going into hospital in a couple of weeks?"

"No. What for?"

"Nothing serious. Just a minor op." As usual Mum's legs were shrouded by brightly striped tights and now she patted one of them, the one she'd so nearly lost in the car crash.

"It's this wretched thing. I had a silly accident in a supermarket a few years ago—someone pushed a shopping trolley into me. The old scar opened up and it's never properly healed. Apparently there's a blocked vein and I've decided to get it sorted out."

"Will you be in for long?"

"They said only for a night or two. Will you come and visit me? It'll be nice to be on the receiving end for a change."

Sometimes I forgot that Mum spent every day in hospital looking after cancer patients.

"I will if you'll come to my wedding," I said.

She smiled. "I wouldn't miss it for the world."

But she did miss it. The hospital treatment that was supposed to involve no more than an overnight stay turned into something much more than that. Mum was admitted to the Middlesex Hospital on the morning of February 20, 1989. That evening I kept my promise and visited her. She was cheerful—her treatment hadn't been too painful and she hoped to be let out in the next day or two.

But a few days later I walked into the ward to find Mum's bed empty.

"I'm afraid your mother's had a bit of a setback," the ward sister told me. "We've transferred her to intensive care for a while."

With my heart in my mouth I followed her to ICU. Charles greeted me at the door looking distraught.

"She's not at all well, Heather."

It was an understatement. Mum was very ill indeed. She seemed to be having trouble breathing and there was an oxygen mask over her face.

"What's wrong?" I demanded. "She said it was a simple operation."

Charles shrugged helplessly. "It was. But there've been complications. They've been using heparin to clear the blocked vein and they say Beatrice has created antibodies to it."

I stared at him in dismay, but it got worse.

It seemed that the risk associated with heparin was well known and Mum's blood had been routinely checked for antibodies but someone had missed one of the checks. By the time they took the next one, the antibody levels were sky high and blood clots had formed in her heart and lungs.

"They're going to operate very soon to try and remove them," Charles said.

It was a nightmare. I couldn't believe this was happening. People didn't come in to hospital for a minor operation and end up having heart surgery. They just didn't.

We went in to see her. Mum was conscious and trying to make light of what was happening.

"Heather, do me a favor? While I'm in theater run out and buy me another pair of pyjamas. My leg's bleeding so get red ones if you can." She smiled weakly. "At least it won't show."

Fiona and Shane arrived and a few minutes later porters came to take Mum to theater and we were sent into the waiting room. Charles looked so devastated I felt a rush of warmth toward him.

Fiona didn't look much better. I told her about Mum's request and we decided to go and look for some red pyjamas.

It proved to be a real challenge. In most shops all we found were rails of frilly white nighties. As we raced up and down Oxford Street we grew more and more frantic. The lingerie department in Topshop was downstairs and when we failed to find what we wanted there, we hurtled back up the escalator and pushed past a group of girls standing in the middle of it.

"Excuse me," I said. "I'm in a hurry."

One of the girls grabbed hold of my hair. "'Ere, who do you think you're pushing?"

It was weird. At the back of my head I knew someone was pulling at me but it was far away, unimportant. The only thing I cared about was getting to C&A and finding some red pyjamas. I reached the top of the escalator and walked out into Oxford Street with the girl still hanging on to my hair. The fact that I was ignoring her seemed to enrage her more: She kicked my legs from under me and we fell in a heap on the pavement. The next thing I knew she was sitting on top of me. She was a big girl and it was like being sat on by a sumo wrestler. I wriggled helplessly underneath her while the precious seconds ticked by.

"My mother's dying!" I screamed. "What are you doing this for?" I wanted to kill her. At last Fiona managed to pull the girl off and we bolted up the road to C&A.

There, finally, we found the coveted red pyjamas and bore them back in triumph to the hospital. But we were too late. Mum had come out of theater and had briefly regained consciousness, but while we were away, possibly even as that girl was delaying me, she had slipped into a coma.

The nurses' faces were grave. One look at the small still figure on the bed surrounded by tubes, dials, and bags of blood told me why. Mum looked dreadful. Her face was so dark it was almost blue. A big white dressing covered her chest. This had been no cautious exploratory operation, I realized—the doctors had cut her open from top to bottom. She was on a respirator now and her breathing sounded really desperate. For the next two hours I sat beside her bed, taking every breath with her until I felt faint from hyperventilating.

Doctors with grim expressions came and went and I could tell they held out little hope. One told us that if Mum came around there was a possibility she would be severely brain damaged. "I think you should consider this when you think about what we should do next," he told Fiona, Shane, Charles, and me.

We looked at each other, appalled. We were all sure Mum wouldn't want to live in a totally helpless state, but it was horrifying to be asked to make a cold-blooded decision about her life. We were all distraught. Shane, Charles, and I left the ward to think, but we hadn't been away more than a couple of minutes when my mobile rang. It was Fiona. "Mum's worse," she sobbed. "The doctor told me to call you all back." We rushed back down the corridor to Mum's bedside. Gradually, almost as we watched, Mum's face swelled up like a football and her skin turned bluer and bluer. Then at seven o'clock she let out one long shuddering breath and lay still.

I couldn't believe it. I just couldn't believe it. Mum was only forty-seven. It was too young to die. I stared at her for a minute, squeezing Fiona's hand as rage welled up inside me. It was so unnecessary. Mum had died because of other people's carelessness. First some stupid person had pushed a shopping trolley into her leg, then someone else had forgotten to do a blood check. And now she was dead. People were supposed to die from cancer, from old age, not from carelessness. *It wasn't fair!* In my anguish I picked up a chair and hurled it on the floor.

Gently, they led me out of the intensive care unit, but I was like something demented. Inside the matron's office I started to kick the furniture. Then I overturned the cupboards, the desk; I flung the telephone at the window. Vaguely I registered Fiona and Shane staring at me aghast.

"Stop it, Heather. Please stop it," Fiona begged. Shane put his hand on my arm. He couldn't believe what was happening. I couldn't believe it myself. This wasn't me. Someone had taken over my body. All my life I'd been the calm person. Whatever went wrong I hardly ever lost my temper. Going berserk was Dad's outlet, not mine.

Slowly my rage died and I started to sob. Shane took me for a cup of tea in the canteen and when everyone else had drifted away we went home. Behind us in the hospital, we left her new red pyjamas, unworn.

The funeral service was held in Pont Street Church in Chelsea. I'd expected there'd be just a few family mourners, but I'd forgotten about Mum's other life. Hundreds of Mum's cancer patients from the Royal Marsden turned up and when Fiona and I walked out after the service, people came rushing up to talk to us, grabbing our arms, touching us, as if we were saints. Shane said afterward it was because we looked so much like Mum.

"It's not right," one old man said. "We're the ones who were supposed to die, not her."

Listening to people's stories about Mum's kindness, of how she'd been their inspiration and had cared for them, I felt a big lump in my throat. Mum might not have mothered us, but she'd certainly mothered her patients. People with tears in their eyes told us how she'd given them acupuncture, aromatherapy, hypnotherapy, and helped with their pain relief.

A woman in a wheelchair took my hand. "She really cared about us, you know," she said. "It wasn't just a job to her. She was a wonderful woman."

I didn't know if it made me feel better or worse to find out that Mum had been able to get so close to other people when for all those years she had been so distant from us. On the whole, I think it made me glad to know that after her dreadful time with Dad, Mum had salvaged some satisfaction and happiness out of her life.

After the service was over Grandma linked my arm. I hadn't seen her for over a year and was shocked to see she was using a white cane now. She patted my hand. "Why don't you come down to the flat and see me some time, Heather? None of us have got much family left now. We should stick together."

I went down to Brighton the following week. I had no reason to delay it since I wasn't working—after the Paris fiasco I'd had no taste for modeling and since Mum had died no urge to look for any other sort of work. I felt really listless and depressed.

Grandma, however, was as lively and bustling as ever. I'd told her I would take her out for lunch, but when I arrived she'd prepared a three-course meal.

"I'm not going to let you waste your money, Heather. I know how much these restaurants charge," she said. "It's daylight robbery." Grandma hadn't changed. I remembered how when we were small she used to trail us through the supermarkets to find the cheapest can of beans.

Now, over roast beef and Yorkshire pudding, she gently encouraged me to talk about Mum, seeming to understand that it would be therapy for me.

"You've kept things bottled up for too long, Heather," she said. "All three of you have."

For the first time it all poured out. All my memories of Mum being bullied and knocked about by Dad.

Grandma nodded. "I used to suspect something like that was happening. But she never said anything to me about it. I never heard her say one bad word about Mark."

I nodded. "I don't understand that. If a man treated me that way I'd call him all the names under the sun."

Grandma reached over the table and patted my hand. "Other people's relationships are always hard to understand. I don't know what went wrong between your mum and dad. When they married I never saw two people more in love. Your mum adored Mark. When he first brought her home to meet us she'd sit at his feet with her head on his knees and he'd stroke her hair. We used to call them love's young dream."

"So, what happened?"

"It's hard to say. I don't think Beatrice found motherhood easy. She'd been all set for a brilliant career, you know, before she married. She was very talented. She spoke half a dozen languages, did you know that?"

I shook my head.

"She wrote poetry too. She'd had things published in Scottish newspapers. I think if she hadn't been married she might have become a writer."

I was stunned. Why had Mum kept these things secret? Grandma was talking about a stranger, someone I had never known. Someone I would really like to have known. And now it was too late.

Two months later, on May 6, 1989, Alfie and I were married—a beautiful big white wedding in the Catholic church at Stanmore. Although Alfie had been married before it had been a register office ceremony, so it didn't count in the eyes of the church and we were allowed the full works. I had three bridesmaids: Joanne, the six-year-old daughter of Alfie's best friend; Dawn, a model friend of mine; and Fiona. It was a wonderful sunny day and the church was packed. Alfie's relatives nearly filled the groom's side of the church. My side was less crowded but most of the important people were there: Fiona and her boyfriend Gus; Shane, on vacation from the London School of Music where he was now a student; Norman; Charles; and Grandma. The only two members of my family who were missing from the celebrations were Dad—whom I wasn't speaking to after the BMW incident—and Mum.

Mum's absence put a cloud over the day and as I walked up the aisle I was already having doubts. It was too soon. I felt emotional and mixed up and I needed time to recover from Mum's death. With every step I took I felt panic growing. Did I really love Alfie or did I just want security? What would happen when I had that security? Would I feel trapped as I'd felt with Stephen? Did love ever last? Grandma said Mum had adored Dad when they got married and look what had happened to them.

But as I reached Alfie's side and the priest started to read the words of the wedding service I knew it was too late for second thoughts. For better or worse, my fate was sealed.

# Chapter 13

When I'd first met him, Alfie had been selling dishwashers, but for two years now he'd been working for a computer firm and had done really well for himself. When we came back from our honeymoon in St. Lucia we moved into a four-bedroom house complete with swimming pool in Hoddesdon in Hertfordshire. It was real commuter-belt country and I think, deep down, Alfie would have liked me to be a real commuter wife but I'd already made it clear I had to work. I was obsessive about my independence.

"I know you think I'm funny that way, Alfie, and it's probably because of my childhood, but I don't want to rely on you for anything," I told him. "I don't want to feel as if I owe you something because you're looking after me. Do you understand?"

Alfie's own parents had a very traditional sort of marriage and I wasn't at all sure Alfie did understand, but he went along with me. He wasn't keen on me carrying on modeling and I didn't mind that. My experience in France had put me right off modeling anyway. Now I had a new dream: to go into business again.

I wanted to open a model agency, a good one, where the models were looked after properly. I'd come across a lot of bad agencies when I was modeling and knew I could do better. I wasn't worried about attracting clients. Loads of girls I knew were fed up with their agents and were looking for a new one.

Dawn, my bridesmaid, had also had enough of modeling and I agreed to take her on as my partner. I sold my precious car—the souvenir of my frozen yogurt business—and used the money to set up the agency. Phillip Goodhand-Tait, who'd become a really good friend, rented me some cheap offices in the West End and, in response to my canvassing, twenty-three girls agreed to leave their current agents and come with me. Six weeks after my wedding, the ExSell model agency opened its doors for business.

Having a partner worked well. Dawn was happy to do the routine office work, which left me free to do what I enjoyed most—banging on the doors of potential clients. The numbers of models on our books soon built up. One friend of mine, an Indian businessman called Sharp, was a big help. He used to accost any likely-looking girls he spotted, whether it was in the hairdresser's, the supermarket, or just walking along the street, and hand them the ExSell card. Sometimes he'd escort them in for an interview himself. It became a sort of hobby for him. Sharp always went for tall girls and it used to make me laugh to see this little short guy dragging in gangly six-footers, but within a month of opening, thanks to Sharp's efforts and our own advertising, we'd recruited nearly sixty girls. It was enough to bring out a "headsheet" (a big poster carrying photos and brief descriptions of all our models) so photographers could make an instant choice of girls they'd like to attend a casting.

In running the agency I drew a lot on my own modeling experience. I made a point of finding out exactly what each photographer needed and only sending girls who met his requirements. When I'd been modeling I'd been amazed how often agencies sent the wrong people to castings, like sending a blond girl along when the specification said brunettes. Some agencies, instead of preselecting, would send all the girls on their books to try to make certain the agency got the job. It wasted the photographer's time and the model's and it was bad for a model's ego. Often she'd go away feeling useless when she just wasn't right for that particular job.

When I was recruiting I never forgot the way agencies had rejected me when I was trying to break into modeling. I realized now that when I'd gone for interviews I'd made every mistake in the book. Instead of going in dressed simply with no makeup as agencies like you to do, I'd always been made up to the eyeballs with long blond curly hair and black leather gear. But not one agency had bothered to try to see past my "glam" image. I resolved that ExSell would be different. Whenever Sharp brought in young girls who wanted to be models, I tried to look beyond the face they were showing me and imagine them with different hair, clothes, and makeup.

As long as her figure and features were okay, then the most important quality in a model was her attitude. She had to be professional, to want to model so strongly that modeling came first, ahead of social life, morning lie-ins, and even boyfriends. I learned that last rule the hard way: A model we'd booked for a catalog shoot argued with her boyfriend the night before and didn't turn up because her eyes were red. Not only did she let herself down, but she let all the other models down because we lost that contract and there was no more work for them.

Modeling is a hard discipline to follow. Strangely, Dawn and I found that the most gorgeous girls rarely had the right attitude. The ones who had to struggle because they weren't physically perfect were often much more conscientious. They'd always turn up on time and you could rely on them to watch their weight, while often the girls who had it on a plate couldn't be bothered to make the effort.

When we'd been going a few months, a couple of photographers asked ExSell to represent them and it soon became an important part of the business. It was through a photographer—Ansell Cizic—that ExSell got its longest-lasting and most prestigious client, Dorothy Perkins. It took me eight months to sign them up and I loved every moment of the chase.

From the start I knew that Ansell was just the photographer Dorothy Perkins needed. The problem was convincing them of that.

Time and again I rang the marketing director.

"Look, you have to see Ansell's book. He's brilliant, perfect for what you want."

He wasn't interested. "Heather, I'm perfectly happy with the photographer we're using now."

But I wouldn't take no for an answer. Every week I rang to ask, "Have you been considering what I told you about Ansell?"

Soon the marketing director gave up being polite.

"Go away, Heather. Go away."

Not long afterward he reached the breaking point.

"Heather, I'm about to go on bloody holiday and you call me. The second I walk back in the door you're calling me. What do I have to do to get you to leave me alone?"

It was just what I'd been waiting for. "Just see me," I said. "Just let me show you his book. If you don't like it I promise I won't bother you anymore."

There was a long pause. "Okay, I give in," he said. "Come down."

"I'll be there in ten minutes," I promised.

He loved the pictures as I'd known he would, but was still reluctant to commit himself because of already having a photographer under contract. But I wasn't about to let him wriggle off the hook now.

"Look, if you're not happy with the pictures then you don't pay for them," I promised.

He thought about it. "Well, I suppose I've nothing to lose."

"Exactly."

I was so excited when I got that deal. I was really getting into business. The salesmanship, the gamesmanship, all the wheeling and dealing gave me a real buzz. So did getting noticed by other agencies. They were starting to regard us as serious competition now. *People in Camera* magazine wrote a flattering article describing me as "the smartest, chicest and toughest agency manager you are likely to meet."

There was just one cloud on the horizon. Alfie wasn't nearly as happy about my success as I was. Since I'd opened the model agency we were having more and more arguments. To me our marriage seemed one-sided. It was all right if *he* was late home from work but if *I* was late it was a problem. I sensed Alfie was jealous of my attention being on something other than him. I never doubted for a minute that he adored me. But I was beginning to suspect that his dreams and mine didn't match.

I was in a real dilemma over what to do. Should I give up my business to try to save our marriage? When, eighteen months after our wedding day, I found I was pregnant it seemed like fate stepping in. If we were going to have children then our marriage *had* to work out. No way was I going to let my kids go through what I'd been through with my parents. I decided to sell the agency and stay at home for a bit while I worked out a new career that would be compatible both with what Alfie wanted and with motherhood.

It was probably the right time to get out anyway. Dawn had fallen in love and wanted more free time and I'd achieved what I wanted to do in getting the agency off the ground. From now on it would start to become routine and humdrum. It was the setting up that I thrived on. Who was to say I couldn't do that again from home? Two weeks after I found I was expecting a baby we sold ExSell to a rival agency and I went home to Hoddesdon to enjoy my pregnancy.

I felt really broody, which I hadn't expected. Although I loved my two little stepchildren, Christopher and Matthew, I'd never before been happy to sit at home and let life pass me by. But now, shopping for baby clothes and planning a nursery, I almost purred with contentment. Maybe this is what I'd wanted all along without knowing it. I kept feeling my tummy, impatient for the day when the world could see that I had this little person growing inside me.

Then one Sunday Alfie offered to take me and the kids out for Sunday lunch. We'd only just set off when I felt a stabbing pain in my back. When we got to the hotel I went to the loo. Five minutes later I staggered back to the table.

"Alfie," I said, "I don't think I'd better have lunch. I'm bleeding."

Alfie rushed me to Enfield Hospital where a doctor told me I was having a miscarriage.

"We'll keep you in overnight and give you a D and C," he said. "You'll be able to try again. It's just one of those things, I'm afraid."

The following day I was discharged and for the next week sat miserably at home wondering what to do with myself. The nurses had told me I'd get over such an early miscarriage quickly because I was young and fit, but I didn't. I had no energy and I also had a horrendous backache. Because I'd always done so much sport I understood my body and I knew it was telling me something was wrong.

I decided to get a checkup from my own gynecologist. After what seemed to be a thorough examination he gave me a clean bill of health.

"You're fine," he said. "You've had a miscarriage and your body is taking a little while to recover, that's all."

But *I* knew I wasn't fine. I asked to see another gynecologist and was sent to see Dr. Yehudi Gordon in the Garden Hospital in Hendon. He gave me a scan and finally confirmed what I'd suspected for two weeks.

"You haven't miscarried at all, I'm afraid, Mrs. Karmal. The bleeding you experienced was from an ectopic pregnancy."

Apparently I was still carrying a baby but instead of growing in the womb where it should be it was growing in my fallopian tube.

It was quite a shock. So was the proposed treatment.

"Normally we remove the whole tube because if it bursts it can be life-threatening," Dr. Gordon said.

"Will that mean I can't have another baby?"

"Well, it'll reduce your chances of conceiving, but you'll still have one tube."

I panicked. I really wanted children. "Do you have to take the tube away? Isn't there anything else you can do?"

He nodded. "Usually not, but in this hospital we do offer another option. There's a chance that if we don't remove your tube your ectopic pregnancy will stop growing in the next few days and your body will resorb it. The only way we'll know is by checking the hormone levels in your blood each day. But it's going to hurt and we can't give you painkillers, I'm afraid, so it's your choice."

I chose to try to save my tube. For a week I walked around in agony trying not to think about what was going on inside me. Alfie gave me the impression he wasn't interested now there was no baby to look forward to and as a result we spent the week being very distant with each other.

Slowly, the HCG levels in my blood went down and the knifelike pain in my side went away and after two weeks the doctors confirmed that the pregnancy—my baby—had "resolved itself." Though my tube was saved I was depressed and filled with a sense of anti-climax. For a while I helped Alfie with administration work in his office but it didn't satisfy me. I needed something more challenging than office work to take my mind off what had happened. Much against Alfie's wishes, I decided to go back into modeling, and inspired by the idea of making a fresh start I also decided to have a breast reduction.

It had been on my mind for a long time. People make jokes about big breasts but mine were no laughing matter. They were so uncomfortable I could never go to bed without a bra on. But apart from the practical considerations, there were sound career reasons too. As a married woman I didn't feel I should fly all over the world looking for work, but to get regular employment in England I had to get away from the glamour look—it was as simple as that. In January I booked into a Harley Street clinic and my bust was reduced two cup sizes to a 32C. Despite the pain I never regretted it for a moment.

Two days after I came home from the hospital I celebrated my twenty-third birthday and Alfie's first wife Annie brought Christopher and Matthew around to see me. Annie and I had become good friends by now and we had a long chat. The boys were excited because Annie was taking them skiing in Yugoslavia. While we were discussing their holiday plans Alfie came in from work and on seeing the presents the boys had brought me clapped his hand to his forehead.

"Heather, I'm sorry, I forgot to get you a birthday present. Is there anything you'd like?"

I thought. In the past two months I'd had two operations and a lot of pain. Really, what I needed before rushing back into modeling was a holiday.

"Annie," I said slowly. "Would it be all right if I came to Yugoslavia with you? I've never been skiing and I could help with Matthew and Christopher."

"Yes!" the boys yelled in unison.

Annie smiled. "Of course. It'll be wonderful. It's not much fun skiing on your own."

Alfie looked relieved it had been sorted out so easily. "Okay, then, that's settled. For your birthday you can learn to ski." He frowned, jokingly. "You'd better be good though!"

I had every intention of being good. Whatever our differences, I'd never been unfaithful to Alfie and I had no plans to start now. In any case, with the stitches in my boobs and the pain of my ectopic still fresh in my mind, the thought of sin of that kind was too excruciating to contemplate. Focusing my mind on business instead, I rang John Davis, a photographer I used to represent, told him of my plans, and asked if he wanted any snow pictures for his library. He jumped at the idea.

Two weeks after my operation we arrived in Bled, a ski resort in Yugoslavia's Zatrnik Mountains. I'd only had my stitches taken out two days before we left, so learning to ski was a painful experience and my technique was different to say the least. I was so busy protecting my boobs that instead of relaxing the poles by my sides, I kept my arms clamped to my chest the whole time. Even so I managed well, moving up from nursery slope to black run in seven days. I fell in love with skiing. It was like being a kid again and discovering a whole new way of enjoying myself. I hadn't felt so exhilarated since I'd won my first race at school. It came as a shock to remember just how much fun life could be.

The weather in Yugoslavia that week was brilliant with blue skies and soaring temperatures. It was so hot that when John Davis turned up I was able to do some swimsuit pictures in the snow for him as well as some family skiing pictures with Matthew and Christopher for his picture library. Most evenings Annie and I took the boys down to the hotel pool bar for a game and a gossip.

I don't know what would have happened if Annie and I had managed to get on the same flight home—my whole life might have turned out differently—but because I'd booked my holiday after Annie, I had to return on a later flight.

We all spent the day on the slopes making the most of our last few hours. Every now and then I sensed one of the ski instructors looking at me. I recognized him as Milos, a little quiet guy who'd bought me a drink one night at the disco. I really didn't want to speak to him. He'd been staring at me every morning on the bus that took us to the slopes and something about him made me uneasy. He had the most incredible penetrating blue eyes that seemed to see right into your thoughts.

I couldn't understand why he disturbed me so much. He wouldn't have been my type even if I'd been available. Not only was he quite short, but with his black T-shirt and drab brown dungarees he had the worst dress sense of any man I'd ever met. There was a real provincial air about him, quite the opposite of Alfie's worldly sophistication. Admittedly he had very nice eyes, but it didn't matter because I was married: married; married; married. I kept reminding myself of it and every time I saw him heading my way I skied off in the opposite direction. At four-thirty I packed up for the day and went to my hotel to change.

Because they had such an early flight the next day, Annie and the boys left the pool bar at eight o'clock that evening. I decided to stay on at the pool table for half an hour more. I'd just taken a shot when I felt a tap on my shoulder. It was Milos.

"Hello," he said. "I have noticed that you seem to be on your own. May I play pool with you?" We played three games. Then he smiled nervously. "I was wondering . . . If you are on your own perhaps you would like to see Ljubljana this evening? We could go in my car. It would be nice for you to see Ljubljana before you go home to England. It is a very beautiful city." He smiled shyly. "You should see something else of Yugoslavia, besides just the ski resort."

He seemed so shy, so sweet. How could I say no? Milos was no lusty womanizer. He seemed genuinely friendly and keen to make my last night enjoyable. Anyway, what was the alternative? An evening on my own in my room or a session at the disco trying to fight off the attentions of some real live womanizers.

"Okay," I agreed.

Milos picked me up outside the hotel in his little white VW Herbie and drove me the fifteen miles to Ljubljana. The weather had turned really cold and he turned the heater on full blast but it didn't seem to make much difference—the Herbie had seen better days. We had a brilliant time. Milos took me on a tour of lovely little pubs and over halves of beer he told me about his girlfriend who'd just gone back to Germany, breaking his heart. In return I told him about Alfie and admitted that I wasn't really happy. On the way home Milos put a cassette in the car radio. It was Spanish guitar music, the Gipsy Kings, who had always been favorites of mine. It turned out they were Milos's favorites too and we both started singing along as we drove back toward Bled. It had started snowing, and great soft flakes were floating out of the darkness and smudging the windscreen. It was another world, a million light years away from Hoddesdon and Hertfordshire and England.

I was so tired I fell asleep. When I woke Milos was still driving steadily through the darkness and I realized with a shock that my head was on his knee. I moved to sit up but his hand stroked my hair and I lay still again enjoying the warmth of his body against my face and feeling so cared for, so safe and protected, I could have cried.

When we reached my hotel he walked me up to my room and at the door I turned and kissed him good night. That was all it was—just a kiss. But it was enough. Oh, God, I thought. Married or not there was no denying it: I had really strong feelings for this man.

He left then, promising to see me the next day. But he came while I was out shopping and we missed each other. He left a note in the hotel for me and I opened it in the bus on the way to the airport. It read simply, *If I never see you again I'll treasure those moments we had together.*

While I was traveling back to England in the plane my mind was spinning. I'm going to leave my husband, I thought. I've kissed someone else. I've been unfaithful. I have to leave because I want to be with Milos: To me it was black and white.

"Heather, you're crazy," one of my girlfriends said when I told her what was in my head. "Holiday romances happen all the time; you only knew the guy for a day. Don't leave Alfie, just go back there first and see if that's what you really want. See if it's what this ski instructor wants. He might be chatting up someone else now for all you know."

For a week I wrestled with my conscience but it was no good.

"I'm going to Yugoslavia again," I told Alfie. "I'm in love with skiing." It wasn't a lie—just not quite the whole truth.

I booked another ten-day holiday and returned to Bled.

I didn't tell Milos I was coming. Instead I rang his hotel when I had settled into my room.

"I'm here again," I said.

He ran down the hill from his hotel and came into the lobby carrying a single red rose. "I'm so pleased to see you," he said. He shook his head and he was laughing. "I can't believe you're back."

That afternoon he drove me to the slopes in his little Herbie and we went skiing. For the next ten days we were like children who'd discovered a soul mate, talking nonstop, learning everything we could about each other.

Being with Milos was so different from being with Alfie, it was impossible not to compare the two men. Alfie would turn the smallest mishap into a major catastrophe. But Milos never got in a panic. He was capable and strong and he gave me the feeling that whatever disaster befell us he would cope. Two nights after I arrived we were driving along in his Herbie in a blizzard when the windscreen wipers stopped working. We couldn't see a thing and I started to get worried, picturing us buried in a snowdrift, but Milos just laughed, got out of the car, and tied some string to the wipers. Then he threaded it through his window and drove back to Bled pulling the windscreen wipers backward and forward with one hand and steering with the other.

The following day we were supposed to be going out in the evening and Milos was late. When he did come through the door of the hotel he was covered in snow from head to foot and his hands were nearly black with cold. His car had broken down completely this time and he'd had to lift the boot and fix it in a howling blizzard. But instead of making a big drama out of it, he just said, "I'm really sorry I'm late. I'll have a shower and I'll be right back down. Okay?"

Incidents like these confirmed not only that Milos was the polar opposite of the man I'd been with, but also that he was the man I wanted. After ten days I knew without a shadow of doubt that my marriage was over. It was out of my hands now. I was in love with this man. I'd never before experienced a feeling like it.

"I'm coming back," I told Milos on the last day of my holiday. I could tell he only half believed me. Romances like ours weren't uncommon on skiing holidays and we both knew they usually fizzled out when the visitor flew home.

But our romance wasn't going to fizzle out—I was determined about that. This time as I returned to England I felt very calm and composed. I knew I was going to change my life. I didn't want the responsibility anymore of trying to be the perfect wife, the perfect hostess, the perfect stepmother. I'd spent my childhood being responsible. Now I was going to find out what I'd missed.

# Chapter 14

Two weeks later I'd said good-bye to the four-bedroom executive residence, the swimming pool, and the BMW and was back in Yugoslavia, living in a single shabby room in a terraced house in Ljubljana. I had no regrets about the material things I'd left behind. I'd have lived in a cardboard box on the street if it meant I could be with Milos.

My marriage hadn't had a pretty ending. When I'd told him I was leaving, Alfie had been first shocked, then angry, then bitter. He'd told me that running away to Yugoslavia was just like running off to the fair when I was thirteen. It was a sure sign, he said, that I couldn't face up to my problems and never would be able to. I didn't argue, but to me there was one big difference between the two situations. This time there was someone waiting for me. Someone who had no idea I was a successful model and businesswoman but who loved me purely for me and whom I loved madly in return.

I hadn't expected leaving Alfie to be easy, but it became even more traumatic when I discovered I was carrying another ectopic pregnancy—I must already have been pregnant the first time I went to Yugoslavia. Alfie tried to persuade me to stay in England and get it sorted out, but now I'd made up my mind to go I wasn't going to postpone it. I decided to take the chance that the pregnancy would resolve itself as it had the first time.

"If it doesn't, they do have hospitals there too," I said to my disapproving gynecologist. "I'm sure they'll cope."

Soon afterward I packed my stuff, bought a cheap £99 ticket, and flew back to the man I loved.

Fortunately the ectopic did resolve itself and the next few months were among the happiest in my life. We lived in Milos's bedsit and when he went off each day to teach skiing I would tag along and spend the day perfecting my own skiing technique. I decided to try to get a teaching qualification so that I could contribute to our income. I had some money left from the sale of ExSell and from selling my car but I didn't want to live off my capital, and I certainly didn't expect Milos to keep me. His pay was so low that by the time he'd given some to his elderly mother it hardly covered his own living expenses let alone mine. Not that living on a shoestring seemed to bother him. That was the lovely thing about Milos. Where Alfie had been a businessman and a capitalist, Milos couldn't care less about money. To him, the important things in life were comradeship, family, and love.

They seemed to be the most important things in the lives of most of Milos's friends too. The Slovenians were lovely people: warm, friendly, and less concerned about what you'd done in life than with the sort of person you were. Even though most of them were hard up by Western European standards they really knew how to enjoy themselves, and the smallest piece of good news would be an excuse for a party. Though people were so poor there was very little crime. Slovenians didn't lock their doors when they went out or hide valuables in car boots like they did in England. I saw little jealousy of the rich European tourists who came flocking into the ski resorts with expensive cameras, wristwatches, and suitcases. Milos's friends and relatives weren't at all materialistic and envy seemed foreign to them. After four months in Slovenia I knew it wasn't just Milos I'd fallen in love with—it was the whole country.

That year I rediscovered the pleasure of simple things: the smell of fresh-baked bread wafting out of the baker's shop as I waited in line for a loaf of hot *krugh,* or the comforting warmth of a blazing log fire on a night when the wind was howling.

At the end of March 1991, I passed the first stage of my ski instructor's certificate, but with the season nearly over, I needed to look for another job for the summer months.

Unfortunately there weren't many suitable jobs in Slovenia for English-speaking ex-models. I knew it would improve my prospects if I spoke the language so in the evenings I got Milos to coach me in Slovenian. I picked it up quite quickly and was soon fluent enough to be taken on by a local model agency. There weren't many professional models in Slovenia and I was given several plum TV commercials as well as some poster work.

During the summer Milos earned his living by running a gym in Ljubljana and giving private tennis lessons. But at the end of that ski season he took a tennis coaching job for a month on an island off the coast of Croatia. I went with him and taught aerobics at our hotel in the mornings. While we were there Milos made it his mission to educate me about his country. Until I came to live with him I'd been so ignorant about Yugoslav politics and history that I'd barely realized we were living in the part of Yugoslavia known as Slovenia. Milos's lessons came just in time. By the time we returned to Ljubljana, politics had become an everyday topic of conversation.

The first clue that everything in the garden wasn't as rosy as it seemed was when I woke one morning to find my old banger had been jacked up and had its two back wheels pinched. I thought it was quite funny: The car was such a wreck by now it hardly seemed worth doing. But everyone else was shocked.

"How can you laugh, Heather?" Milos's mother asked. "This sort of thing never happens in our country."

No one, including the police, had heard of anything like it before. However, it wasn't long before similar things were happening on the streets of Ljubljana every night. There was a rash of break-ins and general lawlessness everywhere in Slovenia. It was generally accepted that the cause of the discontent was the state of the economy.

There was rampant inflation throughout Yugoslavia, and Slovenia was suffering just as much as the other Balkan states, even though the Slovenian tourist industry should have ensured a healthy economy.

When I came to Bled in February there'd been 25 dinar to the pound. A month later you could get 75. What really brought it home to me was that when I'd first arrived in Bled I'd bought a pair of skis and some boots, which came to £250. A month later when it came through on my American Express account it was only £85. It was the main reason the Slovenian government wanted to declare independence. With a separate currency, not tied to those of the other Balkan states, they hoped Slovenia's economy would stabilize. But the overall president of Yugoslavia, Slobodan Milosevic, wasn't happy at the idea because he thought it would encourage Croatia and Bosnia to follow suit.

"We're rumbling toward war, I'm afraid," said one of Milos's uncles when we went around to his tiny flat for a drink one night. "We won't escape it, mark my words."

No one took him seriously.

In June, a week before the date Slovenia had set to declare independence, Fiona paid us a visit. We had a wonderful time touring in Milos's Herbie in the Tirolia Mountains with their beautiful ice-blue lakes and rivers. Among the news Fiona brought from England was a message from Helen that Dad had suffered a severe stroke but had discharged himself from the hospital though he was still paralyzed down the left side and had hardly any speech. "He still manages to get his own way even when he can't speak," Fiona said with a wry smile. Fiona had refused to speak to Dad for years now.

After visiting the mountains I took Fiona to the Croatian coast where Milos had been coaching tennis. I loved Croatia almost as much as Slovenia. The people were just as friendly and welcoming and the coastline with its hundreds of little islands was a real paradise. We had a hilarious time trying to master the water-ski machine at Poreč, but too soon it was time for Fiona to return.

On the morning of the eve of Independence Day, Milos and I had delivered Fiona to Brnik airport and were driving back to the flat when we heard on the car radio that Slovenia had been invaded. According to the announcer the Serbs were at that very moment heading for the airport, apparently with the intention of bombing it.

"Oh, my God! Fiona! . . ." I gasped. Milos stopped at the next public call box so I could ring the airport. They assured me Fiona's flight had left ten minutes earlier.

"Thank God." I hugged Milos in relief.

If I'd known the truth I might not have been so relieved.

Six hours later Fiona rang me from London.

"I can't believe what happened. It was a nightmare," she said. "As soon as we got through customs there was a big panic. They said tanks and planes were coming and they herded us all out of the airport, loaded us into a coach, and shipped us to Zagreb airport instead. You've got to get out, Heather. It's much too dangerous to stay there."

But by now my alarm had been diluted by the general air of confidence around me. Earlier that evening in our local bar, we'd heard people reassuring each other. The media always exaggerated things, they said. There'd been no invasion. Why should there be? Slovenia had no border dispute or clash of cultures like other parts of Yugoslavia.

"The UN won't allow the Serbs to invade," our landlord, Boris, assured us. "Croatia maybe, but not here."

If the army really was in Slovenia, he said—and personally he doubted the radio stories—it was just passing through. Its real target was Croatia.

"Everyone is panicking over nothing." He smiled. "Don't worry, Heather."

I took his word for it. After all it was his country.

To Slovenians the Declaration of Independence was a great excuse for a party and that night there were huge celebrations in the streets of Ljubljana. Everyone was really optimistic. Money problems were going to be solved. Everyone was going to be rich. As the wine and beer flowed people clapped each other on the shoulders and got more and more carried away.

But the next morning I woke to find a different atmosphere in the house. Milos and Boris were sitting in the kitchen and listening to the radio with solemn faces. My Slovenian wasn't fluent enough to understand what the announcer was saying and they both went

"Shhhh!" when I tried to ask so I gave up and set off for the corner bakers for some bread. As I stepped out of the front door I stopped short. The street was full of petrol tankers strewn higgledy-piggledy across the cobbles in both directions.

"What's going on?" I asked a passerby.

"It's to stop the tanks getting in," he told me.

When I came back with the *krugh,* Milos was still hunched over the radio. He looked up as I came into the kitchen, his expression grave.

"They're closing the borders," he said. "The radio says Serbian tanks are gathering all around Slovenia. They're calling on everyone under thirty to go into the army."

No wonder he looked worried. Milos was twenty-eight.

"Where's Boris?" I asked.

"He's gone to work—he still doesn't think it's serious. He said, 'Let them get on with it.'"

"It's all right for Boris," I said. "He's thirty-two."

Milos sighed. "I don't know what to think."

"You're not bloody going in the army," I said. "I know that much. Changing the currency isn't worth dying for. We'll go to Austria."

Slowly he nodded. "But we'll have to take my mother with us." Milos was devoted to his mother.

"Of course, why don't you ring her?" I said.

But Milos's mother didn't want to go.

"She says her home is here," said Milos, putting down the phone. "But she wants me to go. She says she doesn't want to lose her only son to the Serbs."

"Quite right too," I agreed. "Why don't you go and see if anyone else wants to come with us while I get packed."

I was an expert at quick evacuations. In forty-five minutes I had the whole flat dismantled and all our clothes crammed into the boot of my Fiat (thanking God I'd traded in the old banger when it had lost its wheels).

Milos arrived back as I was pushing the last case onto the backseat. He was alone. "Most of the others have already gone." He shrugged. "No one who's left wants to come with us."

He registered what I was doing. "We are taking your car?"

"Your Herbie'll never get us to Austria. We'd be lucky if it got us out of Ljubljana."

Milos grinned and got into the passenger's seat.

"Which border post shall I head for?" I asked.

"We haven't much choice. The radio said the only one left open is Podkoren."

There was a petrol station a hundred meters away and I joined the long queue winding its way out of the entrance. It took us over an hour to get filled up. Afterward we wove our way through the maze of petrol tankers and cars. Twice we found our path completely blocked and Milos got out and helped other drivers use planks to build ramps over the blockading cars so we could drive over the top of them. When at last we were clear I put my foot down and headed down the Jesenice Road. The road was surprisingly clear. Judging by the queues at the petrol station I'd expected it to be jammed with refugees.

It was only sixty kilometers to the border but the journey was so horrendous it seemed like a thousand. Every bridge we came to was barricaded with cars and tractors and we had to drive along the riverbank until we found a place where we could ford it.

Fortunately, in June the water level was low, but it meant we found ourselves off the main road and had to take narrow twisty mountain tracks. It was three hours before we finally crested a hill and saw Podkoren far below us in the distance. We were so relieved we burst out laughing. I shifted the car into top gear and we raced down the hill and then, just as we reached the last little hummock in the road I saw my first tank. It was sitting on the brow of a hill to the right and its gun was trained on us. I knew I wasn't imagining it because as we sped down the road the gun followed us around.

Milos had seen it too.

"We're going to get blown to bits," I said. I couldn't understand why my voice sounded so calm.

"Put your foot down," Milos ordered.

I obeyed but I was sure we were doomed. Any second now, I thought, we're going to be killed. Any second now . . . Some Austrian guards were standing at the border gate and as they saw our car hurtling toward them they raised the barrier.

"Get through, get through, get through!" they shouted, waving us on.

Seconds later it was all over. We were in Austria. We were not dead. We had made it! I skidded to a halt to find myself trembling like a leaf.

Milos had a broad smile on his face. "Nice driving."

We hugged.

Two customs officers came up to the car and I wound down the window.

"Where are you going?" one officer said. I looked at Milos, who shrugged. Up to now our only plan had been to get out of Slovenia.

"England," I said on the spur of the moment. They waved us on and moved away to wait for the next car. But to my dismay, seeing the tank had given Milos second thoughts.

"I feel like a coward, a deserter," he said. "Maybe I should go back."

"Milos, come on," I protested. "We'd probably get killed on the journey back. We can do more to help from the outside. If the Serbs start bombing, people are going to need medicines and food. We can help with that."

Reluctantly Milos saw the sense of my argument. Before he could change his mind again I set off for Belgium and fourteen hours later we arrived at Zeebrugge. I was so exhausted after driving a thousand miles almost nonstop that the minute we found somewhere to sit on the ferry I fell sound asleep on Milos's chest and didn't wake up till we reached Dover. We hadn't eaten for nearly twenty-four hours so our first destination when we got off the boat was a local Indian restaurant where we gorged ourselves on tandoori chicken. Then I rang a startled Fiona and told her to put the kettle on. An hour and a half later we were sitting in her flat in Tooting Broadway recounting our adventures.

"You'd better stay here until you decide what you're going to do," Fiona said. "You both look as if you need a good sleep."

She was right. We slept almost around the clock. But it wasn't restful sleep. I woke exhausted after dreaming about the other sports instructors and friends whom we'd left behind. We tried to ring their flats in Ljubljana but there was no answer. We didn't know if it was because they too had managed to escape or for another, more sinister reason.

Milos's mother did answer our call, but her news wasn't reassuring.

"There have been many airplanes flying very low over the house," she said. "It says on the radio that the Serbs have bombed the airports."

"Have you seen any soldiers?" Milos asked.

"No, none. People say they won't come to our village: It's not important enough."

But Milos wasn't convinced. By the time he put the phone down he was again tormented with guilt at leaving her.

That afternoon we started ringing around London companies and organizations with Slovenian connections to find out if anything was being done to coordinate aid efforts. At Adria Airways, Slovenia's national airline, we were put through to a manager who invited us to come in. At the airline's offices in Conduit Street we spoke to several airline officials. All flights to Slovenia had been suspended, so a lot of the staff had been left twiddling their thumbs and were anxious to do anything they could to help. By the end of the afternoon we had decided to set up the Slovenian Crisis Centre where relatives could inquire about their families back home and refugees could come in and receive advice about jobs and work.

"We ought to try and get the British government to do something as well," I said. "They went to the Gulf. They didn't let the Iraqis get away with invading Kuwait. Why can't they go and stop the Serbs invading Slovenia?"

"Because there's no oil there, that's why," said Milos cynically. Everyone else too seemed to think I was being naive to imagine that Britain would intervene.

I resolved at least to try to get the British press interested in the story. I'd bought a newspaper that morning but there was nothing in it at all about the Serb invasion. Either British journalists hadn't heard what was happening or they were deliberately ignoring it.

Back at Fiona's flat I rang several newspapers and spoke to the news desks. The response was exactly what everyone at the Adria Airways offices had predicted. Three news editors gave me the same line: This was a civil war that the Yugoslav people would have to settle themselves. The only sympathetic response I got was from the BBC, which agreed to broadcast the Slovenian Crisis Centre number on their home and world services.

Over the next few weeks some of the papers did begin to carry stories on the crisis, though they were usually buried inside the paper. The exception was the day when a few papers carried front-page reports that the Yugoslav army (which now, after mass desertions, consisted almost entirely of Serbs) had moved into Croatia and shelled the city of Vinkovci. But there were no pictures and no sense of the reality of what it might mean for the people whose homes were being bombed. It was the death of a pressman, a German journalist killed by Serbs on July 26, that finally made the papers sit up and begin to take notice.

When we phoned her, Milos's mother told us the Yugoslav army had left Slovenia. Boris's predictions had been right—their real destination all along had been Croatia. But Milos's mother hadn't left her village and had no idea what state the Serb soldiers had left her country in.

After three weeks in England, the cost of making phone calls, traveling by tube, and just living had left me very short of money. Most of the nest egg from my ExSell business had been eaten up and if I wasn't careful I was going to go overdrawn, which I'd never done in my life. One day Milos overheard me talking on the phone to the bank manager trying desperately to organize an overdraft. The next thing I knew he appeared in the doorway of our bedroom carrying a tray. On it was a mountain of notes and coins. "Here, take it." He pushed it into my arms. "I don't like to see you stressed like this." It was his life savings—about £4,000 in lire, deutschmarks, and schillings—that he'd received in tips from grateful skiing pupils over the years. I was lost for words.

I decided to do some modeling both to pay Milos back and to help cover our living expenses. It meant I wouldn't be able to work at the Crisis Centre anymore but I wasn't much help there anyway as my Slovenian was only good enough to cope with the most straightforward requests.

At the beginning of August I went along to my old agency and announced I was back in business. It was the first time I'd looked for modeling work in England since my breast reduction and I was amazed at the difference the operation made to my prospects. I was offered jobs I wouldn't have even attended castings for at one time. I still wasn't exactly flat-chested but there'd been a move away from the waif look in England and my new 32C measurement was just what clients were looking for. Earning good money made me feel much more secure and relaxed; it always had. By the end of August, I realized I didn't relish returning to a situation where you had to pay hundreds of hard-earned dinar for a loaf of bread. Much as I loved Slovenia I found myself hoping Milos would stay in England permanently—or at least until the war was over.

But Milos hated England—or rather he hated London. He was a country boy at heart and in a big city he felt like a fish out of water. The traffic, crowds, and noise depressed him and it depressed him even more to think of his friends and family back home. As the summer came to an end he couldn't stand it anymore and went back to Ljubljana. Adria Airways still wasn't flying to Brnik airport (apparently the Serbs had taken a vital piece of equipment from the control tower) and he had to fly to Klagenfurt airport in Austria, then take a bus back to Ljubljana. It was two days before he reached our flat, but the news when he got there was good.

"It's true. The Serbs have gone," he told me on the telephone. "Why don't you come back too?"

I stayed in London for a couple more weeks fulfilling my contracts, then flew out to join him, leaving my car with Fiona. (Some instinct told me I might return to London and I didn't relish doing that drive more times than I had to.)

Back in Ljubljana there was no trace of damage to buildings or roads. The only sign that anything was amiss was the presence of all the skiing reps and instructors from Yugotours. I couldn't understand what they were doing there—the ski season didn't start for months. Renata, one of the reps I'd been friendly with that spring, told me they'd been working in Croatia for the summer season and had fled back to Slovenia when the Yugoslav army invaded.

"It's very bad there," she said. "The Serbs have been bombing all the big cities and they've been massacring whole villages."

For the Yugotours reps, fleeing back to Bled wasn't much of a solution. Although they were safe from bombs and bullets, there was no work for them and the large number of refugees only increased the pressure on the welfare services. Things were reaching desperate straits in the area around Ljubljana, where there were shortages of food, clothing, and accommodation. Some of the ski hotels had been made available for the refugees, but obviously it wasn't a permanent answer.

Staying in Slovenia wasn't a permanent answer for Milos or me either. Neither of us had much money and inflation was still spiraling out of control. It seemed sensible for us to go back to England.

"If you find a job over there you can send money back for your mother," I said.

I had another motive for returning. Besides finding work for myself, I thought maybe I could organize jobs for the Yugotours reps in London.

We returned in October. This time, rather than imposing on Fiona again, we took a flat with Ruth Matthews, an English model who'd done some jobs with me in Slovenia before the war. The plan worked well and Milos quickly found a job as a waiter at the Victoria and Albert Museum. It turned out the manager of the restaurant was one of his old skiing pupils and when he heard the story he offered to find jobs for waitresses too.

I rang Renata and told her to come over. "Don't worry about accommodation. You can stay in our flat."

Over the next few weeks I managed to find jobs for all ten of the Yugotours reps and at night the floor of our flat was crowded with bodies in sleeping bags.

I found work for myself too, signing a deal with Slix swimwear to do showroom work and fittings. When I wasn't modeling I kept up my pestering of the media. From the stories Renata and the other Yugotours reps had told me, the invasion of Croatia had been much bloodier and more barbarous than that of Slovenia. Renata said that in one village, Četekovac, twenty-one villagers had been massacred in their homes by Serb soldiers. In the town of Vinkovci the hospital had been targeted and shelled until it was reduced to rubble. In other villages and towns, any non-Serbs were being forced out of their homes and told to find somewhere else to live. There were even stories of concentration camps. I couldn't understand why we weren't hearing more about these events on the news. I rang newspapers and MPs begging them to give the war a higher profile but I got nowhere. Once again, BBC radio was the only member of the media to give Croatia much prominence.

It was the radio news reports that, by the middle of November, had convinced most of the Yugotours reps to return. They were unable to cope with sitting in England knowing the Serbs were pillaging their way through their hometowns and villages. With most phone lines down there was no way of knowing if their families were dead or alive except by going to see for themselves, and one by one that's what they did.

"I'll be in touch to let you know what's happened," Renata promised as she left.

Shortly afterward Milos too left London. In two months he'd earned enough pounds to bring thousands of dinar when he exchanged them. Now the ski season was due to start and he felt sure there would be work for him at home.

"When people know the war is no longer in Slovenia they will come on holiday," he said. "Nothing stops people taking holidays."

I wasn't so sure.

I stayed on in London until my contract with Slix was finished. During that time Renata managed to telephone me twice from her hometown of Sisak. Her news was depressing. The Serbs had wiped out Sisak's school and hospital. According to Renata it was the same story in every town they attacked. The Serbs were deliberately killing children and sick people in their beds.

With the siege and shelling of Dubrovnik, newspapers and television began to take much more of an interest. But still the outside world was doing very little. There'd been a peace conference in the Hague back in September, but little seemed to have come of it. I tried in vain to get a commitment to help from British politicians.

I rang the Houses of Parliament and Downing Street. Once I even tried to ring Margaret Thatcher. I didn't get very far up the line. I think they thought I was a crackpot.

"We are aware of events in the former Yugoslavia," some third undersecretary said. "We are keeping an eye on the situation." Then the phone was put firmly down.

I couldn't understand the government's indifference. It wasn't as if Croatia was on the other side of the world. It was as close as Portugal; much closer than Greece. Hundreds of thousands of British people had been there on holiday. We weren't talking about Martians here. We were talking about fellow Europeans.

If the public realized that the main victims of this war weren't soldiers but old ladies, children, and simple country people caught in the crossfire I felt sure they would put pressure on the government to intervene for humanitarian reasons. But there was a lack of such information. The trouble was that after the Gulf War the newspapers had had enough of war stories for a while. They wanted some light relief after all those pictures of dead bodies in the desert. It was good timing by the Serbs and bad luck for the Croats.

Meanwhile, my personal problems were causing me nearly as much heartache as the war. I was due to return to Slovenia but I couldn't avoid the fact that I was earning as much in a day in London as I could make in months in Slovenia. A plan started to form in my mind. I'd never minded traveling. What was to stop me traveling back to London to work once or twice a month, or even weekly? Surely it would be worth it if it meant I could spend my time with Milos relaxing instead of both of us working long hours to pay the rent.

I drove back to Ljubljana at the end of the year. It was amazing that after those short ten days of war Slovenia had slipped back into an almost normal life. The one big difference as far as Milos was concerned was that the economy had gone from bad to worse. He and all his family were finding it a real struggle to make ends meet. In the circumstances my plan to commute to England made even more sense. Soon I was spending most of the week in London and flying back to Ljubljana every weekend. It was exhausting but it paid well, which to me was what mattered. However, Milos saw it differently and sadly that difference of opinion spelled disaster for our relationship.

It was becoming clear that though we still loved each other dearly our cultures were too far apart to let us live happily ever after. Milos was too proud to accept being supported by a woman and the poverty all around him made the money I earned as a model seem almost sinful to him. It was understandable. I could earn in a day what he had once collected for a month as a ski instructor. It was when it came to spending the money that our attitudes really divided. He'd see me paying for a manicure or having my hair done or legs waxed and he'd shake his head disapprovingly.

"But, Heather, that would buy food for a whole family for a week."

I didn't blame him for feeling that way but I looked at it from another viewpoint. I wouldn't get work if I didn't look well groomed, so these "luxuries" were expenses necessary to my job.

I tried to draw comparisons to make him understand.

"You know you need to buy the right clothes and equipment if you want to get work as a ski instructor. Well, it's the same for me."

Milos looked blank. "I don't need new skis every week," he said.

Milos's hopes that there would be a normal ski season in Bled were dashed. There were no tourists booked into the hotels at Bled or at any of the Slovenian ski resorts and by the time 1992 dawned Milos was resigned to losing his main source of income for the year.

By now he was having to live off his savings, which didn't help our relationship either. Although he still had the gym job and was doing a little bit of tennis coaching he spent a lot of his time brooding about my "gadding about."

"Why don't you give up modeling and stay home with me?" he asked.

"What would we live on?"

"We'd manage."

"No, we wouldn't. I'd be just one more person to feed. At least this way I'm bringing money into the country."

A couple of months into the season Milos found work as a ski instructor in Bad Kleinkirheim in Austria. I went along for a month hoping to mend our relationship but it didn't work. We squabbled all the time and after only two days we weren't speaking. I put my new teacher's certificate to use and found myself teaching a gang of English kids from Croydon. To my surprise it was the most satisfying job I'd done in my life. To get these kids who had never stood on skis before and help them get from beginner to red-run standard in a week was really rewarding.

The winds that first week were blistering and at midday we'd break and go for lunch to a taverna that had a huge fire in the middle of the room. On the last day I was standing by the fire and the kids from Croydon were all crowding around me competing for praise.

"Heather, Heather, did I ski well?"

"Heather, am I the best?"

As a good-bye present they'd bought me some woolly gloves, a hat, and five bars of milk chocolate. They also handed me a postcard saying *To the best ski instructor in the world.*

I was thanking them when I became conscious of someone's eyes on me and looking across to the other side of the fire I saw Milos watching with tears rolling down his cheeks. I went over and hugged him. I knew just how he felt. We loved each other so much, and it was so sad we couldn't make each other happy. Three weeks later I returned to London and in the quiet of Fiona's flat I forced myself to think honestly about the situation.

I had two choices. Either I could do what Milos wanted—give up modeling abroad, settle down with him, and become a traditional Slovenian housewife—or I could defy him, and carry on commuting, knowing it would mean the end of our relationship. Milos wouldn't compromise. If anyone was going to compromise it would have to be me.

The more I thought about it the more unfair it seemed. After all I was already compromising. I was spending £300 a week flying back to be with him. But it wasn't enough. Milos wanted me to sacrifice more.

I realized I wasn't prepared to do it. My independence was too important to me. I loved Milos more than I'd loved anyone in my life, but I didn't trust him not to change if I became reliant on him.

People did change. Nothing was forever. Dad's love for Mum turned to hate once he was able to control her. If that's what love could turn into there was no way I was going to give up my whole life for it. It was too much of a risk.

Milos took my decision well. He must have been half expecting it. "We can still remain friends, can't we?" he asked.

I put my arms around him. "I hope so. You're my best friend. I wouldn't want to lose you."

Under the circumstances it was as amicable a parting as was possible.

# Chapter 15

Even though we no longer lived together, Milos and I continued to see each other whenever I found myself in Ljubljana, which in the first half of 1992 happened quite often. I was still besotted with the country so whenever I was offered modeling work over there I would take it. I even did some agency work driving English models over to work in Slovenia and transporting them around while they were there.

Often Ruth Matthews, the model I'd shared my London flat with the previous autumn, would drive over with me to share an assignment. She too had fallen in love, not just with the country but with a young Slovenian man. Ruth and Istok had a flat in Ljubljana where I often stayed. Ruth's love life, like mine, was in turmoil, and we weren't a very good influence on each other. Once when we were doing a fashion show we went for a fitting in the afternoon, then came back to her flat for a couple of hours before the show. Unfortunately, we started talking about our relationships. She told me her boyfriend was always criticizing her extravagance just as Milos had criticized mine.

"Istok told me off this morning for buying a pot of jam," she grumbled. "He said it was a waste of money because his mother had a cupboard full of homemade jam . . ."

To show Istok that Ruth wouldn't be dictated to we went out and bought another pot of jam and two loaves of bread and somehow in the next hour I managed to put away a whole loaf and the best part of a pound of jam. It was comfort eating, pure and simple, and the end result was that I couldn't fit into the outfit I was supposed to be modeling that night. When I did finally manage to zip myself up I could hardly breathe. It didn't teach either of us a lesson. After that, whenever we got together and started talking about our love troubles we would end up eating. Hot chocolate, apple strudel, *krugh* spread thick with butter—all we did was cook and eat, cook and eat. In just a few months each of us put on a stone in weight.

But as 1992 went on I found myself spending less time in Ljubljana. Often now when I left London I headed for another destination—Croatia. I wanted to see for myself what was going on there. In April the UN had finally intervened and sent in troops to try to keep the peace but they were reportedly having little success. Every time the Serbs agreed to call a cease-fire they promptly broke their promise . . .

Even so, my first few visits suggested that the stories we'd heard in London might have been exaggerated. Zagreb airport was still open. Along the coast many of the holiday resorts seemed busy and the beaches were crowded with sunbathers though there were no English voices among them.

Inland, however, things were very different. Renata's telephone calls had prepared me for that. The lines to her hometown of Sisak were often down but whenever she could she rang me in London or Ljubljana. Often her phone calls would be interrupted by the sound of plane engines in the background and the dull thud of grenades going off.

"I have to go. I have to go," she'd gasp. "We've got to go under." Then she'd put the phone down to run to the air-raid shelter. Over the months she'd grown calmer about it until eventually, when I heard the whine of plane engines in the distance, she'd just say, "Oh here they come again," and carry on talking.

But one day when I was in London I took a very distressed phone call from Renata. She was sobbing so much I could hardly make out what she was saying.

"I was sitting in the café in town today and a grenade went off. One of my friends was killed. He was sitting opposite me . . ." Her voice broke. She was obviously still in shock.

"Renata, are you all right?"

"Yes . . . no . . . I just got a scratch, that's all. But I feel bad. I wish you were here."

"I will be," I promised. When I arrived at Zagreb airport two days later Renata fell into my arms.

"It's so good to see you," she said. "So good. I thought we would never meet again." She looked drawn and pale but otherwise all right. It was a sobering thought that if she'd decided to sit in a different chair in that café two days before she might have been blown to pieces like her friend Dumboyic.

Another of her friends drove us from the airport to her home in Sisak. It was the first time I'd driven inland since the invasion and the contrast with the coastal area was dramatic. Twice we were stopped by Croatian soldiers wanting to know exactly where we were going and why. UN soldiers in blue berets looked on while we were being interrogated but didn't interfere. At one roadblock, without thinking, I picked up my camera. A Croatian soldier held up his hand.

"Please! Don't take pictures or we must take your camera."

I put it away hastily.

We didn't pass through much evidence of war damage on our way to Sisak but in the town itself it was a different story. It looked an ordinary sort of town of washed-out gray buildings but I remembered from Milos's history lessons that it was a really important place historically because it was the point where the war had stopped when the Turks tried to invade years ago. Perhaps that was what had made the Serbs pick on it. It hadn't been completely flattened—they'd been selective.

Renata pointed to a blackened shell in the distance. "That was my old school. And over there was the maternity hospital. They go for children and women—they're very brave, the Serbs. Have you heard about what they are doing now?"

She didn't wait for me to answer. "They are going through the villages, raping all the women, trying to make them pregnant so there will be lots of Serbian babies. They want to plant the Serbian seed everywhere in Croatia. It happened in Osijek to a friend of my cousin's. She is three months pregnant now and she is trying to get an abortion. Some of the women who've been raped say if they can't get an abortion they'll kill the babies when they are born. You can understand it. They are not human, the Serbs, they are animals. They are worse than the Nazis." Renata spat out the words.

I stared at her in horror. "But we haven't heard anything about that in England. Doesn't anybody know about it? Surely now the UN are here they can stop things like that happening."

"The UN!" Renata shook her head. "My father says they only make things worse. They know the Serbs have ten times more weapons than us but they've put an arms embargo on the whole country. Then they just stand by and watch while the Serbs move into our villages and plant their flag."

Renata had a look on her face I didn't recognize. It was as though her brush with death had brought a shutter down.

"Your friend Dumboyic—the one who was killed—was he a close friend?" I asked.

She shook her head. "Not really, but he was a good honest boy. He didn't deserve to die like that."

Renata took me back to her family's tiny flat to meet her parents. Her father was a historian; while her mother cooked us a wonderful apple strudel he sat me down and using maps and books from his library educated me on the history of Yugoslavia back to the Ottoman Empire. He told me that years before he had written a book predicting the present war. But, in spite of all his knowledge, he couldn't offer an easy solution to the crisis.

"Who knows what will happen?" He shrugged philosophically. "Life goes on."

Renata's family's fortitude in the face of war made me feel very humble as I left their home that night. There was no room in their tiny flat for me to stay and Renata had booked me into a small guest house. It was extraordinary to find people still carrying on the hotel trade when whole houses had been blasted out of existence just down the street.

The next morning Renata wanted to drive me to see the villages where her relatives lived.

"What about land mines?" I asked. I'd read about a couple of vehicles being blown up recently.

"You have to watch out for them but that's one good thing the UN have done," she said. "They have patrols that go out clearing them and they put red sticks in the road to mark where they are. Sometimes they'll divert you off a road if there are mines waiting to be cleared."

Many of the roads we drove along were pitted with craters where shells and land mines had gone off, so our progress was difficult and we were often delayed further by having to slow down for pathetic groups of refugees—small boys carrying huge suitcases and old women clutching blankets and photographs.

"Their villages have been destroyed so they're hoping some relative will take them in at the next town," explained Renata.

Some of the villages she took me to had been literally razed to the ground and where once there had been picture-postcard cottages and farmhouses there were now empty shells or piles of rubble. In one of the villages near the border the attack had been recent and a pile of neatly stacked dead bodies was lying beside the road.

"Renata, you can't stay here," I said. "It's terrible. Why don't you come back to London with me? I can find you another job."

She shook her head. "No. My place is here with my family. When I was in London all I did was worry about them. When I'm here at least I know what's happening."

I felt a desperate need to do something to help. But what? What could one person do in the face of so much need?

After leaving Renata I decided to return to London via Ljubljana and while I was there I discovered I was not the only person anxious to help. I became friendly with a group of students who were planning to drive a convoy down to Croatia taking food and clothing for refugees. They told me that several British charities had sent crates of food and medical aid to Slovenia, which, traditionally, had been the gateway to Croatia. Now, however, the gateway had become a bottleneck and the aid was still waiting for someone to take it across the border.

"Would you be interested in joining us?" asked Boyen, the student organizing the convoy.

I said I would be more than interested. I put my name down for the next convoy, two weeks later, and told Boyen I would share the driving.

We took two vehicles on that first convoy: a van and a big truck. Boyen said that most of the towns and villages that had suffered shelling had set up distribution centers where the donated goods could be handed out fairly. Both food and clothing were desperately needed, but clothing, he said, would be particularly welcome. The weather in Croatia that year had been very wet and cold and many people had lost everything but the clothes they stood up in. I was surprised to see we carried nothing on the side of the trucks to identify us as an aid convoy, but Boyen said that was deliberate.

"If the Serbs know we are taking aid to the Croats, they might decide to shell us just for the hell of it," he said. "Better to be anonymous."

Getting to Croatia presented no real problem though the border crossing was manned by heavily armed soldiers as well as by police. They seemed most interested in whether we were bringing in any expensive gadgets or electrical equipment that might sell on the black market. Two of the students in the convoy had their cameras confiscated and one had to hand over his transistor radio. The activities of the guards were again monitored by UN soldiers but as before they didn't intervene.

UN troops seemed to be everywhere. Twice during the drive to our first destination, a town called Mošćenica, blue-bereted soldiers diverted us off the main roads to avoid mines or snipers. What we saw in the villages that lay away from the main thoroughfares was heartrending. Churches seemed to have been especially singled out for attack. In nearly every village we passed through the church had been shelled and looted. In one village we saw three old men trying to hammer the church door back in place while others nailed wood over the shattered windows. In another village, the heavy iron cross had been knocked off the top of the church and a little old lady was struggling to lean it back against the wall. In the churchyard behind her, graves had been dug up and looted.

"They steal the jewelry that's buried with the dead," said Boyen.

In that village the Serbs hadn't confined themselves to attacking the church. Half the houses were demolished too.

With all the delays the journey to Mošćenica took nearly twenty-four hours. At night we parked our vehicles under some trees and slept in trenches dug by Croatian soldiers beside the road. They weren't too comfortable but they were a safer bet than staying in the trucks. We dropped off our aid of clothes and tinned food at the distribution center where it was warmly received by a large group of waiting families who had somehow heard we were coming. Then we turned around and set off back toward Ljubljana.

From then on we did a convoy nearly every month. Once I drove my car over and used that, filling up the backseat with food. As the fighting around the borders became fiercer so the sights we came across got worse. It became commonplace to get to a village and find bodies lying by the side of the road. Sometimes we'd even have to stop the convoy to move bodies off the road or, worse still, parts of bodies, because often the casualties had been victims of land mines with limbs blown off. I was very conscious of the danger from land mines, particularly when I was driving. Sometimes, as Renata had described, we'd spot a red stick in the road where the UN had located a mine but hadn't detonated it yet. When that happened you just had to drive around it slowly and carefully with your fingers crossed.

We saw all too often what land mines could do. In nearly every town we drove through there were amputees crawling along the pavements or dragging themselves around on sticks. In the hospitals where we deposited medical equipment we saw yet more amputees, victims of mortar shells and grenades as well as land mines. Sometimes they'd be lying two or three to a bed with their stumps bleeding and infected because the hospitals had run out of antibiotics. Everything in the hospitals was in short supply: bandages, painkillers, even anesthetics.

Operations were having to be done on fully conscious patients. All the doctors we saw looked haggard and unshaven from endless hours on emergency duty. Our white plastic boxes of drugs and dressings made some difference to the care they could offer but the need was so great we knew they'd only last a few days.

So much more aid was needed. But it just wasn't arriving fast enough. Although charities like the Red Cross were aware of the situation in Croatia and were making appeals, the public in the rest of Europe weren't responding generously because there was still so little publicity about the war. In the English papers at any rate, very few photographs were being published. That was what was needed, I thought. Only pictures would focus the world's attention on the full horror of this conflict.

On the next convoy I managed to smuggle in my Nikon 35 mm camera and tried to photograph every macabre sight we saw, but it was a fruitless exercise. Both my camera and film were confiscated on the way out. The searches by the border guards were getting very thorough now—on one of our convoys they'd completely stripped down one of our trucks—but while I understood the need to stop arms being smuggled I couldn't see why the border guards didn't want the war atrocities publicized. Still, I didn't feel inclined to argue over the barrel of a rifle.

Renata put me in touch with an amateur photographer from Zagreb called Mladin Knezevic who'd had similar thoughts to mine and had already been driving around taking photographs in the war zones hoping to get them out. He agreed to join one of our convoys. Afterward I went back with him to Zagreb where he had a darkroom. I felt I might be able to smuggle prints out better than film. But sadly I was wrong. The prints from his first trip with us, like the film before them, were confiscated on my way out of Croatia.

As the fighting increased our convoys sometimes became caught in the crossfire, but there was no time to be afraid. Situations arose and we found ourselves dealing with them. Twice we arrived at a hospital caring for shell victims only to find that it too had been bombed and we had to help move the casualties to a safer part of the hospital. In most of the hospitals, beds were a luxury. Often, patients would be lying side by side on the floor. Once, while we were inside a hospital helping move elderly patients down into a cellar, the shelling started again and we had to dive for cover ourselves as glass and bits of masonry flew through the air. That was the closest I ever came to injury: Three people died in the ward I was helping evacuate, but oddly I didn't feel at all afraid. I had a strange sense that Grandad was there looking after me.

Our first job was to deliver aid, not to act as front-line war photographers, so we never set out deliberately looking for trouble but you didn't have to seek it out: It was everywhere. We tried to keep away from active areas but it wasn't always possible because no one knew where the next attack would be. Mortars were falling on bread queues outside shops, in markets, and on churches full of worshipers. If there were no mortars there'd be snipers. There were no safe areas. We arrived in one village to find the Serbs had just taken over and we watched them literally planting their flag in the ground in front of us while UN soldiers stood by and watched. One young Croatian man stood against the wall of his ruined house banging his head over and over against the wall crying, "Why have they let this happen to us? Why? Why?"

In between convoys I would fly back to London or Ljubljana to earn some money so I could carry on helping. It felt odd to be back in London after what I'd seen. Often when I was modeling expensive clothes I'd suddenly remember the convoys and wonder if this was really part of the same world. Like Milos, I began to feel it was wrong to be living at such a trivial level when people were dying and suffering so terribly only a plane ride away. It was hard to come to terms with, but I told myself that it was the money from this consumer society that was helping take aid to Croatia—without it the suffering would be even worse.

Croatia was never far from my mind, even in London. It had almost become an obsession. Twice when I had a free week and there was no convoy due to go out I got together with Mladin and we went in his battered Zastava on another photographic trip. It was my dream to march in to see the editors of the *Sun* and the *Mirror* and plant photos on their desks that would be so gripping they couldn't refuse to publish them. On both these trips we were driving along the road when shelling started up without warning and we had to stop the car and take shelter in trenches. The trouble was that often now the trenches had taken a direct hit and still contained the bodies of soldiers so we'd have to check that they were empty before diving for cover. Once the shelling was so close we had no choice but to dive in anyway and for an hour we huddled next to the bodies of two dead soldiers in camouflage uniform.

On my second trip with Mladin it had been raining for days on end and many of the trenches had filled up with water. With all the mud and bodies and shell craters the Croatian countryside was starting to look like something out of the First World War. One night when we were looking for a safe place to sleep we shone a torch into a trench beside a road only to find that the bottom had become a river of mud. Dark shapes were sticking out of the mud and when I shone the torch closer Mladin suddenly exclaimed, "My God!" The dark shapes were human hands and fingers. Heaven knows how they'd got there. Afterwards, back in London, I had nightmares about that trench.

Everywhere we drove now, the tracks between villages were crowded with refugees wandering with pathetic bundles of belongings, just walking, walking to the next town because they had no village anymore. There were little kids, women, and old men. But there were never any young men, because they had stayed to fight.

Mladin took rolls and rolls of photographs of the refugees. Back in Zagreb he printed the film in his darkroom and gave me copies. They were some of the most disturbing photographs I'd seen. They really captured the reality of what was happening. But it was a picture from another roll of film, taken on our second trip, that seared itself into my brain.

As the fighting got worse Mladin and I became almost immune to grisly sights. We had to, if we were to do our job. That's the only reason I can think of to explain this photograph. It was meant to be a picture of bodies piled up against a fence; I'd been the one who suggested he take it—I thought it might awaken memories of World War Two atrocities and stir British consciences. But when Mladin processed the film back in Zagreb the first thing our eyes focused on as the print came out of the developing tank was a left foot, still with its shoe on, lying in the foreground in the middle of the road. Neither of us had even noticed it when he took the picture.

In the end that photograph too was confiscated, along with all the others, when I tried to smuggle it out. Funnily enough it was the one photograph I wasn't sorry to lose, even though it would have made a really gripping image for the papers. Looking at it had sent a shiver down my spine.

# Chapter 16

By early 1993 my visits to Croatia were getting to be less frequent. Partly it was because my abortive attempts to smuggle photos out were becoming unnecessary. The world in general was beginning to take much more notice of the war and hundreds of professional reporters and photographers were now covering events in Croatia and Bosnia where the fighting was now focused.

But there was another reason. I was no longer able to join convoys at the drop of a hat because my career at home was taking off. In January, after following a strict fruit and veg diet to lose my excess pounds, I'd landed a modeling job for a swimwear company in the Bahamas. It was a really plum contract and I was given five-star treatment: collection by chauffeur, transfer by private jet, and finally accommodation aboard a luxurious yacht for the ten days of the shoot. I'd heard of models who got jobs like this but to date I'd never been in that league. The fee was so incredible I was not only able to finish paying for the Saab convertible I'd just bought on higher purchase, but also to put a deposit on a flat in West Hampstead.

Ruth moved in to share the flat with me—her relationship with Milos's friend Istok had ended too—and we spent the next few months enjoying our freedom. With no man in my life I was able to throw myself headfirst into promoting my career. I got John Davis to take some new pictures for my portfolio and concentrated on building up a solid reputation in the business. I was in luck. The new "busty" look had become really popular and in the next few months I found myself more in demand than I'd ever been in my life, working everywhere from Malaysia and America to the Middle East. In America, being an English model got you a ticket to all sorts of social events and I sometimes found myself brushing shoulders with superstars, the most memorable occasion being one evening in June when I found myself having dinner with Bruce Willis *and* John McEnroe.

I tried to keep my feet on the ground and, usually, wherever I was sent I'd trade the club-class ticket supplied by the client for two economy tickets so I could take Ruth with me. It meant she got a free holiday and I had company.

Work rolled in all summer and I signed good contracts with Marks & Spencer and River Island as well as another really lucrative swimwear deal with Slix. Swimwear was my specialty now. Most models have features that are particularly marketable and in my case those features were my bust and my legs. A good cleavage is obviously important for swimwear shots but equally important is the ratio of leg to body. Nature had kindly given me a relatively short body and an inside leg of thirty-three inches. That inside leg measurement, as long as I kept working out each day to keep my legs in shape, meant my niche in the market was fairly secure.

The excitement of my booming career didn't make me forget about Croatia and I stayed in regular touch with Renata, who told me in April that little had changed in her country.

"One cease-fire follows another," she said. "But children are still getting shot. Some people say it will never end."

Her phone calls always brought me down to earth. After speaking to Renata I was never in danger of getting swimsuit modeling out of perspective. It was a job, that was all. A well-paid job, but essentially a trivial job compared with the business of life and death. I tried to always remember that. Three times that spring I went out to Ljubljana and to Zagreb, but I always came home depressed and dispirited. I was no longer needed as a convoy driver—there were plenty of volunteers now without me—and there seemed little else I could usefully do. By my third visit in May I was beginning to feel like a voyeur of other people's suffering and I decided that for a while at least I wouldn't go back to Croatia.

As I said good-bye to Renata at Zagreb airport we were both tearful, but I promised her that when I could see some way of really helping the situation, I'd be back.

"Don't worry," I said, hugging her. "It's not forever."

Back in London the war sometimes seemed like a bad dream; it was never far from my thoughts but I tried not to brood about it. Life, I told myself, was too short to stay depressed about things you couldn't change.

On the personal front at least, things were looking good. For the first time in years my free time was my own and I could do things simply to please me. I made the most of it. I took tennis lessons, I worked out in the local gym every day, and I even fulfilled my childhood dream and started taking saxophone lessons. And then one day, out of the blue, I fell in love with Raffaele Mincione . . .

It happened despite my very best intentions. Not long after my split-up with Milos, my divorce had come through and both experiences had been so painful that I'd resolved not to get seriously involved again for a long while. I wanted time for the scars to heal first. Time to enjoy being single. It didn't mean I became a hermit though. Two or three times a week Ruth and I would go clubbing, not to meet men, but to dance, which we both loved. Things had changed since I'd last been an unattached girl in London. Six years ago I'd been working *in* the clubs. Now I was well off enough to go as a paying customer. That summer we sampled all the top clubs in London, often staying on the dance floor until the early hours. One of my favorites was Stringfellows, because there was rarely any hassle from men and it always had good music. It was there, on the evening of Friday, July 23, that I was dancing away with Ruth when a tall handsome dark-haired man made his way across the floor and said in a seductive Italian accent, "Would you like to dance?"

I gave him the cold shoulder—recently it had been my automatic reaction when men tried to chat me up.

"No, I wouldn't."

He looked so taken aback I took pity on him.

"Look, it's nothing personal. I just don't dance with men."

He looked even more taken aback by that statement. But it didn't put him off.

Half an hour later he popped up again.

"Would you like to come to a party at Tramps?"

He obviously expected me to be really impressed. You had to be a member to get into Tramps and since membership was around £1,000 any bloke who invited you there had to be well heeled. Little did he know that for me it was the worst chat-up line he could have used because Tramps was the one club I really didn't like—it always seemed to be full of snobby people with plums in their mouths.

"No, thank you," I said sweetly.

But he kept pestering me. Ten minutes later as he passed me on his way to the bar he asked, "May I buy you a drink?"

I refused, but in a few more minutes he was back.

"Would you like to go out for a meal tomorrow evening?"

"I'm afraid I'm going to see *Don Giovanni* tomorrow evening," I said. It was a lie, but I thought it was an appropriate put-down for an Italian.

But he refused to be put down.

"Oh, the opera?" His face lit up and I had to admit he had a really nice smile. "I love the opera."

*Oh, I bet,* I thought. If he was an opera buff then he'd be the first one I'd met at Stringfellows. It wouldn't take long to put this one in his place.

"So which composer do you like in particular?" I asked innocently.

"Oh . . . ," he said. "I love Puccini, Verdi . . ."

Fair enough. Any Italian man would have heard of them.

"What about Wagner?" I inquired.

"Oh, yes. *The Ring of the Nibelung*? Fantastic."

Taken aback I began to really test him, but I couldn't catch him out. He knew all the answers. His favorite opera, he told me, was *La Bohème,* which just happened to be mine too.

I felt the old familiar melting sensation inside and struggled to fight it off.

"Do you have tickets for *Don Giovanni*?" he asked.

"Not yet," I admitted.

"If you have trouble getting a ticket then would you have dinner with me?"

Danger signals were flashing in my head but I ignored them. What harm could it do to have dinner with him? I must stop overreacting when men asked me out. He wasn't suggesting I move in with him. Anyway I hadn't taken a vow to become a nun, just to avoid commitment.

"All right." I smiled.

I didn't bother to find out if *Don Giovanni* was a sellout—it wasn't one of my favorite operas anyway—and the next evening I met Raffaele outside Ed's Diner on the Fulham Road where we shared a chocolate milk shake. Later over pasta and salad at Harvey Nichols I learned that he was a bond dealer for the Industrial Bank of Japan. I also learned that he was twenty-eight years old, the eldest of three children, and that he had been brought up very strictly.

"Until I was nineteen my mother never let me drink tea or coffee," he informed me. It was hard to match this image with the suave young man about town I'd met the night before. He said he had just been on holiday in Bali and had arrived back the previous week. The way he described it in his sexy Italian voice made me want to go to Bali with him there and then.

After dinner he came back with me to my flat in Hampstead for coffee—Ruth was away visiting her mother—and by the time he took me in his arms I knew I was lost.

When I woke up the next morning, though, I had second thoughts. Raffaele was already up, making coffee and chattering on nonstop. He had this really excited way of talking, and hearing this alien voice coming from my kitchen I panicked. *Oh, no,* I thought. *What have I done?* I felt scared. I realized I could fall in love with this guy and I didn't need it. I drove us to a coffee shop for breakfast and then made an excuse about having to go to the gym and left him to catch a taxi back to his flat.

"I'll call you," I said as I waved good-bye, but I had no intention of calling him. I hadn't given him my phone number and since we'd arrived at my flat in the dark and left in a hurry that morning I was hopeful he wouldn't have much idea where I lived.

But Raffaele wasn't to be discarded so easily. Later, he told me he spent four hours driving around looking for me that evening. It was eight o'clock when he rang the bell of my flat.

"Oh, my God," I said when I saw him standing on the pavement like an abandoned puppy that had finally found its way home. I knew I couldn't do it again. Leaving him had taken all my willpower and self-restraint and I had none left.

We went out for a Chinese meal and then drove back to his flat in Beaufort Street where I stayed for the rest of that week—much to Ruth's amusement. We fell into an instant routine; it was as if we'd known each other for years. In the morning I'd wake him up at six and drive him to his office in the City before setting off for work myself. The attraction between us was incredible, but it still felt dangerous. I was very aware of our differences. Raffaele had obviously had an authoritarian upbringing and held very conservative views on everything from etiquette to fashions. For example my current style of dressing in tight tops and short skirts wasn't to his taste at all.

"I like my ladies to dress . . . not so boldly," he informed me one evening as we set off to go dancing. He eyed my cleavage with disapproval. "Why don't you wear a nice blue skirt with a nice blue shirt when we go out? It would suit you."

"Get lost," I told him. "I dress to please myself."

The weekend after our first meeting I surprised Raffaele by presenting him with an air ticket to Greece. Fiona had been working there for six months and I had such strong feelings about this man that I wanted her to meet him.

On Friday, July 30, 1993, we flew to Athens where we met Fiona and her new boyfriend Dimitri and had a nice long weekend, doing all the usual tourist things like visiting the Acropolis and sampling retsina and ouzo. Raffaele wasn't just good company in private. It turned out he could be the life and soul of the party as well and he kept us in stitches the whole weekend.

The trip was a great success. Fiona definitely approved of my new relationship and, as we were leaving on that Monday morning, she announced that she'd be coming to London the following weekend so we could return the compliment and introduce Dimitri to the sights of London. In the middle of that week—which I again spent at Raffaele's flat—Fiona rang to confirm their visit. She said she'd be arriving on Saturday and would meet us outside Covent Garden tube station at ten o'clock.

Early on Saturday evening, at Raffaele's suggestion, we had dinner with some of his cousins. The service was very slow and I started to get agitated. I hate being late for anything, but especially when it means people will be hanging about waiting for me. Raffaele seemed oblivious to the time, so as soon as he'd finished his coffee I nudged him.

"We must leave to meet Fiona," I muttered (under my breath, because his cousins were very correct and the proper etiquette when you finished dinner was obviously important).

"Okay," said Raffaele, and promptly ordered another coffee.

I sat there fuming and the minute he finished I stood up. "Excuse me, everybody," I said between clenched teeth. "I'm really sorry but we have to go."

We arrived at our rendezvous point ten minutes late to find Fiona and Dimitri already waiting.

Sometimes I look back to that night and think what a trivial thing it was to get upset over. What an unimportant thing compared with the events that it set in motion. If only I hadn't got so upset about it. If only I'd overlooked it, put it behind us, and made the most of the rest of the evening. Things might have been so different today.

But *if onlys* are a waste of time. The sad fact is that I didn't put it behind me, and the reason I didn't was that Raffaele and I immediately had another difference of opinion about which club to go to. I wanted to take Fiona to my favorite, Stringfellows. But Raffaele had other ideas.

"No," he said. "I don't like it at Stringfellows."

Considering it was where he'd met me I thought that was an odd statement, and said so.

"So where *do* you want to go to?" I demanded.

"I'd like to go to Brown's."

"Right. Fine. Let's go." I marched off.

We were trapped in that silly situation where everything you do irritates the other person. In my heart, I knew exactly why I was finding Raffaele so annoying. It was because I wanted to be annoyed. I wanted to pick holes in him. I was desperate to find he had feet of clay because I just did not want another heavy relationship. I didn't need that sort of thing just now, when my life was going so well, so I was consciously looking for an excuse to dump him. And Raffaele, bless him, gave me plenty of excuses that night.

No sooner had we arrived at Brown's than his whole entourage of cousins and friends turned up from the meal where we'd left them. Raffaele had obviously prearranged it, and all that stuff about not liking Stringfellows had been a load of nonsense.

*Oh, bugger this,* I thought. "Come on, Fiona," and I dragged her onto the dance floor to get some steam out of my system.

It was hot and after half an hour I was desperate for a drink and went over to the table where Raffaele and his freinds were chatting. There was a glass of mineral water sitting in the middle of the table.

"Is this mine?" I asked.

Raffaele nodded.

"Cheers," I said.

He looked pained. "What?"

"Cheers," I repeated.

He shook his head patronizingly. "It's not 'Cheers,' Heather. It's 'Thank you.'"

I stared at him unbelievingly, as my picture of this wonderful man went bump, bump, bump, downhill.

A moment later Fiona and Dimitri came up. "Heather, we're tired," said Fiona. "Would you mind driving us home?"

The plan had been for me to drive them to my flat in West Hampstead, then return with Raffaele to stay in his flat for the night. But Raffaele was obviously having too good a time to leave so I said, "Look, I'll just drop Fiona and Dimitri off—then I'll come back and get you."

It was a twenty-minute drive to West Hampstead. Forty minutes later I arrived back at Brown's to be greeted with, "Where have you *been*?"

That did it. Something snapped. We were giving a lift to his cousin and I sat behind the wheel of the Saab being very tight-lipped and polite until we'd dropped him off and had pulled up outside Raffaele's flat.

Then as he reached for the handle on the passenger door I said very calmly, "I don't want to see you ever again, Raffaele. Just get out of my life."

"Why? What have I done?" He looked mystified.

I wouldn't even argue with him and eventually he realized I meant it and got out.

I drove home with tears pouring down my face. Ruth was away at her mother's, but Fiona was still up, making a hot chocolate drink in the kitchen.

"Heather? Is anything the matter? I thought you were staying at Raffaele's."

I exploded. "I can't believe that man. He thinks he owns me!"

I was so angry. Much angrier really than his behavior deserved; I knew that. In my heart I also knew that the person I was really angry at was not Raffaele but me. Because I'd left it too late to pull out gently. I'd already fallen in love with him. Cursing, I went to bed where I tossed and turned until, just as it was getting light, I dropped off to sleep.

That would have been it. Usually when I make a decision there's no going back. But when I woke on Sunday morning and decided to go to the gym to take my mind off things, I discovered Raffaele's jacket and wallet in the boot of my car. As I carried them back into the house the phone rang.

"Heather, have you seen my wallet?"

"I've just found it. I'll drop it off on my way to the gym."

His voice was hesitant. "Can't we meet?"

I hardened my heart. "No, I'm not interested. I told you."

An hour later, dressed in my gym kit of vest, cycling shorts, and trainers, I stopped the car outside Raffaele's flat, ran to his front door, and rang the bell. The door opened immediately—he must have been waiting for me—and he looked so penitent and sad that my determination wavered.

"Please, Heather, can't I just talk to you?"

"No, you can't." Even to my ears it sounded childish.

"But it's such a lovely day. Why don't we go for a walk in the park?"

Rather halfheartedly I shook my head.

He caught my arm and looked at me with those melting Italian eyes. "Please? I am so sorry about last night."

I couldn't carry on saying no. I was still determined that I wasn't going to let this thing start again. But I told myself it wouldn't hurt to let him down more gently. If we went to the park I could explain that I wasn't ready for a heavy affair yet. That it was too much for me to cope with after Milos and my divorce. It wasn't good to end our relationship with a quarrel. If I could make him understand my reasons for finishing with him then maybe we could stay friends the way Milos and I had.

"All right, then," I agreed. "But just for an hour. I'm still going to the gym later." I didn't want him getting his hopes up.

I parked the Saab in De Vere Gardens. From there it was just a short walk over the road into Kensington Gardens. The roof was down so I popped out the radio and locked it in the boot, then put up the hood. I felt surprisingly cheerful. Maybe it was the lovely weather or maybe it was the fact that I was about to see Kensington Gardens for the first time. I'd often heard about them. There were supposed to be tame squirrels there, and the statue of Peter Pan. I was looking forward to seeing them. But we never made it to Kensington Gardens . . .

My very last memory of that day, August 8, 1993—my last memory until three days afterwards—is of standing at the junction of De Vere Gardens and Kensington Road with Raffaele just behind me. So far I'd said very little to him. I wanted to wait till we got to the park. I was frightened of casual conversation, frightened of the slippery slope of intimacy it might lead to. While I was driving I'd been busily going over in my head exactly what I was going to say in the park. By the time I'd locked up the car, I had it all worked out. I was going to tell him that while I liked him a lot I had absolutely no intention at all of going out with him again. We were too different. Our cultures were too different. *Italian and Geordie—what a mixture!* I'd laugh. I was going to bring Milos into it—explain how our relationship hadn't worked because of the differences in our backgrounds. *What's the point of making life difficult for ourselves?* I'd say. *Better to call it a day now before we get hurt.* I felt very calm. As soon as we got to the park I intended to find a bench for us to sit down on and then I would tell him.

As we stood at the curb waiting for a gap in the traffic, I heard the sound of sirens in the distance. Steadily the sirens got louder and louder until suddenly two police motorbikes went flying by.

I took a step back. "Jesus, they're doing a speed," I said, more to myself than to Raffaele.

When they'd heard the noise of the sirens all the traffic had pulled over. To my right a double-decker bus had stopped to let the motorbikes go by. Now I saw the bus driver looking in his mirror as if preparing to pull out again. Farther up the street to my left people were once more starting to cross the road. I checked again to my right. Behind the bus the road seemed clear.

"Come on, Raffaele," I said. "Let's go." Still looking right I stepped out. One step. Two steps. And after that I don't remember anything . . .

# Chapter 17

It's only through talking about it to Raffaele and other witnesses that I know the details of what happened next. According to Raffaele I was walking two steps ahead of him and he was looking after the bikes that had just disappeared when suddenly he turned his head and saw a third police motorbike roaring "out of nowhere" and heading straight for me. He says I saw it too and turned to face it, hesitating as if deciding which way to jump. In the end I dived to my left but the bike veered the same way and hit me head-on. The next thing Raffaele saw was the motorbike, the bike rider, and me all flying through the air.

I was hurled ten yards up the road, landing outside the Kensington Palace Hotel, while the bike, with the policeman still clinging on, ended up several yards farther on. For a moment Raffaele says no one moved. Then suddenly there was chaos with people screaming and running about in all directions. Raffaele took a step towards me and nearly stepped on something lying on the road in front of him. He looked down. It was my trainer. And in my trainer was my foot. Attached to the foot was something red and bloody.

"It looked," Raffaele told me, "like a piece of meat from the butchers." He said that while he was staring at it, his mind seemed to float away. "I told myself, *I am not here. I do not want to be here,*" he said. "My mind was saying, *No, No, No, No, No.*"

But the nightmare wouldn't go away. The foot was still there and so was he. Clearly he had to do something. But what? Half his mind was telling him to pick my foot up and half was telling him no, that's stupid, so in the end he left it where it was and ran up the road to where I was lying. By this time a small crowd had gathered around me. He pushed his way through to find me lying on the road, moaning and dazed, while what was left of my leg was pumping out blood onto the tarmac.

"I thought you were going to bleed to death in front of my eyes," he said.

No one seemed to know what to do to stop the bleeding. People were talking about tourniquets and pressure points but nobody had the nerve to actually *do* anything until suddenly a man pushed his way through the crowd and said, "I'm a doctor."

That must have been the moment my guardian angel came back on duty. It turned out this doctor had been picnicking in the park when he'd heard the commotion. He'd brought a first-aid kit with him from his car and he sent someone to a hotel to fetch some ice and made ice packs to stem the bleeding.

"Find something to keep her warm," he instructed Raffaele. "She mustn't get cold."

Up until then Raffaele said he'd just been petrified with horror but now, at the thought he could actually do something to help, he leaped up and ran into a nearby restaurant where he looked around wildly for something suitable to cover me. There was nothing. No blankets, no rugs, no coats even—it was shirtsleeve weather—but there were tablecloths. Frantically he began grabbing them off the tables. It didn't matter that they were laid. It didn't matter that people were sitting at the tables eating their lunch. He grabbed and pulled, grabbed and pulled like a conjurer gone mad.

"I wasn't thinking," he told me. "I couldn't be bothered to explain. I just knew I had to have them."

He had to have them so badly that when a waiter came up and tried to stop him, he spun around and hit him. Then, while the waiter picked himself up off the floor, he stuffed all the tablecloths under his arm, ran back outside to where I was lying, and draped them over me.

Even a gory accident doesn't stop people going about their business for long and by now the traffic was starting to move again, trying to get by. So far, no traffic police were directing the proceedings (the policeman's colleagues were all clustered around him) and when Raffaele glanced back down the road he suddenly froze as he saw that a car was about to drive over my foot.

"No! No! No!" he screamed and ran back down the road waving his arms madly. Just in time the car stopped and the driver got out. When he saw what was lying on the road in front of his wheel his jaw dropped. Looking as though he'd seen a ghost he got back in the car, reversed, and drove carefully around it. Afraid it might happen again, Raffaele nerved himself, picked up my foot, and carried it back to where I was lying.

About ten minutes after the accident an ambulance arrived, but to Raffaele's dismay the ambulancemen went straight to the injured police motorcyclist and took him away without coming over to look at me. Then suddenly he heard the sound of a helicopter landing in the park nearby and moments later an air ambulance doctor and some paramedics dressed in bright orange overalls appeared.

The doctor who'd been pressing ice packs to my leg helped them maneuver me onto a stretcher and then someone produced an icebox and tried to lift my severed foot into it. Raffaele said it got really gruesome then because the foot and the attached bits of flesh that had been dragged from the inside of my calf wouldn't fit into the box, so in the end they had to resort to using a carrier bag. As they ran with my stretcher to the helicopter the air ambulance doctor told Raffaele that they were taking me to Mount Vernon Hospital in Northwood, which specialized in reattaching severed limbs.

A police car took Raffaele, who was still shaking with shock, to Mount Vernon. When he arrived he found I'd already been admitted to the casualty department where I was causing some problems. The nurses were trying to cut my fingernails because they needed to see the nailbed to check what was happening to my circulation. But I was still conscious and I wasn't having any of it.

"No, no, no!" I shrieked. "You mustn't cut my nails. It took me months to grow them." I must have won the battle because I still had my long fingernails when I woke up three days later.

When I'd been taken down for X rays Raffaele said a nurse came over and sat down with him.

"She's very ill, you know," she said. "You must realize that she may not pull through . . ."

In X ray they discovered that as well as minor head injuries, I had crushed ribs, a punctured lung, and multiple fractures of the pelvis. But the most urgent concern was for my leg. So far, everybody, including Raffaele and the paramedics who had recovered my foot and packed it in ice, had been working on the assumption that it could be reattached. But it turned out to be a false hope. When they saw the damage that had been done to the rest of my leg, the surgeons at Mount Vernon decided reattachment wasn't an option. The injury had been caused by the stainless-steel exhaust pipe of the BMW motorbike and was by no means a neat and tidy wound. Somehow my leg must have been trapped behind the pipe so instead of being cleanly cut, it had been literally wrenched in two. The result was that all the muscle and tendons had been stretched and torn beyond repair and there was just no putting it back together. Once they'd recognized that fact the surgeons decided to remove more of my leg in order to leave a clean stump that would heal as quickly as possible.

By the time I recovered consciousness it was all over. A five-hour operation had left me with just six inches of leg below my left knee. In the brief oblivion since my last conscious thought I had become an amputee.

For a week the reality of what had happened didn't come home to me. Although I'd heard Fiona tell me about my leg when I regained consciousness on the third day, it hardly sank in because all my attention was focused on the pain in my pelvis and chest. I'd been so heavily sedated that, after my first brief awakening, I floated in and out of consciousness for several more days. Mostly it was painful physical events that roused me. I was aware of being jarringly turned every four hours by nurses. Of having a cold metal thing like a wheel brace laid against my ribs and screwed into my side by white-coated figures. Of having needles and wires and tubes inserted and removed until I felt like a pincushion. Each time a nurse or doctor came to check me I begged for drugs to dull the pain and each time I was promised, "Very soon."

Not all of my awakenings were unpleasant. Sometimes I'd open my eyes to find Raffaele or Ruth or Fiona sitting beside my bed. Usually one of them would pass on the latest news the nurses had given them about my condition. It was Raffaele who explained that the reason I couldn't be given painkillers was that they would interfere with my breathing. Apparently that was causing quite enough problems as it was. My punctured lung had filled with fluid, which meant they'd had to screw a drain into my side. While there was fluid in my lungs they couldn't risk giving me any more general anesthetic, so the operation to insert a metal plate into my broken pelvis had been postponed. I was already being turned every four hours to avoid bedsores. Now more painful hoisting and turning sessions, this time for X rays on my lungs, were added to my daily routine.

During this time Fiona was a rock: always there, always ready to respond to my demands for help. She moistened my lips, emptied my bedpan, and worked out a way of turning me that didn't hurt nearly as much as when the nurses did it. She also made phone calls for me. I don't remember asking for my Filofax—I've few memories of that week apart from the constant pain—but Fiona assures me I did.

"You kept worrying about your appointments," she said. "You insisted you had to contact everybody so they wouldn't think you'd let them down."

She'd tried to pretend she couldn't find the Filofax but I wouldn't be put off.

"You kept reeling off numbers and making me ring them," she told me. "You didn't need the Filofax. You had all the appointments and telephone numbers in your head."

What I didn't have in my head was any sense of how serious my injury was—of what it actually meant to lose a leg. I was behaving as if I'd had my appendix out.

"You told me to ring Slix and postpone your appointment but not to tell them that you'd lost your leg," Fiona said. "You wanted me to tell them you'd do the shoot in a couple of weeks' time."

In fact Fiona didn't have to lie to Slix because they already knew about my accident. Everyone knew. While I'd been lying unconscious in intensive care the press had been full of the story. Fiona said she'd kept the clippings to show to me when I was well enough.

"Everyone's been really supportive," she said. "One of the papers interviewed a taxi driver who saw it all happen and he told them you never stood a chance. He said the bike was on the wrong side of the road and doing fifty miles an hour."

I still had no memories of the bike Fiona said had hit me. "What about the bike rider?" I asked. "Was he hurt too?"

"According to the paper, he's okay," said Fiona. "Just cuts and bruises I think. They let him go home the next day."

She wouldn't let me see the cuttings myself. "Wait until you're better," she said.

But I knew Fiona too well. "There's something you don't want me to see, isn't there? What is it?"

Fiona hesitated.

"Go on, tell me, or I'll belt you."

She grinned. "Well, I suppose you've got to find out sometime. You know the police were answering an emergency call? That's why they were going so fast with all the flashing lights and everything?"

I nodded. Some of the details of the moments before the accident had come back to me by now.

"Well, it turns out there wasn't an emergency at all. It was a false alarm."

Because of all the press coverage the response from the public had been enormous and cards and flowers were flooding in from well-wishers.

By the end of the week I'd received over five hundred bouquets. I was even sent one by the restaurant waiter whom Raffaele had punched on the day of the accident! Sadly, I hardly saw any of the flowers because the nurses said all that pollen in the intensive care unit would give people asthma attacks, so I agreed they should be handed out to the pensioners in the hospital.

Toward the end of the week as I recovered from my sedation and spent more time awake I began to sense an atmosphere in the room whenever Raffaele walked in. Fiona, I noticed, hardly spoke to him. When I asked her why she looked surprised.

"Well, I thought you'd finished with him," she said. "After all you said about him last Saturday night, I thought you weren't going to see him again. If he hadn't talked you into going for a walk, none of this would have happened."

I was horrified. "Fiona, you can't blame Raffaele."

She sighed. "I suppose not. It helps to blame someone, that's all. It seems so unfair, what's happened to you. I can hardly believe it."

Sometimes I could hardly believe it either. But the pain was always there to remind me. The strange thing was, the pain in my leg was still the least of my worries. It wasn't that it didn't hurt—sometimes I got a shooting sensation up the whole leg as if someone was pushing a hot metal rod up it—but most of the time the pain in my pelvis pushed the leg pain into the background. It was difficult to accept that nearly half my leg was missing. Sometimes I was certain my toes were hurting. But I knew it was no cruel joke people were playing on me. Each time I was turned or lifted onto the bedpan I could see the empty space below the huge white dressing covering the top of my leg. It felt strange to know that I would never see my foot again, never paint my toenails, never massage my funny bent little toe—the result of wearing high heels too young. Sometimes, when I looked down at the empty space where my leg used to be, I felt almost as if someone had died.

As the week wore on Raffaele looked more and more strained. He told me he'd spent the first two nights at the hospital, staying in a bedroom reserved for relatives of seriously ill patients.

"But I didn't sleep very much," he admitted to me.

He didn't seem to have slept much since either. His face looked drawn and he had dark circles under his eyes.

Gradually, as I became more alert, I found myself pondering exactly why Raffaele was hovering over me in the hospital. After all, I clearly remembered telling him our relationship was over. If he knew I wanted us to split up then why was he here? To me, there was one obvious answer: guilt. Perhaps, as Fiona suggested, Raffaele felt somehow responsible for me losing my leg, or perhaps he simply thought, in his gallant Italian way, that it wouldn't be chivalrous to desert me in my hour of need. Either way I couldn't accept it. I was touched by Raffaele's devotion but I didn't want anyone staying by my side out of duty. A fortnight's relationship didn't commit you to a responsibility for the rest of your life.

It was no use pussyfooting around. I decided bluntness was the answer.

"Raffaele, I need space," I told him that night. "Thank you for all you've done, but I don't want to see you anymore."

He looked shocked but he didn't argue. To me it proved that he was relieved to be offered a way out. In fact, as I learned later, he'd already sensed that Fiona and Ruth blamed him for the accident and now he felt that I did too.

After he left I felt really depressed, but an hour later my mind was distracted from the subject of Raffaele by the arrival of one of the doctors. He brought the surprise news that I was judged fit enough to be moved to a private hospital just down the road.

I was transferred to Bishopswood the next morning. It was there, three days later, that X rays finally showed that my lung had drained, and the operation to fix a metal plate into my damaged pelvis was given the go-ahead. I heard the news with mixed feelings. Although I'd be glad to be relieved of the pain I was worried about what the operation involved. I was still working on the assumption that one day soon I would be modeling again, and not just fashion modeling but swimsuit modeling. Throughout the past ten days that was the one thought that had kept me going. I'd never allowed myself to doubt it.

Fiona tried to warn me not to be too ambitious but I wouldn't listen.

"Most swimsuit shots aren't full length," I told her. "They're cut off at the knee so no one will be able to see below it anyway."

It was my swimsuit modeling that made me so worried about the pelvic operation. I wanted to be able to model not just one-piece suits, but bikinis as well.

"Where will the scar be?" I asked Mr. Belham, the surgeon who was to do the operation. "Front or back?"

A scar at the back would be easier to hide, but Mr. Belham said he had to go in through my abdomen.

"Okay then, I've got just one request," I told him.

He raised an eyebrow. "And what's that?"

"Please don't go over my pubic hairline."

I thought his chin was going to hit the floor.

When I came around after my trip to theater the difference was incredible. The horrendous pain had been replaced by a dull ache. Almost as welcome, the terrible feeling of paralysis had disappeared, and I could move again and even, with help, sit up. I couldn't wait to get out of bed.

Two days after the operation I persuaded the nurses to let me have a Zimmer frame so I could walk to the bathroom. Though *walk* wasn't quite the word. I couldn't walk anywhere anymore as I soon realized. The best I could manage was a sort of hopping shuffle. Still it meant I was on the road back to independence.

"Don't you dare try and have a bath or shower though, Heather," the ward sister warned. "You mustn't get your residual limb wet." The nurses always talked about my "residual limb." I suppose they thought it didn't sound as upsetting as "stump."

I found my way to the bathroom where I washed and cleaned my teeth and did my hair. Everything went well till I decided to have a pee. Sitting down on the loo was no problem but when I stood up I forgot to take hold of the handrails and toppled forward onto the floor. That, I think, was the moment I really grasped what had happened to me. As I pulled myself painfully up on the handrail a mass of emotions was churning around inside me. I felt shocked and cheated and angry. But most of all I felt sad.

It was the first time I'd asked myself, *Why me?* The first time I'd faced up to what losing a limb was going to do to the rest of my life. Of course I wouldn't be able to model again. Who did I think I was kidding? I wouldn't be able to dance or ski or play tennis or swim either. I wouldn't even be able to wear short skirts. No men on building sites would wolf-whistle and shout "Nice legs" again. All at once the thought of losing all these things, even the trivial ones, seemed unbearable and I felt tears running down my cheeks.

Worse than the sense of loss was knowing that I faced a future of dependence. For most of my life I'd been the one doing the caring. When Mum left us I'd learned to be self-sufficient, not to depend on other people. Coping on my own had become such a habit for me that even when I met someone who wanted to take care of me I wouldn't let them do it. I liked to be the strong one in relationships.

But the other side of the coin was that I'd always found it very hard to take or to be in anyone's debt. It terrified me. Now I would have no option. From now on people would have to help me take every step on the road to recovery. I wasn't sure how I was going to cope with that.

I felt sad and weepy for the rest of the day. It took till suppertime for me to get sick of my own misery. I knew by then I had to pull myself together. Self-pity was something I'd always disliked. From what I'd seen, once you fell into that trap you couldn't get out of it.

*Come on, Heather,* I ordered. *You've managed to cope with what life's thrown at you so far. Don't let it beat you now.*

I had to be positive. My life was about to change direction, there was no escaping that. But it had changed direction before and I'd always coped with it. Why look at this latest change as a disaster? Why not treat it as an adventure instead? I had no idea what my new life had in store for me but who was to say it wouldn't be something even more rewarding than modeling? One thing I did know. It was up to me to make the most of it.

# Chapter 18

I was allowed more visitors now and for longer. At first only Fiona and Raffaele had been allowed into my room, and then only for restricted hours. Now that Raffaele was no longer visiting, Fiona stayed for most of the day. Dimitri had gone home to Greece but Fiona's employers—she was PA to the boss of a Greek shipyard—were fantastic. Her boss had actually flown over to see me while I was in intensive care and was giving Fiona indefinite compassionate leave on full pay. It was Fiona who told me that Shane was abroad, playing in a concert tour. We decided not to tell him about my accident until he returned.

One of my first visitors after I moved to Bishopswood was Grandma. Her cheerful common sense was just what I needed at that time. Later on some visitors got so distressed at the sight of my leg that I ended up comforting them, but Grandma was such a strong character there was no chance of that. The first day she visited one of the nurses led her into my room and she sat on the chair beside the bed, shook her head, and gave a little laugh.

"I just can't believe the things that have happened to this family," she said.

She stayed for two hours talking about everything under the sun. As she left she took hold of my hand. "I know you'll get through this too, Heather," she said. "You're going to cope with it like you've coped with everything else."

Every day now my "residual limb" was being cleaned and redressed with heavy white bandages. The whole leg was still very swollen from the thigh down and the severed end, what I could see of it, looked awful: It was just a mess of pus and blood. Mr. Morgan, the doctor looking after my leg, told me the problem was a cavity on the inside of the leg where the flesh had been drawn out in the accident.

"I think we'll end up giving you a skin graft," he said. "But I want it to heal a bit more first."

The cavity was presenting nursing problems because it was trying to heal up but it had to be kept open so it could drain and heal from the inside out. It meant they had to keep poking things in it and putting dressings inside and then pulling them out. I'd expected to be squeamish when I saw them, but to my surprise I wasn't. Pretty soon I was even helping with the dressings.

Eventually Mr. Morgan announced that he thought I was ready for the skin graft. Again I proved to be a troublesome patient. "Where will you take the skin from?" I asked him suspiciously.

"We'll take a big square off your right thigh," he said.

"No, you'll bloody well not," I said. "I'm not having a scar there."

He raised his eyes to the heavens. "It won't scar any more than I can help, I promise you."

"Can't you take it from anywhere else?"

"Not really. We need a big area. The only other possibility would be to use your buttocks, but that's out of the question because of your pelvis operation."

"Why?" I persisted.

"Because you'd have to lie on your side until the site on your buttocks had healed and it would be very painful because of your pelvis."

"Do it," I said.

As far as I was concerned a bit of extra pain was preferable to a scar that would destroy my career.

On the morning of the operation I got Fiona to bring in a pair of bikini pants. She helped me wriggle into them, then, following my instructions, she drew a line in felt tip all around the edges.

"Now write *Don't go past this line* all around my bum," I said. Giggling, Fiona obeyed.

I had just had my pre-med and was feeling nicely woozy when Mr. Morgan came in to give me a final examination. When the nurse pulled up my gown and he saw Fiona's artwork Mr. Morgan burst out laughing—but he followed my instructions to the letter.

The next day as I lay curled up on my side in bed, wincing and moaning and thinking, *Oh, God, have I done the right thing?* Mr. Morgan appeared in my doorway. He shook his head at me but there was a twinkle in his eye. "Satisfied, Miss Mills? Did my handiwork meet your requirements?"

I nodded.

"Does it hurt?"

"Yes."

He smiled. "Serves you right. Don't say I didn't warn you."

Mr. Morgan was a great guy. Recently, he'd performed an eye operation on a boy from Bosnia and we had long discussions about the war over there. He was also very musical and was interested to meet Shane when he came in and to hear of our experiences with Wagner. I asked him if Fiona could bring my saxophone in but he said because my punctured lung was still healing it wasn't a good idea. However, the day after that conversation he reappeared in my room.

"Here . . ." He handed me a small set of drums. "I found these on my travels in India. See what you can do with them."

It was as well I was in a private room because for the rest of that week the air echoed with jungle rhythms.

A week after my skin graft my leg really started to hurt. I propped it up with a pillow to help the blood circulate but it didn't seem to do much good and before long the graft was showing signs of being rejected. Mr. Morgan explained that there was still residual infection underneath the graft.

"These things take time," he said. "Try not to be impatient. We'll get there in the end."

. . .

Every day I'd been asking the nurses if Raffaele had rung and every day they'd told me he had. Then one morning they announced he'd asked if he could visit me. I hadn't the heart to say no.

When he walked in I felt such a sense of relief I could have cried. I didn't though. In fact I didn't let myself show much emotion at all, because I didn't want to put any pressure on him. "I'm sorry if you don't want to see me," he apologized. "It was my brother's idea I should ask. I told him I was missing you like crazy and he said, 'Tell her you want to see her. She can only say no.'" He smiled. "Are you pleased to see me?"

My face must have told him the answer.

Raffaele pushed me out into the hospital car park in my wheelchair. I could feel his strong hands pushing my chair and the closeness of his body and I wanted him so much to kiss me but I daren't let him know it. I didn't want to drag him back into a relationship if that wasn't what he wanted. He'd brought me a present, a little oblong wooden box, and now he opened it to reveal a set of brown and cream discs.

"Do you play backgammon?" he asked.

I didn't but he devoted that afternoon to teaching me, sitting on a bench in the car park beside the chair. By the time he wheeled me back into my room that afternoon I was hooked on the game.

"Is it all right if I come again?" Raffaele asked.

"If you like." I was still trying to stop my feelings from showing.

"I would very much like to," he said. Then he leaned over the wheelchair and kissed me gently on the back of the neck.

After that Raffaele came to see me every day after work, always bringing a present with him—usually something to eat, like fresh cream chocolates or pizzas from Luigi's—and every evening after supper we'd play backgammon. Northwood was so far out of London it didn't make sense for Raffaele to go back to his flat at ten, so he started to stay in my room overnight, sleeping in my bed. It was so comforting to have his arms around me, but it can't have been at all relaxing for him. I was still sleeping on my side and I would get him to lie flat on his back so I could rest my left leg on his. When the nurses came in the morning they'd find Raffaele wide awake, afraid to move, while I was always sound asleep. The nurses never said anything. I think they realized that having Raffaele there was a bigger tonic than anything they were doing for me.

Until Raffaele started staying over, the nights had been my worst time. I could cope with the day, when there were people around, but I'd never needed much sleep and often I'd found myself awake at three in the morning, staring at the ceiling and thinking gloomy thoughts. Now all that was changed.

Mr. Belham was the only one to look disapproving when he found out that Raffaele was staying the night.

"You do realize it will be months before you'll be able to make love, don't you?" he said. "It would cause far too much pressure on your pelvis at the moment."

I couldn't resist it. "I feel sorry for your wife if that's the only position you know," I said.

He wasn't amused.

One day Raffaele came in holding an envelope in his hand. "I've two tickets for *La Bohème* at the Barbican this Friday night. Do you think you can make it?"

I knew I could make it. I also knew the staff wouldn't let me go, so I didn't ask them. The farthest they'd allowed me to go in my wheelchair so far was to the park over the road. I planned every detail of the evening like a military operation.

By now, for getting around inside the hospital, I'd progressed from the Zimmer frame to crutches and I was determined to use them rather than a wheelchair for my first night out. I got Fiona to drive me secretly to Stanmore where I bought a beautiful tight blue dress with slits up the side so that when I was on crutches it would flare out and I'd be able to swing my legs. I also bought a matching blue and gold Chanel scarf to tie over the white dressings on my stump.

On the evening of the opera I told the nurses I was going out to sit in Ruth's boyfriend's house, which was just around the corner. Then I locked the door of my room while Fiona helped me into my dress. When I was ready I draped a long dark coat over my glamorous gown, picked up my crutches, and hobbled down the corridor to the lift. Raffaele had arranged to meet me in the West End so Fiona drove me there, transferred me to Raffaele's car, then took her leave like a true fairy godmother.

The opera was absolutely wonderful, though if it had been dreadful it wouldn't have mattered. To me, just being there was enough. It proved I could still enjoy myself. My life wasn't over. I could still look good. I could still go out on the town and have a good time like anyone else.

It was one in the morning and I was high as a kite when Raffaele and I drove back to the hospital. Luckily the nurse wasn't at the central station so when I came out of the lift I was able to slip into the bedroom and quickly get undressed. Five minutes later, when she came in to give me my antibiotics and sleeping tablets, the nurse found me in bed, though it was just as well she didn't decide to have a look at my leg—it still had the Chanel scarf tied around it. She looked at Raffaele in his tuxedo and frowned suspiciously but she didn't say anything. As she closed the door we collapsed in giggles like schoolkids.

# Chapter 19

The press had been taking a tremendous interest in my accident. The clippings Fiona had cut out to show me carried headlines like *Crash Tragedy of the Model Who Had a Golden Future* and *Bike Cop Who Hit Swimsuit Girl Did 50 mph.*

While I was unconscious, newspaper reporters had been hounding Fiona and Raffaele for quotes but since then they had transferred their attention to me. I was constantly getting phone calls from journalists and one German reporter had even sneaked into my room.

"Miss Mills, Miss Mills?" He'd waved a tape recorder at me. "Can I have an interview please?"

Fiona threw him out. At first I was in too much pain to be remotely interested in giving an interview, but I'd had so many cards and flowers from people all over the country that, after my pelvis operation, I decided it would be a good way of saying thank you since I could never reply individually to the hundreds of letters. I agreed to do a short interview for GMTV. However, on the morning it was due to be broadcast, Fiona brought in the morning papers and in one of them there was a full-page "exclusive" interview with me with quotes lifted from the interview and even a picture taken straight off the videotape.

I stared at it in dismay. I knew that normally the paper would have paid me several thousand pounds for a photograph and an interview. Now by lifting it from television they'd got it for nothing.

I felt cheated. The truth was I could really have done with the money. I had hardly any savings because I'd always spent my money as fast as it came in: on my new flat, on trips to Croatia, on new cars. Now the harsh reality of my situation was beginning to come home to me. I hadn't earned a penny for weeks and it was likely to be months before I could work again. My belief that I'd be back modeling within weeks had long since collapsed. Mr. Morgan had told me it might be six months before the infection in my stump cleared enough for me to get my first artificial leg. In the meantime I had a lot of expenses to meet, as not only was I paying off my mortgage but I was helping Fiona buy a flat. In addition, very soon I was going to have to pay for physiotherapy and for help around the house, as well as find several thousand pounds for an artificial leg.

That morning, as on most mornings, Fiona said there were reporters in the hospital lobby downstairs wanting to speak to me.

"Shall I send them away?" she asked.

Up until today I'd always said yes but now I had a change of heart. If the press were going to print my story anyway I might as well give them an interview. At least that way I'd get paid for it. It was time to put my entrepreneurial skills into practice.

"Tell them to come up and see me," I told Fiona.

"Who do you want to talk to first?"

"I don't," I said. "Tell them I want to see them all together."

Five minutes later I smiled up at the six reporters grouped expectantly around my bed.

"Look, I know you want this story, but you're not getting it for nothing. Go back to your editors and tell them that whoever comes up with the most money will get the exclusive interview, pictures, the lot. I'll cooperate in every way I can. But not until there's money on the table. It's as simple as that."

There was a bit of a stunned silence and I saw them exchange looks, but they dutifully shuffled out and went off to ring their editors. It's funny how once you take control of a situation people become more respectful. After my little announcement no more reporters tried to sneak into my room. In the end it was the *Sunday People* that came up with the best offer and Ruki Sayid, their reporter, and a photographer came around the next day. The photographer took a picture of me in a white shift standing on my Zimmer with my stump just showing under the shift.

The *People* ran their feature the following Sunday. I was pleased with the way Ruki had written the story. Her article was forward-looking and positive instead of just concentrating on my loss. Other people liked it too. A few days later the *Sun* rang me and asked if they could have a second exclusive. They ran the story at the beginning of September on three successive days. Their reporter went into my background in more detail, even going into my days at the fair and Mum's own accident.

Both papers' photographers wanted to take a picture of Raffaele as well, but he wouldn't play ball. He didn't give me any hassle about it, but when he saw me organizing the press and revealing all my past history I sensed he didn't really like it. He was a very private person and it was against his principles to divulge things for money. I respected that in him but it caused a few arguments especially when reporters asked about our love life. They'd asked me something like, "Do you feel men will now find you unattractive?" and I'd replied, "Of course not. Ask Raffaele." The next day the headline screamed, *I Lost a Leg but Sex Is as Incredible as Ever.* He was mortified, particularly as a photographer had managed to take a sneaky shot of him and they'd put it in under the headline.

"What will people say?" he asked, horrified.

"I can't control what they write, Raffaele," I said.

Raffaele didn't go on about it because he could see that organizing the press coverage was giving me a buzz. In a way it was keeping me going. The only time I ever got down now was when it was quiet. With all the people coming in and out of my room I did get very tired, but to me it was worth it. Instead of concentrating on my phantom pains or the ache in my pelvis, I woke up every morning thinking, *What am I doing today?*

By the end of August I had enough money tucked away to be confident I'd be able to manage financially for the next year. But it wasn't only money that came out of my cooperation with the press.

After the newspaper features were published I gave interviews to four TV stations. I found I was quite relaxed in front of the cameras—probably because of my modeling experience—and afterward two TV companies expressed interest in using me as a presenter.

The idea of working in television held many attractions, not least the fact that being an amputee would be no real drawback in that career. With every day that passed my confidence that I would return to full-time modeling was weakening. I was becoming more realistic. However well I coped with it, an artificial leg was always going to be a handicap. My movement, the angles cameramen could use, even the clothes I could wear, would all be restricted. Model agencies and photographers weren't charities. Why should they bother with me when they could find able-bodied girls who didn't present these limitations?

There was no point in getting maudlin about it. If I had to look at alternative careers then why not TV? Hosting a chat show would suit me down to the ground. Different guests every night. Different topics to get to grips with . . . It would be a real challenge.

With new avenues beckoning I was itching to get out of the hospital now. The nurses used to allow Fiona to push me outside in my wheelchair for a breath of fresh air each day, but by the end of August it had become a bit more than that. "I'm just going to the park with my sister," I'd say, as we wheeled past the nurses' desk. But out in the car park Fiona would help me into her car and we'd drive thirty miles to London where we'd go to Harvey Nichols for lunch. I had to be really careful I wasn't seen by reporters because I'd promised the *Sun* an exclusive photograph when I officially left the hospital. I'd be hobbling out of the lift at Harvey Nichols on my crutches and Fiona would suddenly say, "Watch out—there's a guy with a camera there," and I'd have to duck behind the counter.

Moving about was still very painful because gravity made the blood rush down into my stump and it would throb madly, so Harvey Nichols was the only place where I got out of the car. After lunch Fiona would take me down the King's Road to shop for clothes and I would simply look in the shop windows as she drove slowly past and point to what I wanted to try on. What I was looking for was a pair of trousers that were tight-legged to the knee and then flared out so that when I was on crutches it would look as if I'd only lost my foot rather than the whole leg. Fiona would get the shop assistant to bring trousers out to the car for me to look at. The first pair of size tens I picked out drowned me when I got back to the hospital and tried them on and we had to go back the next day and exchange them for a size eight. I couldn't understand it, but the physio explained it was because I had lost a lot of hip and thigh muscle from not working out.

There wasn't much else they could do for me in hospital. What my leg needed more than anything now was time for nature's healing process to work. That could happen just as well at home, so on September 10 I was discharged. I wanted to give the *Sun* their money's worth for their exclusive photo and I got Fiona to bring in one of my favorite dresses, a very short blue velvet shift with a low-cut top. Unfortunately, I'd lost so much weight it hung off me like a tent but we managed to arrange it so it looked passable. My plan was to let the photographer take a picture of me sitting in Fiona's car, but he had other ideas. He wanted me to throw my crutches away and balance on one leg with a bunch of flowers in one hand and the other arm waving in the air as if I was some kind of trapeze artist. I felt quite cross but I wasn't really surprised. His attitude was common among newspaper photographers: anything for a shot. He seemed quite unaware that standing on one leg when you've just shattered your pelvis is a bit like biting on an abscessed tooth. However, I did what he wanted and then Fiona drove me home.

It was so wonderful to walk into my flat again. It had been five weeks since I last saw it. It was suppertime and Ruth had a pot of chili con carne bubbling on the stove and a great big treacle sponge with custard to follow. After supper she ran me a hot bath with scented oils and I sank into it, draping my left leg carefully over the side. I was still forbidden to get it wet.

For the next few weeks I had to attend an outpatient clinic every day to have my dressings changed. The graft had been rejected and the hole was still infected. A wonderful doctor called Mr. Angel was in charge of me now and he was optimistic it would sort itself out in time, but while we waited for it to do so the pain went on. Two or three times a day Ruth would massage my stump, which not only eased the pain but was a great comfort. It meant a lot to me that she wasn't afraid to touch it.

I also started to go to a Chinese woman called Susie Lung for professional massage. She concentrated her treatment on the top of my left leg, which helped the pain a lot by getting the circulation going; I hoped it would help clear the infection too. Susie also had a faradic pulse machine, which she used on the quadriceps muscles in my left leg to try to stop them wasting away before I got an artificial limb.

My dream of being a TV presenter was close to becoming reality. I'd been asked to help film an item for LWT about my recovery and to do the voice-over myself. Two weeks after I left hospital they filmed me doing my first postaccident modeling shoot. It was set up for the purpose of the film so it wasn't a genuine job but it gave me confidence to know I could still do it even without a leg.

For the last section of the item the director wanted to film me taking part in a sport. I came up with what I thought was the ideal answer. While I'd been hospitalized I'd had a letter from a man called Mike Hammond who'd lost a leg himself and now ran an artificial ski slope at Harlow where he helped train the Paralympic ski team. He'd read in a newspaper that one of my dreams was to ski again and he'd invited me to Harlow to have a go.

Now I rang him and asked if the TV crew could come and film him giving me a lesson.

He was cautious. "It's a bit soon really, Heather."

"I'll chance it," I said. People were always telling me to wait, to take my time, not to be so impatient, but this was something I really wanted to do. I had to get back into life.

Skiing on one leg felt very different from using two; because I was afraid of falling on my stump I was cautious, but Mike was brilliant. He had to ski on one leg because he had no knee. But though I was pleased to know I could do it, I hoped it wouldn't be necessary for me once I got my artificial leg.

Mike was right though. It was too soon. I'd overlooked the fact that it wasn't just my leg I had to look after, but my pelvis too. The next day I went shopping with Fiona. I'd just climbed back into the car when I heard a click and realized I couldn't move my pelvis. My whole groin area felt weak and numb. Fiona drove home in a panic and she and Ruth carried me into the flat and laid me on the bed. I telephoned Mr. Belham but was told he was away on holiday so in desperation I rang Susie, my masseuse.

"Get yourself to the chiropractor, Heather," she advised.

Fiona drove me to the Marble Arch clinic of the chiropractor Susie recommended and he came out to meet us. Michael Durtnell wasn't a big man but he lifted me out of the car as if I was a feather and carried me all the way up the stairs to his consulting rooms where he laid me on the couch.

"Now," he said. "Tell me what you've been up to."

I told him about the skiing and he shook his head in disapproval.

"No doubt you've been hopping around without your crutches too?"

"A bit," I admitted sheepishly.

"Well, don't." He looked stern. "Use crutches or else crawl on the floor. It's really important."

"But it's quicker to hop," I argued.

"Not in twenty years it won't be. Your arthritis will be so bad you won't be able to walk at all, so do as you're told."

His lecture over, he began to crack me back into place. He'd warned me to expect agony and he wasn't joking.

"After twenty-four hours it should start getting better," he predicted. Fortunately he was right about that too.

I went back for more manipulation every two days for two weeks and by the end of that time my pelvis felt better than at any time since the accident. When Mr. Belham came back from holiday he was amazed.

"Perhaps it's as well I was away when it happened," he said. "If you'd come to me I'd have taken you down to theater and put another metal plate in."

Three weeks after I came out of hospital, Fiona went home to Greece. We were both tearful the day she left. Over the past two months we'd grown closer than we'd ever been in our lives.

"I'll ring you every day," she promised as she hugged me goodbye. She did too and her amazing bosses footed the phone bill.

With Fiona gone I needed someone to drive me, and Toni stepped into the breach. She and Gill had been constant visitors while I was in hospital. Their off-license had been sold now and Toni was out of work so she was happy to act as my driver for as long as I needed her. It was Toni who drove me to my first major public engagement after I left hospital.

The *Daily Mirror* had rung up inviting me to help judge the Miss UK contest, which they were sponsoring. It was to be a very grand affair at the Grosvenor House Hotel, Park Lane. Caroline Charles, who designs dresses for royalty, loaned me a wonderful dress for the occasion, a long purple velvet creation with a fitted bodice to show off my bust and a very full skirt that allowed me the freedom I needed to swing my legs when I used my crutches.

My fellow judges were Mike Reid, John Fashanu, Annabel Croft, and Richard Branson. They all seemed to have heard my story and were really nice to me. Richard Branson was particularly thoughtful. The prejudging round, where the finalists were selected, took place upstairs and when we stood up to move downstairs again Richard decided my lovely billowing skirt looked a bit dangerous.

"Hang on, Heather, I'm afraid it's going to get caught in your crutches," he said. With that he swung me up in his arms and carried me down the grand staircase to the ballroom where the judging was to take place. Of course, the photographers loved it. Next day, to my embarrassment, the papers were full of pictures not of the poor girl who'd won the contest but of me in my Caroline Charles dress.

I'd hoped I would be fitted up with an artificial leg in October, but it was looking increasingly unlikely. The infection in my stump just wouldn't clear up and the disgusting daily dressings went on and on. At Mr. Angel's suggestion I was doing my own dressings now.

"Hospitals are full of germs and there's less chance of infection from your own hands than from a nurse's," he explained. "But keep your eye on it. You're not out of the woods yet. If it ever comes up in an angry red lump get straight to the nearest hospital."

Over the next few weeks I tried everything I could think of to get that leg to heal. Antibiotics, acupuncture, homeopathy—you name it, I tried it. Every time I sat down I propped the leg up in the air to try to stop blood pooling at the bottom of the stump. It wasn't very good for my pelvis but that was just too bad—my leg had to take priority. At least three times a week I went to Susie Lung's for massage. Unfortunately, the steps outside her rooms were not only very steep but were often slippery with autumn leaves and one day as I was coming down them my crutch slipped. Automatically, I put out my left leg to save myself and crashed down onto my stump. The pain brought tears to my eyes.

During October I fell several times and each time I made the same stupid mistake. I would just forget my left leg wasn't there and try to save myself with it. A week after the Miss UK contest I went to Germany for a TV interview with my makeup artist and friend Tanya. I was sitting in my wheelchair in Bonn airport when I leaned forward, not realizing Tanya had gone to buy a paper, and the wheelchair tipped forward so that I went right down onto my stump again. I did the interview in absolute agony: My leg was throbbing so hard I couldn't think about the questions.

All the falls did nothing to help my infection. It was getting steadily worse and soon I had to go into hospital again to get the cavity syringed out and dressed with iodine.

On the weekend following the German trip, Raffaele took me to Rome where he had some business. We stayed in a beautiful hotel, met his mum and brother, and I was able to do some early Christmas shopping. I had a really good time—that is until Sunday, when I got food poisoning from some mussel soup. I was violently sick for a couple of hours before we left and by the time we got on the plane I was as white as a sheet.

We were twenty minutes into the flight when my leg started to throb. I could see it swelling up above the dressing almost as I watched. I asked Raffaele to pass me my crutches and hobbled to the loo so I could take a peep at what was going on.

"Oh, Jesus," I said out loud when I peeled off the dressing. On the front of my shin was an angry red lump with a yellow head on it.

Mr. Angel had given me his paging number for emergencies and the minute we got off the plane at Heathrow I rang it. When he called me back and heard my symptoms he didn't hesitate.

"I'd better see you straightaway," he said. "Can you get to Bushey Heath Hospital?"

Raffaele called a cab and we went home, picked up his car, and drove to Bushey Heath where Mr. Angel was waiting for us.

He took one look at my leg and called in a nurse to help him clean it up.

"What you have here is a nasty abscess," he said. "We're going to have to drain it. It's going to hurt a bit I'm afraid."

By this time I'd done so much draining and swabbing myself that I knew the procedure better than the nurse. When she was reluctant to apply enough pressure I gritted my teeth and squeezed the abscess myself while Mr. Angel syringed it out. Every time he seemed set to finish I squeezed again—pain was a price I was quite prepared to pay if it gave my leg a better chance of healing. But it was all in vain. A week later the same thing happened again.

"I've a feeling the infection has spread into the bone," Mr. Angel said when he examined me this time. "If that's the case it could be very dangerous. It rather looks as though I'm going to have to amputate again."

"Again?" I stared at him in disbelief. "How much will you take off?"

"A couple of inches should do it," he said. "It's a dilemma because the leg might heal up in time even if I don't amputate, but it might not, and until it heals you're not going to be able to get your artificial leg."

I didn't relish the idea of losing yet more of my leg, but Mr. Angel was reassuring. "In some ways it will actually be an advantage. With a shorter residual limb you'll get a better fit of prosthesis," he said.

The following day I went into the Garden Hospital in Hendon for the second amputation. This time Mr. Angel kept a flap of skin from the shin and brought it around to cover the bottom of the stump to avoid having to do another skin graft. When I came around after the op, he told me that his guess had been right. The bone had been full of infection, so it would never have healed on its own. The crucial question now was whether he had amputated enough and in time to stop the infection spreading even further.

After the second amputation I felt really low. I seemed to be getting nowhere. Sometimes I wondered if I'd ever get an artificial leg. All my dreams of playing tennis and skiing and dancing were beginning to seem like pie in the sky. What was really worrying about the delay was that the muscles in my left thigh were literally wasting away because they weren't being used. Every day I did isometric exercises to try to keep them toned but it just wasn't enough. I *had* to get a leg soon or I wouldn't ever be able to walk without a limp.

Since I'd come out of the hospital Raffaele had been living with me in West Hampstead, but with Ruth living there too it was crowded and we'd decided to buy a flat in Queensgate. It was only just around the corner from where I'd had my accident, but because it was central and convenient for Raffaele's work, we didn't let that put us off. We moved in on the last day of October. I'd hoped that with a change of scene my luck might change too, but two weeks after our move the infection flared up yet again. Mr. Angel looked grave as he examined me and I was sure he was considering yet another amputation. This is ridiculous, I thought. The motorbike had only cut off my foot. If they carried on chopping bits off at this rate I was going to lose my whole leg . . .

The evening after I'd been to see Mr. Angel I had a visit from a girlfriend who'd recently recovered from breast cancer. When she heard the saga of my infections she was horrified.

"Heather, I went to a clinic in America that specializes in natural cures," she said. "It's a wonderful place and it certainly worked for me. Why don't you give it a try?"

# Chapter 20

A week later I was installed in the Hippocrates Institute in West Palm Beach, Florida. It wasn't cheap—it took a big chunk out of the money I'd got from the newspapers—but by this stage I wasn't counting the pennies. I saw the Hippocrates as my last resort. Sophie, the friend with breast cancer, had booked in with me because although she was in remission she felt another stay in the clinic would benefit her too.

The institute was a beautiful place: a white-pillared Spanish-style building at the end of a long landscaped drive. It didn't look much like a hospital, but most of the people there were very sick. The other patients suffered from all sorts of conditions: cancer, diabetes, rheumatoid arthritis, even AIDS—and most of them, like me, had come to the Hippocrates after conventional medicine had failed to cure them.

The institute's treatments were based on holistic or whole-body healing, and the staff were evangelistic about raw organic food and pure natural products. The first thing the doctors there did was to take me off all my antibiotics and drugs (my doctors in London would have had fits) and put me on the Hippocrates diet, which was based on wheat grass juice.

As soon as we got up in the morning we had to drink a glass of this juice, which was bright green and tasted disgusting. Then, for breakfast we were given more green juices made from things like celery, buckwheat, and sunflower seeds. During the morning there were two lectures on diet and looking after your body. Then we'd have lunch, which might be something like raw mushroom and pepper loaf with an avocado sauce. In the afternoon there'd be another lecture. It was all very hard work, centered on learning how to look after yourself.

Sometimes instead of the afternoon lecture there'd be a psychotherapy session—they called it centropic integration—when you talked about your relationships and especially about your childhood. The idea was that you regressed right back to your earliest memories, sometimes even to before you were born, to try to understand how your experiences then affected your feelings today. I'd never had psychotherapy before, though most of the American patients seemed to be old hands at it. I found it difficult at first to dig down into my innermost feelings but, after hearing some of the others open up, I slowly began to talk. I'd never properly discussed my childhood with anyone before and I found it a painful experience.

I talked first about Dad's violence and about my constant attempts since I'd left home to make peace with him and start again. Although he hadn't made contact with me once since I'd lost my leg, I even felt guilty that I hadn't been to see him for over a year. Recently I'd heard he'd had another stroke and I'd been thinking about getting in touch once more.

Andy, the therapist, nodded as if he'd heard it all before.

"You can't seem to accept that it is he who has the problem, can you, Heather? Something inside you is telling you it must be your fault. Isn't that why you keep trying to begin again?"

Speechless, I stared at him, feeling such a sense of relief that I knew he'd hit the nail on the head. From that moment on visiting Dad was wiped off my list of things to do.

At a later session I told Andy about Mum going off with Charles when I was nine.

"So she abandoned you, Heather. How did that make you feel?"

I felt my hackles rise. "No, she didn't *abandon* us. You don't understand. It wasn't her fault. She just couldn't take any more of my father."

He persisted. "Heather, why won't you face it? She abandoned you. Why are you making excuses for her? Why are you taking the guilt on yourself? Allow your anger. You're entitled to be angry. She abandoned you to the care of a man she knew to be violent. Why didn't she take you with her?"

I gaped at him, feeling as if my whole world had been turned upside down. It was the very first time I had been made to face the truth about Mum. Because she'd looked after people with cancer, and had been so loved by her patients, and had cooked for the old people at church, I'd always thought of her as a sort of saint, incapable of doing wrong.

Now, hearing Andy's words, I was nine years old again, feeling betrayed and hurt and unloved and *angry;* Mum shouldn't have done it, I thought. She should have taken us with her. The only reason she didn't was that Charles didn't want us. A stranger she'd known for just a few months had meant more to her than her own children. I was entitled to feel angry about that. The knowledge came as such a relief that I burst into tears.

I couldn't believe how wonderful it felt to be told my childhood wasn't my *fault:* It was as if an enormous weight had been taken off my shoulders. Afterward, I rang Fiona and told her about my therapy session.

"You can't believe what this man said," I told her. "It made me feel incredible."

Fiona gave a little laugh. "Heather, we had shit parents. I always wondered how long it would take you to realize it . . ."

Sophie was great. She helped me juice my wheat grass and carry it upstairs to my room and even helped with the wheat grass enemas that were another part of the weird Hippocrates regimen. She was a real convert to their philosophy. But for the first week I was a bit dubious about it all. I couldn't believe anything as disgusting as wheat grass juice could possibly be good for you. After only five days on the treatment, however, an amazing thing happened. Almost in front of my eyes my whole leg healed up. The cavity I'd been fruitlessly cleaning and swabbing for three and a half months suddenly closed over with clean pink skin.

The day Hippocrates doctors finally pronounced my leg clear of infection, I was ecstatic. The first thing I did was to have a hot bath. For the past four months I hadn't been allowed to put my left leg in water at all and whenever I bathed I'd had to hang my leg over the side of the bath to keep it dry, which hadn't been too good for my pelvis. Now I soaked in bubbles for over an hour. It was sheer bliss.

The second thing I did was to order an artificial leg. The Hippocrates doctors had advised me to wait for a month or two but I'd waited long enough. I wanted my leg now.

I looked up *Prosthetists* (the official name for limb makers) in the local directory and dialed the number of someone who went by the unlikely name of Rick Shaw.

"What's the cheapest leg you've got?" I asked.

"What do you mean?" Rick said; obviously this wasn't the way most of his clients began their calls.

"I need a leg now," I said. "My boyfriend's coming to see me next weekend and I want to surprise him."

Rick chuckled. "Well, I guess you'd better come in and see me right away. How does 10 A.M. tomorrow sound?"

I told him it sounded fine.

When I'd put the phone down I went to fetch Sophie. There was one other thing I wanted to do to celebrate my recovery. Go for a swim. The clinic had a huge oxygenated swimming pool, warm and bubbly with loudspeakers in each corner playing classical music. I'd been itching to try it ever since I arrived. Sophie escorted me into the pool area and helped me to the side. She wanted me to sit down and slip in gently but I was too impatient for that and simply jumped in at the deep end. I bobbed up to the surface like a cork and started to breaststroke. It was a strange feeling because I didn't go in a straight line but got a sort of wobble on. Front crawl was easier. It was a great sensation. I felt like a beached whale back at sea and for over half an hour I bombed up and down the pool not at all self-conscious about how my leg looked. There were no perfect bodies among the Hippocrates patients: Accident or illness had taken its toll on all of us.

The next morning I went to see the prosthetist I'd located in the directory. He was laid-back and friendly. "Call me Rick," he said by way of introduction.

When he examined my stump though, he looked doubtful. "Hmm. It's only freshly healed, isn't it?"

I admitted it, though I didn't tell him how freshly . . .

"The trouble is it'll change shape quickly as it heals, so if I fit you now you're going to need another leg in a month or so, and they're not cheap. Is that all right?"

I nodded. I'd cross that bridge when I came to it.

He took another good look. "Actually I think it's quite a good idea that you get moving on it. You've got a lot of muscle wastage there."

He wasn't telling me anything I didn't know. I'd been getting quite worried about it. My left thigh now measured three inches less in circumference than my right and the muscle was so weak it felt like cotton wool.

Rick took a plaster cast of my stump and told me he'd do his best to get a leg ready in time for Raffaele's visit. He'd sensed how important it was to me.

"This is a pretty special boyfriend, I guess?"

"Very special," I agreed. Since I'd been in Florida, Raffaele had been calling me twice a day and now he was coming all the way to Miami just to see me for two days. You couldn't get much more special than that.

Rick was as good as his word. The leg I collected from his workshop two days later was a very basic wooden one that attached to my stump with a long rubber over-the-knee socket. It was shaped more like a cylinder than a leg but under trousers it looked passable. The first time I tried to walk on it (still using crutches) it felt really strange. It was much stiffer than a real leg and because my thigh muscles were so weak it felt very heavy, so it was a real struggle to swing it forward. But after ten minutes' practice, I felt much more at home on it. It might not look great but it was a million times better than just having empty space below my knee.

"Now don't keep it on for longer than an hour at a time to start with," Rick cautioned. "And whatever you do, don't try and walk on it without crutches. You're not ready for it yet. It'll damage your stump."

I was aghast. "Can't I just use a walking stick?"

He shook his head firmly. "No. In a couple of weeks maybe, but not yet."

But I was harboring a secret dream and crutches were not a part of that dream. I persuaded Rick to sell me a trendy walnut cane. "Not for now. I want to take it back to England," I lied. Raffaele was due to arrive the next day so I had only twenty-four hours to prepare my surprise. On top of getting used to my new leg there was another problem to overcome. I hadn't brought any pairs of shoes with me, just a caseful of right shoes, because when I set off for Florida I'd never dreamed I'd heal quickly enough to get an artificial leg. That afternoon I went around the local shopping mall with Sophie and bought ten pairs of flat shoes in every color under the sun. The next morning I got dressed up in a tight cropped jumper, then Sophie helped me maneuver my blue jeans over the new leg. I put on a pair of flat black shoes, picked up my walnut cane, and I was ready.

When Raffaele came through the arrivals door at Miami airport and saw me walking toward him behind the barrier with no visible means of support his face was a picture. I could see him thinking, *Hang on a minute, didn't she lose her leg?* Then, as he reached the end of the barrier, saw my stick, and realized what had happened, he just grabbed hold of me and kissed me; he was so excited.

We had the most wonderful romantic weekend. We talked and talked. We went to the cinema to see *Mrs. Doubtfire,* and we went on a hilarious shopping trip when Raffaele took me aback by buying me a pair of purple Rollerblades.

"Hang on," I said. "I'm still supposed to be on crutches."

He smiled. "You will Rollerblade again one day, though, I know it."

It seemed a long way off, but Raffaele's confidence was infectious. Suddenly nothing seemed impossible. Not even driving. I hadn't driven since the accident and I felt dubious about getting back into the driver's seat but Raffaele wouldn't let me duck out. He'd hired an automatic convertible and on the way back to the clinic I put my foot down and went for it.

Afterwards, exhausted and relaxed by the warm Florida wind in our hair, we slept like babies. It had given me just the boost I needed.

As I waved Raffaele off at the airport on Sunday evening, I felt totally revitalized. At long last I could walk again. Nothing was going to hold me back now. If I could walk and swim, then what was to stop me dancing again? Or skiing? Or Rollerblading? In fact why shouldn't I do anything that people with two normal legs could do? I didn't have to stop having fun just because I was disabled.

Now that I had my artificial leg I vowed nothing would be impossible until I'd tried it and failed. And I intended to try everything. The sky was the limit.

Over the next few months I must have had a go at nearly every sport and pastime known to man. After only three weeks I discarded my cane and crutches and soon afterwards I was dancing, swimming, and playing tennis. Early in the New Year, when Raffaele and I went on holiday to the Maldives, I tried scuba diving.

The American leg had its limitations. It was quite inflexible and looked very unnatural. At Mr. Angel's recommendation I went to see a prosthetist from Bournemouth who had been working on improving the design of conventional artificial limbs. Over the years Bob Watts had developed several types of legs, each one suitable for a different purpose. He could, he said, make me a general sports leg, a skiing leg, a scuba leg, or even—though he was still working on this one—a cosmetic leg made of silicone, suitable for wearing with short skirts and high heels.

The reason so many different types of legs were needed, Bob explained, was that different human activities require different movements of the joints. One day it might be possible to replicate all the complicated movements that the human ankle and foot are capable of in one artificial leg, but until then the best prosthetists could offer was a series of different legs. At my first appointment Bob measured me up for a basic NHS leg, which, though more attractive than the American leg, still had its limitations.

Since I planned to do a lot of sport, Bob recommended I order a flexi-foot or "scuba" leg as well, which had an "active" ankle that could be used in two ways—released or locked—depending on which sport I was doing.

"For swimming you'd release it but for something like ice skating you'd use it locked," he said.

*Or for something like Rollerblading,* I thought.

The drawback to Bob's legs was that they were expensive—between £2,000 and £4,000 each—which put them way out of the reach of most amputees who tended to be pensioners and whose only option was the general-purpose National Health Service leg.

After wearing my NHS leg for a couple of weeks I decided to take Bob's advice and go for a "scuba" or flexi-foot, though I was very tempted by the idea of a cosmetic leg. I hated wearing the American or the NHS leg with a skirt because they both made me look so obviously disabled. The last thing I wanted was for people to look at me and think, *Poor thing . . .*

Each of Bob's legs was custom-made. He not only took a cast of the stump to ensure a good fit but matched them in size, shape, and if possible skin tone to the remaining leg, so it was quite a time-consuming business. But eventually, in the first week of February, my scuba leg was ready. The difference was amazing. Even the color was exactly right. Bob carefully fitted a special white cotton sock over my stump, then slid it into the socket and pulled the rubber sleeve up over my knee. It felt really secure, almost like part of me; by the time I'd put my trainers on it actually looked a part of me too. A casual observer might think I just had a bandage over my knee. It was much easier to walk on than my previous legs and after a couple of practice attempts I was striding up and down Bob's workshop with hardly a limp.

I'd waited for this moment for two months. I walked outside, unpacked Raffaele's Rollerblades from the hold-all, strapped them on, and set off down the road. It felt fantastic. "No problem." I grinned at Bob as I slid to a halt.

"Now don't keep the leg on for longer than four hours at a time to start with," Bob warned. "And be careful not to kick anyone with it! It's made out of carbon graphite so it won't get chipped or cracked but if you play any sort of contact sport you'll have to wear padding or you could inflict some serious damage!"

But it wasn't contact sport I was hankering after, it was something else. Two weeks after I'd taken delivery of my new leg, I set off with Ruth to Val d'Isère to fulfill my most cherished ambition—to ski down a black run. It took me some time to build up to it. On my first day I had to start in ski school all over again, but by the third day I was once more classed as intermediate, and on the fifth day I finally skied a black run. There were problems though and I soon realized that, as Bob had already warned, the scuba leg wasn't ideal for skiing. For a start the foot wasn't set at the right angle. But more importantly there was nothing holding the leg in place except the tight rubber sleeve that fit around my stump. For most sports the grip of the sleeve was enough to keep it in place but with skiing the combined weight of the boot and ski, especially when you unweighted a ski to turn, required a more secure attachment. Although I strapped it on halfway up my thigh with masking tape I lived in constant fear of the leg falling off.

I was on a chairlift when the inevitable happened. My companion on the lift was a stout German man. We'd got about halfway up the mountain when I felt a weird sensation in my left knee and realized that the masking tape holding my leg had given way. As I watched helplessly, my left leg, complete with ski and boot, eased its way out of the leg of my ski suit and fell twenty feet to the snow below, nearly hitting a passing snowboarder. The German man's eyes were like saucers as my leg shot off down the slope, gathering speed as it went.

"Stop that leg, it's worth a fortune!" I screamed at the snowboarder.

*"Mein Gott!"* The German guy's face was as white as a sheet. He must have thought I'd been the victim of acute frostbite.

"It's all right," I soothed him. "It's all right. Look, there's no blood. It was off before . . ."

By the time we reached the top of the chairlift he'd realized what had happened and was uttering loud guffaws.

I was in a dilemma over what to do. I could stay on the chairlift and go back down the mountain but if I did that how would I be certain of getting my £2,000 leg back? It could have come to a halt anywhere on the slope. It was a red run from the top of the chairlift but I decided I had no option. The time had come to put last September's lesson in one-legged skiing into practice. Miraculously, Mike Hammond's coaching tips had stayed with me and though I wobbled a bit I managed to stay upright. At the bottom of the run I discovered my leg, stationary now, amid a crowd of interested spectators. It had apparently slithered to a halt in the middle of the ski school to the consternation of some nervous beginners. That night, my leg was the main topic of conversation in the Pacific Bar and a fascinated crowd watched me dancing, obviously hoping it would fall off again!

I realized now that Bob had been right. I needed a proper ski leg—one that had a special corset lacing up my thigh—to avoid a repeat of the fiasco. I resolved to order one before the next season.

Later that month I skied again, this time in Chamonix. Mike Hammond, who had coached me in September, was training the Paralympic team there and for three days I trained with them. Mike was complimentary about my ability. Because I'd done so much skiing before I lost my leg he thought I stood a good chance of making it to the British team for the next Paralympics in 1996.

"Why don't you come and train with us on the dry-ski slope at Harlow?" he suggested. I was tempted but when I learned that the training squad met three times a week I had to say no. Sadly, I just couldn't afford the time.

Since my return from America life had been hectic. Back in August, I'd told a reporter that although one door in my life had closed I was sure others would open. I don't think I really was sure at the time—I was just trying desperately to show a brave face—but my prediction had proved to be true. I might not have any modeling jobs lined up, but I had plenty of other engagements to keep me busy.

One of the first people to contact me when I came out of hospital had been the Olympic gold medalist Duncan Goodhew.

"Heather, I'm helping organize something called the Swimathon in March next year," he said. "I wondered if you'd be interested in helping us."

The Swimathon, I learned, was a fund-raising event that aimed to raise £2 million for a basket of British charities including Barnardo's and Help the Aged. The idea was that during March, thousands of people up and down the country would do a sponsored swim of five thousand meters, or about two hundred lengths.

"Say yes," Duncan urged. "The more celebrities we can get to do it the better the press coverage we'll attract." I was flattered to be regarded as a celebrity but I didn't commit myself then. It was too soon after leaving hospital. At that time I hadn't even been allowed to get my leg wet, let alone swim two hundred lengths. However, after I returned from America it suddenly seemed a real possibility and I decided to accept the challenge, for my own self-confidence as well as for the sake of the charities. Duncan offered to help me train and we did it in style because as their contribution to the Swimathon the luxurious Champneys Health Spa let us train in their pool. I must say it beat the Washington Baths, which was the last place I'd done any swimming training, hands down.

Duncan was a lovely man and gave me some helpful tips. I'd decided to swim without my artificial leg as I felt freer, but my breaststroke was still erratic. Duncan taught me to push harder with my residual limb than on the other so I got a more balanced forward movement. It felt odd at first, but at least it meant I went in a straight line. One of my disadvantages as an amputee was that I used up to 50 percent more oxygen than able-bodied swimmers, so I had to breathe more often during each length than I had before my accident. Duncan was able to help me synchronize my breathing so I didn't end up gasping.

For the official launch of the Swimathon in March, I went to Gateshead Baths with Duncan. It felt really strange to be there. A load of kids from Usworth Grange Comprehensive had come with an old swimming teacher of mine to meet me. It appeared I was now a famous "old girl." A lot of water had passed under the bridge in twelve years! The last time I'd swum at these baths I'd been a pupil at Usworth too. It was the day Dad had thrown Fiona through our glass front door. I half expected to turn around and see Dad standing among the spectators, though I knew that was an impossibility: Since his last stroke Dad had been virtually housebound. Still, it was an eerie feeling.

A week later I made my own Swimathon effort at the Oasis Club in the West End of London. In the end, at Duncan's suggestion, I did the swim relay with three others so only had to do fifty lengths. I felt a bit disappointed as I knew I could have done two hundred. But as Duncan predicted the press turned out in force and I realized that my new status as a celebrity was worth more to the charity in terms of publicity than the actual effort I put in. After my swim I was invited to appear on the BBC program *How Do They Do That?* with Desmond Lynham, and as a result twelve million viewers became aware of the Swimathon. It also meant twelve million viewers became aware of me, which brought its own problems.

I was beginning to get used to being recognized now. It had started soon after I came out of hospital when I was still on crutches and my leg was obviously missing so I was pretty easy to identify. But after *How Do They Do That?* people started to come up when we were having a meal to ask for my autograph or say something encouraging. Raffaele found it hard to handle but it didn't really bother me. After all, I'd benefited from the press's interest in me, so I could hardly complain if their publicity was successful. Often the people who came up had their own stories to tell of friends or relatives who'd lost limbs. Sometimes they said they'd been inspired by reading about me or seeing me on TV because it had helped them realize losing your leg needn't mean the end of the world. Raffaele found it hard to comprehend.

"I could never get inspiration from reading a newspaper story!" he said.

It took one particular couple to make him realize that reading about and seeing programs about other people who'd survived a real tragedy could be a real help. This couple were a young man and his wife who had each lost a leg when a taxi did a U-turn in front of their motorbike. They had two young children and the effect on their lives was going to be enormous. Yet when she saw me walk into her hospital room I thought Mandy's face would crack in two she was so delighted. Raffaele and I visited twice and each time I came away feeling really humble at the effect my visit produced. When Mandy's friend Vivienne presented me with a poem she'd written to thank me for visiting, even Raffaele conceded that sometimes the press had its uses.

Whenever I was asked to visit people in the hospital who had recently lost limbs I always tried to go along, even if it was on the other side of the country. If I couldn't visit I would write. I hadn't forgotten my own time in hospital and I knew how much I'd appreciated encouragement from other people when I was feeling low.

A couple of days after the Swimathon I had another official engagement—I'd been awarded a *Daily Star* Gold Star Award and was invited to go to Downing Street with the other award winners to meet John Major before attending a gala evening at the Savoy Hotel where my award would be presented to me by Michael Howard. It isn't every day you get to meet the prime minister and the home secretary. When I'd received the invitation I'd decided to push the boat out and ask Bob to make me a cosmetic leg for the occasion. I'd been dying to get one for months. I couldn't wear high heels with any of my legs and I hardly ever wore a short skirt with them either.

Two days before my appointment at Downing Street, I took delivery of my new leg. It was incredibly lifelike. Bob had made it of silicone that not only looked natural but felt natural, soft, and warm, quite unlike the cold, hard carbon graphite leg. Bob had offered to put hairs on it as well but I'd said no thanks. I wasn't going to pay to wax an artificial leg! He had given me some lovely toenails though: Each one was individually stuck on so it looked natural and could be painted with nail polish.

I felt like a million dollars as I shook hands with John Major. He was charming and chatted to each of us as he gave us a guided tour of Number Ten. The presentation ceremony in the evening was even more overwhelming with each award recipient being placed at a table of celebrities. My neighbors included Terry Wogan and Jim Davidson.

The Gold Star Award was just the first of a string of awards I received from newspapers and national organizations. Later in the year *The Times* presented me with their Human Achievement Award while the British Chamber of Commerce not only voted me their Outstanding Young Person of the Year but also named a new award in my honor—the Heather Mills Award—to be presented "in perpetuity" in my name to a young person who had overcome some hardship or handicap.

It was a great honor, but at the same time all the adulation I was receiving was starting to make me a bit uneasy. I couldn't put my finger on what the problem was. Being presented with awards and honors and having people shout at me in the street when they recognized me was fun. It wasn't that I wasn't grateful, I was. But somehow, I just felt that something was missing.

Grandma and Grandad *(right)* and my dad, aged seven *(below)*.

My mum just before
she died.

My mum and dad on
their wedding day.

Me with my mum and Fiona as a baby *(above)* and with Shane *(left)*.

(*above*) Shane (four years old) pushing me (fifteen months) in a stroller.

*(left)* Me and Fiona.

*(opposite)* An early modeling picture.

Me playing saxophone in hospital.

(*below*) With Fiona in my Saab. (The *Sun*)

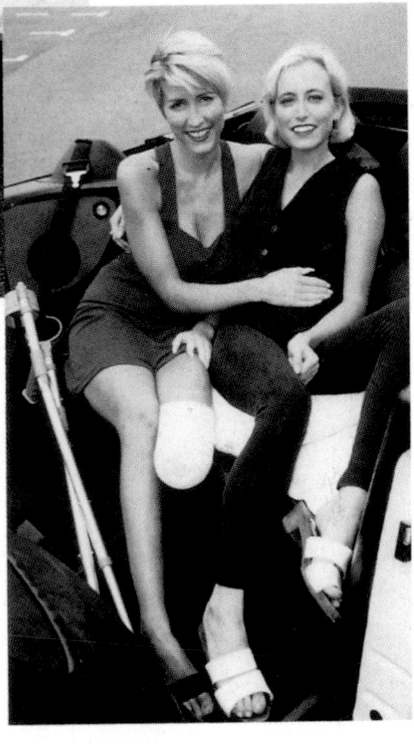

(*above*) Here I am surfing after my accident .

(*left*) British Telecom Swimathon , 1994.

Me horseback riding in 1996.

*(right)* With my sister Claire at Grandma's funeral.

With my beloved Oliver.

Learning to Rollerblade with an artificial leg.

My first ski-school lesson (I'm fifth from the left).

Me, Fiona, and some friends on a day trip to Paris.

(*top*) Fellow amputees and prosthetist Bob Watts (*second from left*) with Chay Blyth.

(*above*) Me and Martina, an eight-year-old Croatian amputee, and truck drivers Dave Nix & Co., in 1994.

(*right*) Me in a minefield, raising awareness of the land mine problem in Croatia. (*Ken Lennox*)

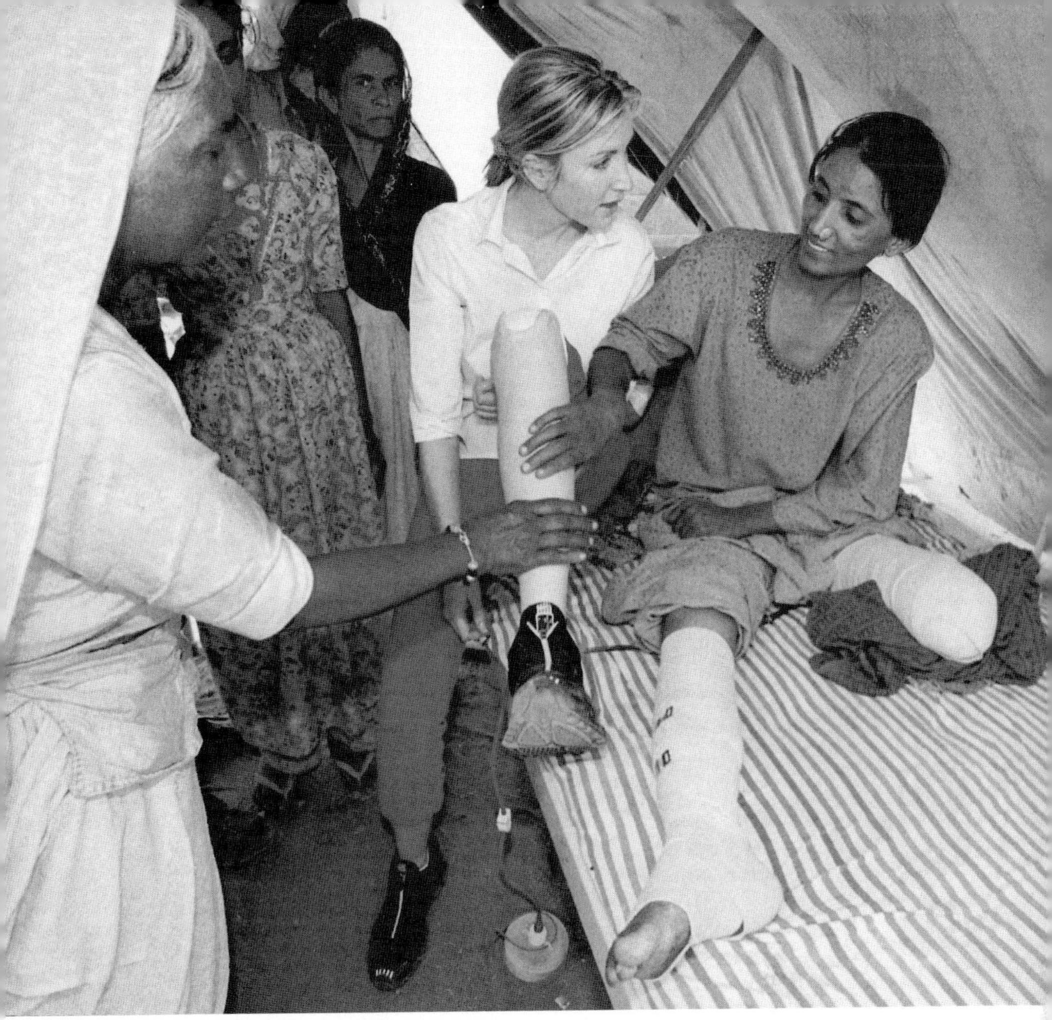

In an Indian hospital with Halima Magdie, a mother of four who lost her leg in an earthquake. (*Ken Lennox*)

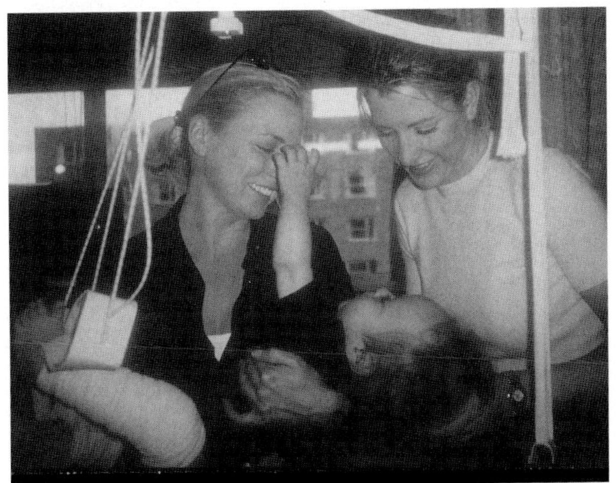

Me and Fiona in hospital with baby Alex.

(*above*) With John Major at the Daily Star Gold Star Awards at 10 Downing St.

(*above*) At the Miss UK contest with fellow judge Richard Branson.

(*left*) With naval personnel collecting the Heather Mills Award for outstanding achievement.

(*above*) Addressing the UN in Geneva. (*John Rodsted & Landmine Action*)

(*right*) With Paul and Colin Powell at the State Department, Washington D.C., after a discussion on the land mine problem.

(*this page and opposite*) Modeling with a conscience. Combining commerce with charity. (*Heather Mills McCartney photos courtesy of I.N.C. International Concepts.® Photographs by Walter Chin.)*

(*right*) Painting my toenails before a modeling shoot. (©*Tim O'Sullivan/Katz Pictures*)

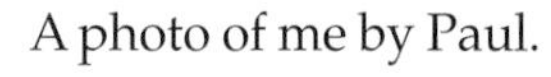

A photo of me by Paul.

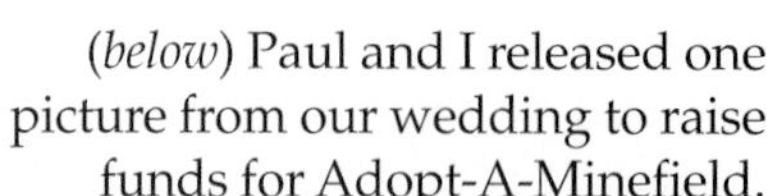

(*below*) Paul and I released one picture from our wedding to raise funds for Adopt-A-Minefield.

# Chapter 21

Back in September 1993, I'd told Pascoe Watson of the *Sun,* "Something good is going to come out of this accident. It seems like fate's way of telling me there is something else in store."

I'd really believed it. All the strange coincidences in my life: my mother's own accident to her left leg, her death as an indirect result of that accident, that strange materialization of a severed left foot in Mladin's photograph of Croatian war victims, had conspired to give me a strong belief in fate. I knew that fate did not intend me to spend my time collecting awards. There was something else I was meant to do, I was sure of it. But what?

I believe now it was fate herself who dropped the clues that led me to the answer to that question.

Ever since I'd returned to England from the Hippocrates Institute I'd been religiously following their raw-food diet. Since November I had eaten virtually no meat, very little cooked food, and had been growing wheat grass in window boxes at home in Queensgate and putting it through a juice extractor to provide my morning "green drink." Like Sophie, I'd become a convert to the Hippocrates way of eating. Since I'd adopted the diet not only had I had no more infections in my leg, but I'd had so much energy and needed so little sleep—in spite of my hectic schedule—that I felt like a different person.

The *People* newspaper had written about my "miracle" diet and as a result I'd been flooded with mail from people wanting to know more about it. To save myself having to write the details out several thousand times I'd put together a leaflet of raw-food recipes and had it photocopied. As covers for the leaflet I'd used some of my color Z-cards: the promotion cards with color photos and vital statistics that most models have printed.

It was when people started writing back offering to pay for the booklets or sending me money to pass on to "a charity of your choice" that an idea began to crystallize in my mind. For some time I'd been itching to return to Croatia. The trouble was, I'd promised myself the last time I left that I'd only go back if I could make a real contribution. Now it occurred to me that if I charged money for my booklet I could buy something useful to take out with me. The question was, what? As I tried to think of things that were in short supply in Croatia, memories came flooding back. Memories of the straggling lines of refugees; of the old lady struggling to lean the cross against the church wall; of the little kids whose legs had been blown off by land mines, squatting helplessly in the street.

Of course! The answer came to me like a bolt from the blue. That was what I could take to Croatia: artificial limbs! They had transformed my life. Imagine what they could do for the hundreds of Croatian people whose arms or legs had been blown off by land mines and mortars.

I started to make inquiries and discovered I had stumbled on a need so great it was almost inconceivable. There were not just hundreds of amputees in the former Yugoslavia, I learned. There were an estimated three hundred thousand! Of these, only a tiny proportion had been fitted with artificial limbs, not because there were no trained prosthetists—apparently there were plenty—but because along with the general shortage of all medical equipment there was a desperate scarcity of limbs. More and more I became convinced that it was my mission to remedy that situation.

In May 1994 I paid a preliminary visit to Croatia to assess the need and to obtain permission to organize a convoy. I flew into Zagreb where I met up with Renata, who had come up from Sisak especially to act as my interpreter. My first port of call was the Institute of

Prosthetics in Zagreb where staff confirmed that the need for artificial limbs was every bit as great as I'd imagined. They said that thousands of maimed refugees were having to manage without any limbs at all while many of those who had been fitted were having to make do with primitive "wire-and-pulley" type legs.

"We fit only one or two limbs here most weeks," one of the technicians told me. It wasn't that the prosthetists in Croatia weren't competent—they'd had more practice than most—it was purely and simply lack of materials that was holding them up. The institute staff welcomed my offer of help but their enthusiasm for my scheme seemed cautious. I got the feeling they'd been let down too many times to get excited. However, they assured me that if I told them my legs were on the way they would produce the amputees to receive them.

Having confirmed that the need was real I had one other task to perform: to arrange for the necessary permit papers to allow our convoy trucks into the country. My experience with the convoys from Ljubljana had taught me how necessary the correct papers were. It had also taught me the snail-like pace of Croatian bureaucracy.

Even so, I was taken aback by the complete lack of interest that greeted my inquiries at the Ministry of Health. For days I tried without success to get an undertaking that my artificial limbs would be allowed into the country. In the end I decided to bypass the civil servants and go straight to the top. The next time I visited the ministry I requested an interview with Dr. Vladimir Tonković, the minister of health.

To my surprise my request was granted and later that day Dr. Tonković welcomed me into his offices. He was a short tubby bear of a man, who showed me the first sign of humanity I'd seen in his department. He was a real eccentric, chain-smoking throughout our interview and talking nonstop, in funny broken English, accompanied by extravagant hand gestures, about the history of Croatia.

"You have to *understand,*" he said. "We are giving our hand out in Croatia and *nobody* is taking it. The Serbs are chopping us down. And nobody *cares.*"

After ten minutes of lecturing he suddenly smiled, revealing a row of nicotine-stained teeth.

"So. You are bringing new legs for our people. That is good, I think that means you care. Eh?" He arched an eyebrow. "Don't worry. You will get your permission. Leave it to me."

I smiled back. I was sure that if anyone could get the apathetic clerks in the ministry to shift, then this man would.

I returned to England confident the paperwork wouldn't be a problem. But other things about this trip were beginning to worry me. My main concern was that the economics of my planned convoy didn't make much sense. By now I'd collected nearly £8,000 from donations and from sales of my health food booklet but though it seemed a lot, it was only enough to buy eight legs at the very most. Compared with the need in Croatia it was a drop in the ocean.

But another link of fate's chain was about to fall into place. At the beginning of June I had an appointment at Bob Watts's clinic in Bournemouth. Bob knew all about my plans for Croatia; he'd agreed to come with me on my convoy to help fit a few people up for limbs and to train local technicians in his techniques.

I'd gone down to see Bob to be measured for a new socket for my cosmetic leg, which no longer fitted properly: It kept falling off. The final straw had been when Raffaele had taken me out to dinner to a posh restaurant in Chelsea. I'd stood up after the meal and had taken three steps when I heard a clunk and the leg had fallen on the floor. That would have been bad enough but unfortunately I had tights on so I was standing there with no leg and my tights all stretched out and trailing on the floor with the crotch bit coming down under my miniskirt looking like Nora Batty. Raffaele tried to pick me up but he couldn't because we were both giggling so much, and in the end I'd had to tuck my leg under my arm and hop out of the restaurant. It had been quite a cabaret act.

When I told him about it, Bob explained that the trouble was, my stump had shrunk yet again. "It was still quite swollen when I fitted you the first time in February and I'm afraid it won't have finished shrinking yet," he said. "A new socket will do the job this time, but if it shrinks any more I may have to make a whole new leg."

"How many more legs am I going to need?" I asked, because by this time I already had two legs in the back of my cupboard that didn't fit anymore.

"It could be a few I'm afraid," Bob replied. "It's inevitable in the first year or so after an amputation because the residual limb takes time to stabilize."

In my brain something started to tick. "So that means most amputees have legs that don't fit them anymore. What happens to them?"

"Well, with NHS legs, nothing. They either get put into store or thrown away."

It seemed an awful waste.

"Can't they be used again, by someone else?" I asked.

"Not really. They're made to measure so even if you found someone with the right-size residual limb they might need a longer leg or a smaller foot. It'd be difficult to find a perfect match. Anyway you'd never persuade people to take secondhand limbs."

My mind was still ticking.

"What about taking them apart? Couldn't you use the components again? All the joints and levers inside?"

Bob nodded. "In theory, yes."

"Only in theory? Why not do it?"

He shrugged. "Because it's just not government policy. I suppose the labor cost of dismantling them makes the powers-that-be think it's not worth the effort."

"So you're telling me that every amputee in the country probably has a couple of spare legs that don't fit anymore?"

Bob nodded. "Probably."

"And how many amputees are there in Britain?"

Bob had statistics like that on the tip of his tongue. "Sixty-three thousand."

I grinned at him "That's it then—that's what we'll do. We'll collect up all the spare limbs in England and Wales, and we'll take them to Croatia!"

. . .

I wasted no time setting my plan in motion. My first idea was to put out a general appeal via the press asking any amputees with spare legs at home to contact me. However, after two minutes' thought, I realized that I'd end up collecting legs from Land's End to John O'Groats if I did that. It would cost a fortune in petrol even if I was able to arrange transport. A better answer would be to contact hospitals to see if they had any stores of obsolete limbs. I started ringing around all the hospitals I could find in the yellow pages. The first orthopedic hospital I contacted admitted to having a couple of hundred old limbs but said they weren't sure if they could make them available to me. When I asked if they could act as a collection point if I launched a public appeal for unwanted limbs they were even more noncommittal. I got a similar response from all the other hospitals I rang and some of my excitement evaporated. This wasn't going to be as easy as I'd thought.

I had a radio interview scheduled for the next day and, hopeful that it might unlock some doors, I mentioned my quest for limbs to the reporter. The response was immediate. No sooner had I arrived back at the flat than the phone rang.

It was someone called Darren Lucas.

"I heard you on the radio talking about legs," he said. "I've located four hundred fifty at the Withington Hospital, Manchester, if you're interested."

It turned out that Darren was a brewery worker who in his spare time was involved with a charity called Siloam that specialized in collecting surplus and obsolete medical supplies for sending to Third World countries. He knew all the ropes for dealing with hospital bureaucrats and within a couple of days of his phone call the Withington legs were liberated and waiting for me to collect them. I'd already arranged with Bob's firm, the Dorset Orthopaedic Clinic, to store them. All I had to sort out now was a method of transporting them.

Once again the long arm of coincidence came into play. On the night I'd collected the British Chamber of Commerce award, I'd been introduced to both the chairman and marketing director of TNT transport. They'd given me their cards and said if they could ever do anything to help me to give them a ring. When I picked up the phone they proved to be as good as their word and a TNT truck took the legs down to Bournemouth for me the next day.

Over the next couple of months, with the help of Darren and his friends from Siloam, we managed to cut through all the red tape and collect nearly five thousand legs from hospitals all over the country. In addition, we obtained several hundred artificial arms as well as some redundant wheelchairs and crutches. One of Darren's friends, Dave Nix, had contacts with lots of charities, including an organization for the disabled called Moneybear, which had several lorries. Moneybear cooperated with TNT in organizing the transport of all the limbs down to Bournemouth.

The next problem was how to dismantle the legs. At Bob's suggestion I'd decided to leave some of the more standard legs intact since, with three hundred thousand amputees to choose from, the chances were high they would fit somebody. When the alternative was no leg at all I was sure people wouldn't be fussy about them being secondhand.

But the majority of legs needed to be taken to bits so that the parts could be used in making new limbs. The dismantling could have been left to the prosthetists and technicians in Croatia, but it would save valuable time if it had been done for them. Making a new leg was a lengthy enough process as it was. Taking a cast for a socket and molding a foam or plastic cover or *cosmesis* took four or five days; if the old legs had to be dismantled first the process would be even more time-consuming. It would also be easier to pack and transport boxes full of parts rather than whole limbs, which were rather cumbersome. The question was, Who could we get to dismantle them? Bob said it wasn't that difficult a job but it did require instruction. We needed to find not only volunteers but also suitable workshops where the dismantling could be carried out.

This time it was Simon Wynn, the marketing director for the London Events Agency, which had organized the Swimathon, who came up with the answer. I found myself sitting next to him on a flight up to Birmingham where I was booked to do an interview for the *Good Morning* program. I started talking about my plans for a convoy of limbs and when I told him about our dilemma over disassembling them he looked thoughtful.

"You know, when we were doing the Swimathon a lot of prisons got involved. They seem very keen to give back to the community. Maybe they'd be interested in helping you."

It seemed an ideal solution: After all, not only did prisons have workshops but they quite literally had a captive workforce.

"I don't suppose there's any way you can introduce me to one of the governors, is there?" I asked.

"No problem," Simon said.

Within days he had set up an appointment for me with Dr. Andrew Coyles, the governor of Brixton prison.

At our meeting Dr. Coyles was very cooperative and said he'd be more than happy to help. The only problem he could foresee was that dismantling the legs required tools like screwdrivers and chisels.

"Obviously they could be put to undesirable uses in the wrong hands." He smiled dryly. "It means supervision will have to be tight."

After our talk he gave me a guided tour of the prison. It was quite an eye-opener to see prisoners playing pool and watching videos. I put the idea of dismantling legs to several groups of prisoners. All the men I spoke to said they'd be very happy to do it but, as Dr. Coyle predicted, the warders in charge of each unit were less keen because it meant keeping a strict eye on the tools and what they were doing with them.

"Leave it to me," Dr. Coyles said as we left. "As long as we select the right prisoners and arrange suitable security measures I'm sure it won't be a problem."

It wasn't. Once the workshop managers had approved the project I arranged for the hospitals to send their legs direct to Brixton and later to the Wolds prison on Humberside, which had also agreed to help us. In August, Bob spent a day at each prison teaching the men how to take the legs apart. We decided to put the parts into big plastic boxes donated by Moneybear, labeled *Shins, Feet, Knee Joints,* et cetera.

Everything was working out brilliantly. By the end of August we had already dismantled about two thousand legs. The only problem was that nearly all of them were for adults. Bob explained that this was because 83 percent of Britain's amputees were over sixty-five: mainly the victims of cancer or diabetes. But I knew that a high proportion of those needing limbs in Croatia were kids—often very small kids—who, while out at play, had wandered unwittingly into minefields. Once again the solution was at hand. I still had the money from the sale of my booklet. Now I resolved to use that money to buy brand-new components for kids' legs.

The convoy had been receiving a lot of publicity and I'd been appearing every week on either radio or television programs to talk about it. I'd never had a problem talking; the difficulty sometimes was getting me to shut up! Obviously Bill Bradshaw, the editor of the *Newcastle Journal,* had seen me in full flow the day he rang to ask me to meet him for lunch.

"Heather—you seem to have an opinion about everything," he said. "How would you like to write a weekly column?"

I started the column the following week and plugged the convoy whenever I could, knowing that any donations that came in could be used to buy more parts to make children's limbs.

To my disappointment I'd heard no more from the television companies who'd wanted to employ me last September, but that job with the *Newcastle Journal* proved to be the proverbial foot in the door as far as my media ambitions were concerned. A few days afterward a BBC producer, Quentin Smith, rang me up. "How do you fancy presenting?" he said.

I was tempted to confess that it had been my dream for the past year, but instead I said demurely, "Yes, I'd love to."

"Well, we're just casting for the Anne and Nick morning show," he said. "And it came into my mind that you'd be perfect as a guest presenter. Could you come up to Brum and meet the producer?"

Two days later I had signed a six-month contract with the BBC.

It was the icing on the cake from the point of view of my convoy plans, because the BBC decided to make a short feature about it and they sent a cameraman with me to Brixton to check how the dismantling was going. He filmed me chatting and having a laugh with the prisoners and it went down so well the BBC said they would send a team to film both the arrival of the convoy and Bob's first few fittings in Croatia. It was really good news. I was hopeful that this would be the first of many limb convoys. If we were to have sufficient funding to make regular trips and to buy children's limbs we needed to keep the public interested and aware of what we were doing, and no one could do that better than the BBC.

The BBC's commitment to film the convoy meant we now *had* to go on the date we'd tentatively set for our departure—October 30. I rang the Institute of Prosthetics in Zagreb and warned them that a mountain of artificial limbs was about to descend on them and asked them to start locating potential candidates for Bob to fit with legs. Everything started to come together. Siloam agreed to lend us some old trucks to use for the convoy, while three of Dave Nix's friends volunteered to help him drive them over there.

There was just one problem: a big one. The permit papers for the lorries still hadn't arrived. I was getting really worried. Without the papers there was no point in even setting off. In desperation I rang Vladimir Tonković's office and asked to be put through. To my amazement I was.

"Dr. Tonković," I said. "I'm sorry to bother you but I still haven't had a response from your ministry."

"What?" His voice was incredulous. "I can't *believe* it!" There was a pause, then he said softly, "I will become crocodile. I promise you, Miss Mills, I will become *crocodile.*"

His crocodile impression must have scared the pants off his clerks because on October 20 a neatly typed envelope arrived from Zagreb containing all the documentation we required.

Ten days later the two thirty-eight-ton trucks supplied by Siloam, laden with nearly five thousand artificial limbs, five hundred wheelchairs, and hundreds of pairs of crutches, set off on the twelve-hundred-mile journey to Zagreb.

# Chapter 22

The day before the convoy left England I flew to Zagreb. Bob was due to follow me on the Monday. Hopefully, by the time our two lorries with their load of limbs arrived on Tuesday, November 1, we'd have organized the formalities and smoothed the way so they could be put straight to good use.

For the first time the responsibility of the massive task I'd undertaken was starting to get to me. What if it all went wrong? What if they wouldn't let us in through the border after all? What if the amputees who the hospital had promised would be ready and waiting didn't turn up to be fitted? The BBC crew were due to arrive on Tuesday and that knowledge put extra pressure on me. If I botched it now, in front of the cameras, there'd be no hiding it. If it all turned into a fiasco there'd be no more limb convoys. It had to work.

The one thing giving me courage was the knowledge that I had an appointment with Dr. Vladimir Tonković on the evening I arrived. Shortly before I left I'd rung his office to thank him for organizing my papers and to finalize details of the convoy. He'd been too busy to talk for long.

"Excuse me, Miss Mills," he said. "The pope is arriving here tomorrow: One million people are coming to Zagreb to see him and everything is going *mad* here! Every*body* is going mad! Do you know what I think? The whole *world* is mad." I heard him strike a match and inhale deeply. "When do you arrive, Miss Mills?"

"On October 29."

"Good. I will meet you at your hotel at eight o'clock on the evening of the twenty-ninth. If you will honor me by dining with me we will talk about the final arrangements for your convoy then."

I was looking forward to our meeting. I liked Dr. Tonković. He might be eccentric but at least he was passionate: He was the sort of man who got things done.

At a quarter to eight I was dressed and waiting in my room at the Panoramic Hotel. At eight-fifteen I was still waiting. At eight-thirty I rang Dr. Tonković's office. There was no answer. I wandered down to the hotel lobby in case he was waiting there, but there was no sign of him. At nine o'clock I gave up and went to bed. I felt lower at that moment than I'd felt at any time since I'd lost my leg. I felt sure everything was about to go wrong. Maybe the Croatians didn't want the legs after all. Maybe all my information was incorrect. Perhaps Dr. Tonković had just been humoring me all the time.

The next day Renata arrived and did her best to dispel my gloom. "Don't worry," she said. "It won't be anything personal. You couldn't have chosen a worse weekend to arrive. There's been a lot of fighting in Bihać. I bet you that's why Dr. Tonković didn't turn up."

There was nothing we could do but wait. Sunday was hopeless. With no government offices open there was no chance of organizing anything. It was simply a question of killing time till the next day. That evening as Renata and I wandered gloomily down the street outside our hotel we heard music. Then we saw people dancing in the street and realized that there was a pop concert going on in the conference center opposite. A pop concert! In the middle of war-torn Croatia! The star of the concert turned out to be David Byrne, the lead singer of the group Talking Heads, and since both Renata and I were fans we decided to go and watch. It passed the time and took my mind, at least briefly, off the subject of artificial limbs.

On Monday morning Dr. Tonković rang me at my hotel apologizing profusely. Renata's guess had been correct.

"I'm really sorry, Miss Mills. How can you ever forgive me? I was called elsewhere without warning. Sixty thousand refugees from Bihać turned up on the border so it was an emergency. Didn't anyone ring you? Someone in the ministry should have let you know. It's been a nightmare: Everybody is in complete panic."

I gave an inward groan. As Renata said, what a weekend to choose.

"I know you must have a lot to think about, Dr. Tonković," I said hesitantly. "But the thing is, Bob Watts, the English prosthetist, is turning up today and we need to get into the workshop at the Prosthetic Institute to get started and set everything up to take castings."

"Don't worry. It's all arranged," Dr. Tonković said. "They're expecting you tomorrow morning."

Bob's flight arrived at midday on Monday and as soon as he'd cleared customs Renata drove us to the workshop.

"Yes, we know all about you. You can start work tomorrow morning," a technician confirmed. "How many patients would you like to see?"

I looked at Bob who pursed his lips thoughtfully. "Let's not be too ambitious. We've only got five days. Three fittings should be plenty. If we're training people it's important we don't rush it."

The technician nodded and smiled. "Good, we will have three patients waiting for you tomorrow morning."

Everything seemed to be going smoothly after all. I breathed a sigh of relief but it was premature. The following morning when we got to the workshop we found our way barred by a stony-faced policeman.

"You are not allowed in," he said.

"But Dr. Tonković himself said we are," I protested.

He gabbled away to Renata in Croatian and she turned to me and shrugged helplessly. "He says someone higher up than Dr. Tonković says you can't go in. He says today is All Saints' Day. It is the day of the dead when we pay respect to those who have died. No one can work on All Saints' Day. He says you will have to come back tomorrow."

I exploded. "Pay respect to the dead? And what about the living? What respect is he showing them?"

I only had Bob for five days and it took that long to prepare a leg, so every day was precious. Was there a conspiracy against us? How was it no one had mentioned All Saints' Day yesterday?

Renata pleaded and argued but the policeman was adamant. No one, but no one, was permitted to enter the workshop on November l.

Seething with frustration we went back to the hotel only to find that Bob and Quentin, the BBC director and producer, had turned up. They were going to Reuters to employ a local cameraman and wanted to know when they could start filming. Unfortunately, the two convoy lorry drivers who had left London forty-eight hours ago had *not* turned up. They'd telephoned to say they were being delayed at the border because officials there weren't happy with their papers.

This whole thing was turning into a nightmare. It was the most stressful thing I'd ever done in my life. To think that all those people were waiting for our limbs and their own people were standing in the way. I was beginning to wonder if fate had led me up the garden path. Surely she hadn't brought me all this way only to sabotage my plans at the last minute?

The thought acted like a spur. Well, I decided, if that was fate's plan I was going to overrule her. I was damned if I was going to be foiled now.

"Can't we take casts in the hotel room?" I asked Bob.

He thought. "I don't see why not. I've brought some plaster of paris in my luggage in case of emergency. It would be better to have an oven to bake the cast but I suppose beggars can't be choosers. Let's get started." He hesitated. "Just one question, Heather. Where do we find a patient?"

"I can help you there," Renata broke in. "I've got a very good friend in Zagreb. I only spoke to him yesterday. His name's Srpak and he's a commander in the army. He lost a leg a year ago. He has an artificial leg but it's not a good one. He says it hurts him so much he can't wear it. Would he do?"

"Sounds all right to me," Bob said. "Fetch him in."

Renata drove off to find her friend and reappeared forty-five minutes later with a bemused-looking man in Croatian army uniform. He was on crutches and had abandoned his old artificial leg altogether.

Bob spent an hour taking a casting of Srpak's stump. One casting didn't really make much of a difference but it was better than sitting around twiddling our thumbs. The rest of the week was still going to be a rush, but, psychologically, getting started cheered us all up and got us thinking more positively.

"Tomorrow," Bob promised Srpak, "when the workrooms open and the convoy lorries arrive, we will start putting your new leg together."

The convoy arrived at two o'clock on Wednesday morning having finally persuaded the border guards that they were on a genuine mercy mission and had no Kalashnikov rifles hidden away in the artificial legs. The four drivers had driven in shifts since setting off on Sunday and looked exhausted.

After a few hours' sleep at the hotel they were up again and helping us unload a selection of limb parts at the Prosthetic Institute. When Bob had picked out what he wanted they set off again, this time to deliver the remainder of the limbs to an unfinished hospital on the outskirts of Zagreb. Dr. Tonković had persuaded his ministry to make available a vast storage depot for us there. From this central point the limbs could be distributed all over Croatia to wherever they were needed.

The drivers were incredible. They were shattered after their drive but they didn't want any glory. They wouldn't even let the BBC film them. All they were interested in was getting the job done. The four of them did let me take them out to dinner that evening as a thank-you gesture, then they turned around and set off back to England. I was humbled by their dedication. All of them had jobs: Two were firemen, one a policemen, one a full-time driver for TNT, yet all of them had taken the time to drive the convoy as part of their annual holiday. It wasn't the first time they'd done it—most of them also drove regularly to Romania—and it wouldn't be the last. To me, people like Dave, Alex, David, and Peter were the real unsung heroes of charity work.

Next day, when we were finally granted permission to enter the workshop, we found it spacious and quite well equipped, with lathes, ovens to bake the plaster casts, and most of the tools Bob would need. The only things that were missing were limb parts and the orderlies were remedying this already, carrying in the boxes the drivers had deposited.

We found our amputees sitting patiently waiting for us in an anteroom. The minute I saw them I forgot all the frustrations of the past three days. This was what we'd come for.

Bob had asked for three patients, but the staff at the institute had been a bit cunning because one of them was a double amputee. Her name was Smelinja, a pretty dark-haired girl of nineteen who had lost both her legs in a grenade attack. She was wearing a smart red top and was sitting behind a table and as she smiled happily at the television camera it wasn't immediately obvious there was anything wrong with her. I asked if she'd mind showing her injuries to the people in England who had sent the legs. Completely unembarrassed she lifted her skirt and revealed that her body literally ended four inches below her hips. She was so brave: She told me she was learning computer studies and hoped to find a job in an office when she'd taken her exams. If ever there was living proof that amputation needn't mean the end of hope it was there in Smelinja's smile.

It was a real challenge for Bob. Smelinja had so little residual limb that attaching artificial legs would require great skill, but he was confident he could do it and that by the end of the week she would be walking again. "Maybe one day she'll even manage to get about without crutches," he said. "She's certainly determined enough."

The institute technicians watched Bob's every move with rapt attention. Their participation was actually the most important part of the whole operation. In the few days he was here Bob would only have time to fit a few legs but by watching him the technicians would be able to fit hundreds more over the next months.

When, later in the morning, Bob started to construct a leg for Renata's friend Srpak the interest became even more avid. One of the prosthetists told me they used a similar casting procedure to Bob's, but the details of his construction technique were new to them because in Croatia they'd been using mainly Ottobach limbs while most of the parts we'd brought over were made by Blatchford, a British firm. Bob knew both makes and explained the differences carefully.

While Smelinja's cast was baking, Bob turned to his next patient. Sasha was a soldier, also nineteen, who had lost his left leg when a shell hit his armored vehicle. He was quite a different proposition from Smelinja. She had been optimistic and cheerful. But though his injury wasn't nearly as disabling as hers, Sasha gave the impression he felt his life was finished. He didn't seem excited at the prospect of a new limb at all, showed little interest in the casting procedure, and answered Renata's questions with monosyllables.

On Thursday, as Bob was measuring him up for a second time, I suddenly realized his residual limb looked exactly the same as mine. Up until now I hadn't mentioned the fact that I had an artificial leg to anyone in the institute. I hadn't thought it was relevant. Because I was wearing jeans and didn't limp when I walked, I don't suppose anyone had any idea that I was an amputee. Now, looking at Sasha's gloomy face, I decided shock tactics were called for.

I was wearing a white lab coat and under its cover I slipped off my trousers and sat down beside him.

"Look, Sasha," I said, pulling off my leg. "Your stump is just like mine."

His face was a picture.

"How did you lose your leg?" he asked in Croat.

The cameras were filming so I replied in English with Renata helping translate. He nodded. Traffic accidents happened in Croatia too.

"Do you like sport?" I asked.

Sasha gave a noncommittal shrug.

"I can do sport," I told him. "With this leg I go skiing and running and roller skating, so you'll be able to do the same."

He threw me a disbelieving look.

I nudged him in the ribs. "Come on, cheer up. It's not the end of the world."

When Renata translated he laughed—a cynical laugh, but still, a laugh. His first.

But it was little Martine, Bob's last patient, who made the biggest impact. Martine was eight years old, a bright little girl with big brown eyes and long eyelashes. She too had lost her left leg, in a land-mine explosion two years earlier. Since then she'd had to hobble around on crutches because the institute had no artificial leg small enough to fit her. Her parents had brought her in for Bob to take a cast. Her father was a young soldier in Croatian army camouflage uniform, her mother, a worried-looking young woman with tired eyes. Through Renata, they told me how for the past two years Martine had been forced to sit and watch while her friends skipped, chased balls, and played tag.

I asked Martine what she was most excited about doing when she got her new leg and she whispered shyly that she wanted to ride her bike again with her brother.

Her mother rubbed her eyes. "That is the most important thing for her," she said. "She is very close to her brother."

There was no need to ask about the pain Martine's parents had been through. It was etched on their faces.

On his last day at the clinic Bob finally pronounced himself satisfied with Martine's leg. He had made it from the new parts I'd bought, specially for children like her, with my booklet money. It looked fantastic. Even the color matched her other leg perfectly. She stared in wonder as Bob adjusted the padding over her stump and pushed her new leg gently into place. Her mum helped her pull down her jeans leg and laced up a left-footed trainer for the first time in two whole years.

"Now." Bob took her hand and helped her to her feet. "Are you ready to have a go?" I offered her my left hand for support and holding it tightly Martine walked up the length of the workshop, the effort of concentration wrinkling her brow. At the end she turned and walked back on her own to Bob with hardly a limp. I looked over to where her mother and father stood, she in the same blue coat she'd worn to the clinic each day, probably her only coat, he in his combat uniform. Tears were running down their faces.

"Heather?" Martine had walked back to where Renata and I were standing and was looking up at me. I bent over and she threw both her arms around my neck and squeezed me tight. Then she whispered something in my ear.

I looked at Renata. My Croatian was still pretty ropy.

"What did she say?"

Renata smiled. "She said, 'Thank you for helping me to walk again.' "

I blinked hard and squeezed her back.

"Thank *you,* Martine," I said. "Thank you for helping my dream come true."

# Chapter 23

Life is a jigsaw puzzle made up of lots of different pieces. At the beginning you've no idea what the final picture will be. It's only as you get older and little bits of your life begin to fit together that you suddenly say, *Oh yes—now I see what it's all about.*

Going to Croatia with my convoy of limbs was a key piece in my personal jigsaw puzzle. When that fell into place, a lot of my other experiences started to make sense. Everything that had happened in my life up until then seemed to me to have been leading up to this task. If I hadn't had to make my own way when I was young, and if I hadn't had to fight so hard to make my name in modeling, then maybe I wouldn't have had the determination to get a convoy of limbs through. If Mum hadn't gone on to dance and defy the doctors after nearly losing her leg, then perhaps I would have thought amputation was the end of my life. Even my impulsive skiing holiday in Yugoslavia seemed now like something more than pure chance. After all, if it wasn't for that I would never have known anything about Croatia.

Whichever way I looked at it, I couldn't avoid the conclusion that my whole life had been preparing me for work with amputees. By the time I returned home I felt I had no choice. I had to keep going with my charity work and build on what we had learned from our Croatian trip.

There was one big problem. How was I going to fund future convoys? Our volunteers were fantastic, but there were some expenses we couldn't avoid: fuel to go in the trucks, food and accommodations for the drivers, telephone calls, faxes, and wages for an assistant to help me deal with paper and office work. After the television film came out, several people had sent me donations to help the cause. However, there wasn't nearly enough money in the kitty for the vision I now had of setting up amputee clinics in every country with minefields. As usual in my life, however, the answer to the problem was just around the corner.

After I first wrote about my life in 1995, I began to be offered lots of public speaking engagements. My talks went down well and before long I was taken on by a major agency. Over the next few years the fee they asked for me to address companies and organizations went up by leaps and bounds. Usually my talks would be about my childhood, my life generally, and my charity work. Then I'd go on to say a bit about the importance of positive thinking. The angle I took would depend on the audience. I found men were often more blasé and less responsive than women and took more warming up. Sometimes, if it was a load of business guys, you could almost hear them yawning before you started and you knew they were thinking, *Oh yeah, another blond bimbo. What's this one going to tell us?* I quite liked that sort of audience. I took it as a challenge to wake them up and make them listen. If I got a standing ovation at the end of my speech, I'd think *yes!*

My public-speaking fees went a long way toward paying the cost of the continuing limb convoys to Croatia. But the convoy funding was also helped by the increasing amount of radio and television work I was being offered. The BBC documentary on my trip to Croatia had been given a good reception and soon afterward I did several TV items, including some pieces for the BBC's holiday program and ITV's *Wish You Were Here,* where I hunted out holidays suitable for disabled people.

On one of these assignments I went to a holiday center in Devon, run by the Calvert Trust. I was really impressed by their work. There were quite a few places that did respite care for the disabled, where families could leave their children while they went somewhere else. But I always felt that sort of holiday was based on the idea that the disabled were a burden. The Calvert Trust took a different approach. Their centers organized holidays for the whole family where they could ride, rock climb, and do lots of outdoor activities together. The idea was that people could enjoy their disabled kids' company without the day-to-day hard work usually involved in looking after them. I thought it was a brilliant idea and after the program I did quite a bit of fund-raising for them.

Toward the end of 1997 I was offered the chance to present *The General,* a major new daytime TV hospital documentary series. The program was to be based in Southampton General Hospital and filmed five days a week. The idea behind it was to make people feel more comfortable about going for operations and treatments on the NHS. It was supposed to be inspirational and educational. I thought it would be right up my street. The only slight qualm I had concerned the new man in my life: Oliver, a soft-coated wheaten terrier. I had bought him as a puppy in 1996 and already he had lived in four different homes. I wasn't sure how he'd take to being uprooted again to a flat in Southampton. But I needn't have worried. Oliver is the most easygoing dog in the world. In some ways he adapted to his new life better than I did.

Filming began in March 1998, and my life turned into a hectic rush of early-morning starts. By five-fifteen I'd be on the beach taking Oliver for a walk. At six-thirty I'd be at the studio, reading through the update of illnesses and new patients. At eight o'clock I'd have my hair and makeup done, and from nine-thirty to ten we'd be on air. To begin with we did a lot of live links where I'd have to go and chat to someone in bed about their illness and what treatment and operations they'd had. It could be a bit daunting, but I made some good friends among the patients, some of whom I am still in touch with today. One woman who made a big impact was Kirsten, a gutsy single mum whose young son Alex was very disabled. He had severe curvature of the spine, which had resulted in one leg being shorter than the other, and he was waiting for a hip replacement. He was also profoundly deaf and Kirsten had been told he would never walk or talk. She was absolutely determined to prove the doctors wrong. Four years later Alex can not only walk, he can run. In addition, he speaks as well as any other boy of his age. The only complication is that because of his hearing problem he is sometimes so loud that his friends accuse him of being bossy!

Making friends like Kirsten was the upside of working on *The General.* But by the time the first series ended I was becoming a bit uneasy about the program. Sometimes it seemed to me as if scheduling was more important than the welfare of the patients. One incident in particular upset me. On the morning in question I was supposed to interview someone who was seriously ill after an operation, but when I saw him he was having trouble breathing, and answering questions was obviously causing him a lot of pain. He really looked at death's door. I suggested to the director that maybe I should talk to someone else instead. However, the powers-that-be wouldn't hear of it. It was a live program, and that was the schedule, so I was told to get on with it.

I began to have serious doubts about the ethics of turning real people's lives and deaths into a soap opera. I was also concerned that the program had started to focus more and more on behind-the-scenes gossip and nurse-doctor romance. I felt *The General* was losing its way and patronizing the audience. All in all I was quite relieved when the series came to an end.

I didn't have time to twiddle my thumbs. In October 1998 I took over Lorraine Kelly's 6:30 A.M. show on *Talk* radio for a few weeks. This meant a three or four o'clock wake-up call to get to the London Oxford Street Studios in time. It was more heavy-duty stuff than *The General* had been. It involved talking to politicians and public figures and I had to go through all the morning newspapers before we went on air, so I would be on the ball. Working on radio was very different from TV, but I loved it. More importantly, the lighter work schedule left me more time for charity work and counseling than *The General* had done.

Counseling had become a big part of my life by now. Every day requests came in for me to visit new amputees and talk to them.

Sometimes the contact came via my Web site, other times from personal meetings, but the largest number came directly from hospitals. By this time many of the hospitals in the country had my number and whenever they had an amputee who they thought would benefit from meeting me, they'd ring and ask me to pay a visit. Sometimes they'd ask me to speak to the patient's relatives as well. They were often in shock, just like the patients, and needed to be told that it is possible for people to recover from an amputation and get on with their lives again.

Some of the people I met at that time also made a great impression on me. Laura Giddings was an eight-year-old British girl who'd been on holiday in 1998 with her parents in South Africa when the Planet Hollywood restaurant was bombed and she lost her left leg. I went to her house and met her parents, who said she'd been very depressed. When she talked to me, I realized at once that part of the reason was the ugly and uncomfortable NHS prosthesis she had to wear. I introduced her to Bob Watts and he made her a new leg that didn't hurt, with pretty toenails. It meant she could ride her bike, paint her nails, and feel like a normal little girl again.

Shortly after that I met Helen Smith, a young Ph.D. student who had recently lost both legs, an arm, and a hand to meningitis. She'd been studying to be a biochemist and had also been a very good pianist, so her whole life had been devastated. She too was having trouble getting the right treatment because of the NHS funding crisis. When I looked into it, I was shocked to discover that since 1985 the amount allocated to supplying and fitting a new prosthesis had actually gone down, rather than increased. In the mid-1980s the NHS had allocated £2,500 per limb. By the late 1990s this had dropped to £750 a limb. Was it any wonder that people found them unsatisfactory? The color was unnatural, the texture looked completely unlike real skin, and the shape was standard for everyone and wasn't altered to match the other limb. Helen had even been given a sort of claw attachment to replace one of her hands. She knew from meeting Bob Watts and from seeing legs like mine that better things were possible, and wanted to be allowed to try them.

I encouraged her to make a nuisance of herself to the authorities who were treating her as if she didn't deserve anything better. It didn't win either of us any brownie points from the NHS, but the publicity did pay off. Eventually a benefactor paid for her to get new limbs from the Dorset Orthopaedic Clinic. Today Helen has state-of-the-art, natural-looking arms that respond to pulses sent when she flexes her remaining upper-arm muscles. Her new fingers open and close so well that she can even apply her own makeup. Not only that; she has a flourishing career as a presenter for Anglia Television.

Indirectly it was Helen who was responsible for my move into another form of counseling. I was asked to appear with her on *This Morning with Richard and Judy* talking about Helen's new limbs, the difference they'd made, and our campaign for more funds to be allocated to the NHS to spend on better-quality prosthetics.

Without any warning, after my item with Helen was finished the producers asked me if I'd like to take over their advice slot for the morning as their usual agony aunt, Clare Rayner, was ill. I was a bit taken aback. "What do I have to do?" I asked.

"Well, we can't give you the questions beforehand because people just ring in," they said. "You just have to do it off the top of your head. We thought you'd be good at that sort of thing."

It was a baptism by fire. The first woman who rang in said that her boyfriend was holding her in his flat against her will—he'd basically kidnapped her and was forcing her to take drugs. "He makes me stay in all day," she said. "He won't let me out."

"Does he lock the doors?" I asked.

"Yes."

"What, even the windows?"

"No, but we're in a high-rise flat."

"Well, you can obviously get to a telephone to ring us, so why can't you ring for help? Just call the police."

"I'm frightened," she said—"I'm frightened that if I leave, he'll come and get me."

I was trying to be patient with her because I knew abused women do get very scared, but I have to admit I didn't feel terribly sympathetic.

I couldn't see why anybody would just sit and be a victim. "Well, is it worse living with him and having him beat you up every day or taking the chance of getting out and getting to a safe house?" I asked. "Get out. Get the police to take you to the local women's refuge and then go to your doctor and ask for help to deal with the drugs you've been taking."

There was a long pause before she promised she would. Somehow I wasn't convinced.

I'd never listened to the agony aunt session before so I hadn't known that the usual *This Morning* approach was about tea and sympathy and offering a shoulder to cry on. I'd been a bit more direct than that. However, some people must have liked it. At the end of the program they said they'd never had so many calls and e-mails, and would I come in the next week and do it again?

The following week I was waiting in the studio for my slot when a middle-aged couple came in to be interviewed. They were talking about how their eighteen-year-old daughter Melissa had gone to prison for burglary and after her release from prison had simply disappeared. They were desperate to find her again. I happened to have seen a program called *Jailbirds* about a women's prison the week before and realized I had actually seen this girl they were talking about. I remembered liking her character—she was very ballsy. I don't know why, but I felt I knew her. When I realized the connection, I started to take more of an interest. When we went on air, her parents were talking about what it was like to have a daughter who went off the rails and you had no control over. Melissa had been stealing goods to sell so she could buy drugs for her heroin addiction and for her boyfriend. Her parents said she had started on marijuana when she was thirteen after the boyfriend forced her to try it and it had gone on from there. Hearing that, I got even more interested. I've always had huge arguments with my friends about marijuana. I think there are certain people who can smoke it and it doesn't affect them, but if anyone has a slight mental vulnerability it can bring out huge long-term paranoia problems. I don't believe it should be called a soft drug. I certainly don't believe it should ever be legalized except for medical purposes.

I was sitting on the couch opposite Richard and Judy and on the spur of the moment I butted in. "Look Melissa," I said. "If you're listening, your parents love you. I know it's hard but we'll all help you. We can get you away from this horrendous guy. Just call us up, this is the number . . ."

We never thought we'd hear from her. I'd made appeals before and nothing had ever happened. But the program had just gone to break when a voice called, "Quick quick, quick! Melissa's on the phone."

I spoke to her for several minutes. Her voice was a monotone and she sounded numb. I guessed she was pretty drugged up. But from what she said it was obvious that she desperately wanted to come home. The trouble was, she was afraid to. "My parents will get really awful with me," she said. "It will all turn out the same as before."

I thought quickly. Oliver and I had just moved again, this time to Hampshire, where I had rented a big old barn in the middle of the country, well away from any nightlife, low life, or drug culture. "Melissa," I said, "if you want, you can come and live with me for three months, and we'll get you off drugs and sort you out."

Before she could answer, I told her there was one condition: She had to spend the first two weeks with her parents. I was no drug expert, but I knew that the first ten or twelve days of cold turkey were the worst. I didn't know Melissa well enough to supervise that and I couldn't guarantee to be in the house twenty-four hours a day, which is what she'd need. "We'll talk after the program about how your parents will behave toward you during that time, because it will be difficult for all of you," I said. "Will you trust me and give it a try?" To everyone's delight, she decided she would.

Not long after the program, her parents rang me, over the moon because she had returned. Twelve days later, as arranged, they drove her up to Hampshire. When they arrived and I opened the door Melissa took one look at me and started crying. I'm sure she thought I was some horrible, sadistic headmistress type who was going to give her the slipper. Luckily, Oliver broke the ice. Melissa obviously had a soft spot for animals and after her parents left, she settled down with Oliver curled around her like a security blanket.

Over the next few weeks I hardly talked to Melissa about drugs at all. Instead I used to say, "Right, I need you to give me a hand with that." "I need you to do this." "When that person calls do so and so." And I got her working alongside me.

At night when the shaking started, I'd put her in her room. "I'm here if you need me," I said. "Come in anytime in the night, but you can't get out and there's no access to any drugs here. So we're just going to have to go through this."

It worked. Probably because I've never taken drugs I didn't empathize with her when the cravings came. I couldn't imagine what it felt like, so I wasn't tempted to go soft on her. Over the next few months she just got better and better. The turning point came when she started to show a natural talent for helping others. If I was busy when the phone rang, Melissa would answer it. Often it would be someone with a problem who'd say, "I'm so depressed," and Melissa would reply, "Oh I know how you feel. Tell me all about it." She could relate to people who felt they were at the bottom of life's pile and it improved her sense of self-worth to realize she was helping them.

By the late spring of 1999 Melissa was completely clean of drugs and I felt she was ready to get out into real life again. I was still in touch with the Calvert Trust and asked if they could find her a job in one of their holiday centers. When it was arranged, she went up to their center in Keilder Forest, Northumberland. It turned out better than any of us could have hoped for. Melissa loved animals and as a child had learned to ride on a friend's pony. She started working at the horse-riding section of the center, where she was an instant hit with the kids. A year later I experienced one of the best moments of my life when I watched a documentary filmed at the Calvert Trust and saw a young, very disabled girl rocking backward and forward and gazing adoringly up at her, lisping, "I love Melissa. I *love* Melissa."

Early in 1999 I was asked to visit Ireland to talk to survivors of the Omagh bombing. I was used to seeing war-torn countries by now, but not so close to home. Sue Prenter, the counseling coordinator at the hospital, drove me down into Omagh, a lovely little market town, and pointed out the shop windows, all still boarded up. "Imagine doing your ordinary weekly shopping around here when suddenly a bomb goes off," she said. "It was just utter devastation."

Meeting the survivors was very moving. One girl's face had been almost completely destroyed by the blast. She'd been planning to get married and was still determined the wedding would go ahead. Several people had lost legs. I counseled a couple of girls, one an above- and one a below-knee amputee, and promised I would get them referrals to the Dorset Orthopaedic Clinic so they could get cosmetic legs like mine. Some of the older victims seemed to be coping with it better than the younger ones. One beautifully dressed gray-haired lady who must have been nearly seventy was only concerned about whether she could still go on holiday. "Will my leg look real, so I can put my swimsuit on?" she wanted to know.

"Of course," I said. "But you don't want to get one of those legs straightaway because your residual limb has to reduce first."

"And will I be able to walk up hills? Because I go to the same place every year in Spain and it's quite hilly." I assured her she would. But she had one final question. "I go to Spain with my girlfriend Ethel, and we usually get a double room because it's cheaper. Should I get twin beds from now on, because I'm afraid I'll kick her with my artificial leg and hurt her." I burst out laughing. "No, no, you take your leg *off* when you get into bed," I told her. She was so relieved.

The biggest challenge in my counseling career came when I had a phone call from a woman asking me to visit her niece Samantha, who was a cancer patient at the Middlesex Hospital. By now I'd counseled in hospitals all over the country, but strangely had never been asked to go to the Middlesex. Because it was where my mum had died, I had always dreaded a call like this—the hospital held such horrible memories for me. But I knew I had to do it, for myself, as well as for Samantha.

Sam was only sixteen and was in the children's cancer ward. She'd had her leg amputated near the hip and was still getting high-dose chemotherapy, so her main problem was the cancer more than losing her leg. From the moment I met her, my own fears about the hospital disappeared. She was truly inspiring. She was one of the few people I met whom I knew immediately would deal brilliantly with losing her leg if only she could overcome the cancer. We had quite a laugh together. Although she was eventually allowed to go home on weekends, she continued to be treated at the Middlesex. Over the next year I went back several times to see her and we became really close.

Around the time of my first visit to Sam, I had my biggest TV break yet when I appeared as one of two disabled presenters on Esther Rantzen's new Sunday show *That's Esther.* I'd already worked as an undercover reporter on *Esther Investigates,* helping expose quacks who offered "cures" for AIDS, cancer, and ME (myalgic encephalomyelitis) in return for vast amounts of money, so I was used to her style of program. The idea of her new show was to focus on inspirational people who had overcome adversity or done something major to help the community. One of the first stories we covered made a big impact nationally. It featured a woman called Sue Parkin from near Sheffield who'd had four young kids. She had put the chip pan on one day, then fell asleep on the couch for a few minutes, and the whole house had set alight. Her two girls were downstairs with her, but her young son and his baby brother were upstairs, and she wasn't able to save them. She had decided to salvage some good from her tragedy by publicizing the dangers of chip pans. She was a very motivational person.

*That's Esther* decided to support her by launching a crusade to "ban the chip pan." I had no idea that twelve thousand fires were caused each year by chip pans overheating. Lots of them ended up with serious burns or death. We got firefighters all over the country to put up posters saying *Please hand in your chip pan* and arranged for them to hand out £10 discount vouchers for deep-fat fryers with thermostatic controls. It was a typical *That's Esther* campaign and I found it a lot more rewarding than my role in *The General.* The impact it made soon helped the program transfer from Sundays to a prime-time weekday evening slot.

The production team encouraged me to come up with ideas of my own and I was able to publicize several causes that were close to my heart. In April 1999 we filmed Bob Watts's work at the Dorset

Orthopaedic Clinic. Shortly afterward I was given the go-ahead for a trip to Cambodia with the Duchess of Kent to follow the work of Voluntary Service Overseas with land-mine survivors. I was really excited about it. I hoped the publicity would help raise funds to pay for more artificial limbs for Third World countries.

Since 1995, with the help of my public speaking fees, we had been able to carry on running our regular limb convoys to help the land-mine survivors in Croatia. We had also shipped out limb parts to other war-torn countries that were farther afield, such as Cambodia.

By 1999, though, we were coming up against a problem. The supply of spare NHS limbs was drying up. In a roundabout way I had only myself to blame. Through my TV and counseling work I had come into contact with dozens of people like Helen Smith and Laura Giddings who had suffered from badly fitted NHS limbs. Trained prosthetists were in such short supply that it wasn't unusual for people to have fittings canceled or delayed and all too often discomfort was treated as inevitable. Unless they could afford to pay for private treatment, people had to make do with what they were given. I campaigned avidly to get the NHS to refer amputees to the Dorset Orthopaedic Clinic. Every time I met a politician or NHS executive in the course of my work, I would point out that cutting the budget for artificial limbs was not the economical option they seemed to think. It was actually much more efficient to supply comfortable cosmetic prostheses from the beginning than to have to refit people every couple of weeks because their limb was chafing them or they couldn't get about on it. Also, if people couldn't function normally, they couldn't work and they would get depressed. Then they would need more NHS treatment and, often, expensive home care too. Gradually the message seemed to have got through. More and more people were getting referred to the Dorset Orthopaedic Clinic by the NHS. The downside was, those people did not end up with a collection of discarded limbs at home. It was becoming clear that we were soon going to have to look elsewhere for a source of limbs for our clinics abroad.

Early in 1999 I'd had a letter from someone called Ed Pennington-Ridge, an inventor from Somerset who ran a company called Elegant

Design and Solutions. He'd read about my work in Croatia and thought I might be interested in a project he had been working on. His idea was to develop a low-cost basic artificial limb that could be built almost entirely from materials that were plentiful in Third World countries, like wood and rubber. He had even been using old car tires for the rubber component and was working on developing a very cheap silicone sleeve to give the limb a more lifelike appearance. He couldn't afford to copyright his idea and he wanted to know if I would be interested in helping to fund the development of his limbs, which he wanted to use in a charitable way.

I went to meet him and was instantly won over. Ed was a complete eccentric. He had wild frizzy black hair and used his hands like windmills while he was speaking, as if he was trying to keep up with his thoughts. He was like a young Einstein. Both his enthusiasm and his prototype limb really impressed me and at the end of our meeting I agreed to fund him. It wasn't just that the supply of NHS limbs was drying up. My ideas about helping land-mine survivors were changing by this time. The more I learned about underdeveloped countries, the more I realized that charity projects there often overlapped. As a result, a lot of money was being wasted on administration. I felt that if only charities cooperated more, far more people could be helped.

A lot of the inspiration for my new approach had come from James Ruddy, the deputy editor of the *Eastern Daily Press,* who had recently contacted me. He was an enthusiastic campaigner for child victims in war zones and had just written a best-selling book about his work called *The Kindness of a Stranger.* It was James who had told me of the horrific mutilations that had gone on during the civil war in Sierra Leone. As well as the land-mine victims in that country, there were now hundreds of children who'd had their hands and arms hacked off with machetes in night raids because the rebels objected to their parents voting for the government. Thus the majority of amputees in Sierra Leone were now upper-limb amputees. Although charities like World Hope International were working on the problem, they could only give help to a fraction of the children who needed it because the prostheses they used were so expensive.

What I hoped now was that when Ed's limbs were perfected I could send him out to Sierra Leone to work in conjunction with the World Hope International Clinic. While they concentrated on their expensive £300-a-pop limb, Ed could work alongside them, supplying his basic £30 limb, at least as an initial stopgap step. It would enable children to begin to function normally again and adults to get back to work. On top of that he could train local people to make them and they could become more independent and help themselves, which is always a better option than depending on outside charities.

Exciting as this project was, for the time being I tried to focus my mind on my forthcoming trip to Cambodia with the Duchess of Kent. It was planned for May 22 and everything was on schedule when, at the beginning of May, a spanner was thrown in the works. A routine health checkup discovered I had some precancerous cells of the cervix. I was told it was important to operate straightaway before they got a chance to develop. "But I'm going to Cambodia!" I protested. Luckily, Yehudi Gordon, who'd been my doctor since I was eighteen and had discovered my ectopic pregnancies, came to my rescue yet again. I was booked in for a quick day operation and a small piece of cervix containing the sinister cells was removed. I could go ahead with my trip, Dr. Gordon agreed, provided I came back for checkups every six months. "I'm sure we've caught it in time, so don't worry," he said.

I had no intention of worrying about it. I had far too much to do before I popped my clogs.

# Chapter 24

Since 1995, with my TV career and charity work running flat out, my personal life had been more or less on hold. Sadly, although Raffaele and I were still very good friends, we had recognized that we had grown apart and had agreed to call it a day. Since then, I'd had a couple of relationships but ended up being quite badly hurt in both of them.

So when, on May 20, 1999, I attended the *Daily Mirror* Pride of Britain Award ceremony at the Dorchester Hotel, meeting the love of my life was not remotely on my agenda. Fate, of course, had plans of her own.

My job that afternoon was to present a bravery award to Helen Smith, who though still in a wheelchair had made a lot of progress since her appearance on *Richard and Judy.* When Helen's turn came, I ran up on stage and gave a little speech to the assembled audience. "Imagine waking up one morning thinking that you'd had a bad dream, but discovering it's real," I said. "You've lost both your legs, an arm, and a hand, and they're never going to come back. Imagine you were going to be a biochemist and you play the piano brilliantly, and you'll never be able to finish your studies or play again. And then you deal with it and become an inspiration to others. Well, that's what Helen Smith has done for me and for many other people. . . ." By now her story was well known, and when Helen came onto the stage in her wheelchair to give her acceptance speech, lots of people were crying. What happened next was so typical of what disabled people have to put up with that it might have been planned. The microphone was fixed at head height for a standing person, so when Helen started to speak, no one could hear a word. I was so cross, I just yanked the microphone out of the lectern not caring if I broke it and pulled it down to her. She gave a lovely speech, and I glanced down at the front-row VIP guests to see Richard Branson, Piers Morgan, the editor of the *Mirror,* Queen Noor of Jordan, and Sir Paul McCartney, all staring up at her, obviously very moved. I had met all of them previously, apart from Paul McCartney. He was there to present an award in memory of his late wife Linda to the president of a vegetarian charity called Viva.

Although I recognized him I didn't know much about Paul McCartney, or indeed about the Beatles. Thanks to Dad my musical education had consisted of *The Ring of the Nibelung* rather than "She Loves You." At home we'd had hundreds of records and tapes, but I didn't remember any Beatles record among them (though Fiona says now they were there—I just wasn't interested!). So that day, although I knew Paul was an icon to lots of people, I didn't really appreciate his status. I do remember thinking how nice looking he was, though, and saying as much to my friend Verna when I left the stage and sat down next to her. However, I had to run off early to a meeting, so we weren't introduced and didn't speak to each other.

The following couple of weeks were even more frantic than usual for me. The day after the award ceremony, I dropped Oliver off with his doting "foster parents" Mary and James, who were neighbors of my friend Rudi. Early the following day I set off for Cambodia with the Duchess of Kent and an ITV team to make our film on VSO work for *That's Esther.*

It turned out to be a really enjoyable trip. The Duchess of Kent wasn't at all as I'd imagined royalty to be. Right from our first meeting she was very warm and spontaneous. The ITV team flew economy class, which we always did when we made charity-based programs, but the duchess, who was flying incognito under the name of Mills, was in first class. She got very excited as we were queuing to climb the steps into the plane and saw it was a 747. She said that she'd never been "upstairs" in an airplane before.

Once we arrived in Cambodia it became obvious that she genuinely cared about the children whom Voluntary Service Overseas were helping, and about the whole situation there. We traveled around a lot and she fell in love with the country, just as I had on my first visit there to help land-mine survivors in 1996. It seemed incongruous that a country with such a horrific past should be so beautiful. Some of the cases we came across during filming were heartbreaking, but we also had lots of laughs—and not just when we were off duty. One day I was interviewing the duchess as we traveled along in a jeep when she suddenly abandoned what she was saying and pointed. "Oh my God," she shouted. "There's an elephant! I've never seen an elephant before." She had the most lovely childlike wonder at new experiences. By the end of the trip we were all captivated by her.

I returned home from Cambodia on June 6 feeling absolutely exhausted and collapsed into bed, where I slept for about twelve hours. It wasn't until the next morning that I opened my post and checked my calls. When I did, I found a curious message on my answerphone. "Hi, Heather. It's Paul McCartney here. Would you give me a ring?" With my mind still full of Cambodia it was a minute before I remembered the award ceremony and the penny dropped. *Yeah, right,* I thought. *Of course. Verna's set me up here because I told her I thought he was good looking. Very funny.*

I made up my mind to get back at Verna and ignored it. The next day I came in to find a second, identical message on the machine and thought, *Hang on a minute.* Warily I rang the number, and sure enough it was Paul McCartney's office. A secretary answered. When I gave my name she said, "Oh yes, Sir Paul's been trying to get in touch with you. He's not here today, but I'll tell him you rang."

The Cambodia film was shown on *That's Esther* on June 19. Five minutes before the program started, the phone rang. It was Paul. I didn't want to miss seeing the film, so he probably didn't get the reaction he expected.

"Have you got the telly on?" I asked.

"No, why?"

"Well put it on," I said. "Watch *That's Esther* and call me back afterward to tell me what you think."

Half an hour later he rang back and said how much he'd enjoyed it. "Actually, it sort of relates to why I've called you," he said.

He told me that a few days after he'd heard me speak at the awards ceremony he'd seen an item on the *Tomorrow's World* program about bionic arms that took nerve impulses from the residual limb and translated them into hand and arm movements. "I thought maybe you would be interested in that sort of thing for your land-mine survivors," he said. "If you were, I'd like to offer some help with funding it."

I wasn't as instantly grateful as he might have expected. As it happened I had strong views on these bionic limbs that overcame any awe I might have felt at talking to Paul McCartney. "That's all well and good for the Western world," I told him. "An arm like that might well help someone like Helen Smith, but I don't think it's a starter for Third World countries. In places like Sierra Leone and Cambodia they need limbs that aren't expensive, that they can make themselves and become self-sufficient. For the price of that one arm I can fit at least fifty kids with artificial limbs in places like Sierra Leone. They might not be bionic, but they can make the difference between dependence and independence. I don't want to seem ungrateful. I'd like to talk about it, but it depends what you want me to do."

There was a pause. "Well," he said, "let's meet up about it."

So the next week I went up to Paul's offices in London. His secretary invited me in and I sat on the couch and had a cup of tea while I waited. After a couple of minutes Paul ran down the stairs and sort of floated toward me and shook hands. The main thing that struck me about him was the energy he projected; he walked like Fred Astaire, almost as if he was dancing. We went into his office, sat down, and started talking. I told him mostly about Sierra Leone and the maimed children there, and what I was hoping to do in terms of working with clinics that already existed to fit Ed's economy limbs. The Sierra Leone project, I explained, was the main funding I needed help with at the moment.

"Okay," he said when I'd finished. "Why don't you put a proposal together of what you'd like to do and what it will cost. Draw up a detailed business plan and we'll meet again to discuss it."

He said good-bye and I walked to the lift. As I stepped in, I turned around and saw him peering at me around the corner. If it had been any other man I could have sworn he was looking at my bum, but this was Paul McCartney. I dismissed the suspicion instantly.

As I traveled home, my mind was focused on what Paul's donation would mean. He hadn't mentioned how much money he was thinking of. And I hadn't liked to ask. I hoped maybe twenty grand. Thirty if we were lucky. It was very exciting; it would really set us up. But at the back of my mind I knew it would also mean a headache for me. Although I'd had a little help financially, I had always funded most of my charity work myself. A big donation would mean I'd have to become a registered charity. I had mixed feelings about that prospect. Up until now, when I wanted to do something I had just gone on and done it. But I knew life wouldn't be that simple when we were a registered charity. There'd be lots of rules and regulations. Everything would have to be voted for by trustees and approved in triplicate before I could move. I didn't object in principle. I knew it had to be done to ensure funds were properly spent, but I didn't relish all that bureaucracy slowing my work down.

I went home with my head spinning with ideas for the business plan I had promised to draw up. The next day it continued to spin. It wasn't long before I realized that actually I didn't feel very well. Later that week I was in the studio with Esther Rantzen when she suddenly said, "Are you okay, Heather? You look really white." Thinking I was about to faint, she insisted on getting me to a doctor there and then. As soon as I told him I had been to Cambodia, he diagnosed what was wrong with me. I had dengue fever. The doctor only recognized it because he had once had it himself. He told me it was a tropical viral disease, a bit like malaria, that is carried by mosquitoes. He ran a blood test that confirmed his diagnosis. "Are you feeling depressed or suicidal?" he asked.

"No, I just feel a bit weak," I told him.

He looked disbelieving. "Well, your blood test shows you've got virtually no serotonin in your body. If you're not depressed, you're not normal."

I laughed. "Tell me about it."

I wasn't laughing the next day though. By that time I was in bed in the barn and literally couldn't move. Every joint in my body ached and my neck and shoulders were so stiff I thought I was paralyzed. I stayed in bed for five days, not eating, and sweating and freezing by turn. I didn't even have the energy to ring to ask someone to come and look after me. Fortunately my lady gardener fed Oliver and let him out and brought me bottles of mineral water, which were all I could face. When I did finally get up, my head was spinning as if I'd drunk too much wine and I felt as weak as a kitten.

It meant I had to delay my next meeting with Paul until the beginning of July, but it gave me time to reflect on my whole situation. Being so ill brought home my own mortality. The doctor had warned me that a second dose of dengue fever could kill me, so traveling in Asia would be hazardous for me from now on. And if I wasn't around anymore, what would happen to my work for amputees? The more I thought about it, the more I realized that Paul's offer of a donation had come at exactly the right time. It was going to force me to do something that was actually very sensible. Once I'd registered the Heather Mills Health Trust as a charity, the aid for amputees would be able to continue no matter what happened to me.

My illness brought something else home to me as well. I needed to delegate more. For ages Fiona and my friends had been telling me that I was doing too much and warning me of the dangers of burning the candle at both ends. First my cancer scare and now the dengue fever seemed to be telling me to listen to their advice. Also, being ill in bed at home with nobody to look after me had not been a pleasant experience. At the very least it seemed sensible to find someone to help me at home until I got stronger.

I didn't have to look far to find the ideal person. When I had worked on the TV show *The General,* although my makeup artist was a lovely girl, she'd been terrible at doing hair. So bad, in fact, that eventually I bought a wig, but that wasn't much better, because I was scared to turn my neck in case the wig fell off. I started to look like a wooden puppet when I was interviewing someone, switching my head from side to side like Orville, the ventriloquist's duck.

Luckily I then found a brilliant beauty therapist and hairdresser in Southampton called Sonya Chapman. She used to give me a secret shampoo and blow-dry every night so all I had to do was lift my hair with rollers before I turned up for work. Chatting away to her, as you do at the hairdresser's, I'd discovered Sonya was full of hidden talents. She played the trumpet, read and transposed music, and jived and tangoed at competition level. She had also been a head scout and was a very good target shooter. With all her skills, I couldn't believe she had ended up working for peanuts in a small back-street hairdressing shop. Eventually she went to work in the local ASDA store because it paid better money than the hairdresser's, but I had stayed in touch with her. In fact she only lived fifteen minutes down the road from my place. On the spur of the moment I rang her up and asked if she'd be interested in coming to work for me as a girl Friday. To my immense relief she jumped at the offer. She gave the supermarket a week's notice and at the end of June she started to bring some much-needed organization into my life. Three years later Sonya is still with me and not only does my hair and makeup as needed but is now a computer buff and has become the linchpin of my office.

Over the next week, as I recuperated, I put together the business plan about the Sierra Leone project. I was helped in this by James Ruddy of the *Eastern Daily Press,* who had first made me interested in the country. I had, in fact, been planning to travel out with him to see Sierra Leone for myself but the dengue fever episode meant I wouldn't be allowed to go there for quite a while. However, James's knowledge and enthusiasm were a great help in drawing up the proposal.

By the time I met up with Paul again the business plan, although still in outline form, was looking quite impressive. Paul was enthusiastic and asked me to find out more about various aspects. A couple of days later I went back to his office once more with the results of my research. Paul asked more questions. Gradually, during the first half of July, every small detail of our plan to send Ed out to Sierra Leone was finalized.

After one of our meetings I had an appointment to see Richard Branson and couldn't resist spilling the beans. "I've just been to meet Paul McCartney," I said. "He's helping me with the charity."

"He fancies you," Richard said.

"No, he doesn't," I protested.

"He does." He grinned. "Don't forget I was sitting next to him at the *Mirror* awards."

"Don't be ridiculous," I said.

I wasn't being coy. I truly didn't believe at all that Paul fancied me. It wasn't that I was naive. Normally I have a pretty good idea if someone's giving me the eye. But he hadn't given me any clue at all, apart from that moment in the lift. At least, not the sort of clue I was used to picking up on.

The only thing I'd noticed was that once or twice while I'd been talking, I'd caught him looking at me with a funny smile. At the time I'd thought, *Is he listening to me or what?* I just imagined he must have so many things on his mind that he was thinking about something else. In spite of Richard's comment, that's what I still thought.

Every last wrinkle in the plan was now ironed out. Ed would spend the next few months developing his limbs and with luck would be ready to go out to Sierra Leone early the next year. Finally the day arrived when Paul was due to hand over his check. It was in a sealed envelope. I took it from him. "Thank you very, very much."

"Aren't you going to open it?"

I was puzzled. Why did he want me to open it there and then? Did he think I expected it to be £1,000 and wanted to see my face when I found out it was £20,000 instead? I decided to tease him. "No that's okay." I smiled. "I'll open it later."

I said good-bye and left, trying to look cool. But really I was itching to find out the amount and as soon as I was safely in the taxi I ripped the envelope open. The check was for £150,000. *Oh my God,* I thought. This was beyond anything I'd dreamed of.

In a panic, I grabbed my mobile and rang up my girlfriend Rudi. Her reaction was instant. "Well, that's it. You've no choice. You're definitely going to have to become a registered charity now." Rudi said that it would probably take about six months to formalize, so I agreed that she should set the wheels in motion straightaway and asked her to become one of the trustees.

When I got home I naturally called Paul to thank him. I imagined that would be the end of it. But some time later he rang and suggested another get-together. A bit puzzled, because I'd thought he was happy with the way things were going, I arranged to fit in another meeting. I prayed he hadn't suddenly found a glaring mistake in the plan. I could do without that. That particular week had been bad enough for me already. My resolution to reduce the stress in my life wasn't making much progress. While I had been filming and editing for *That's Esther* and working flat out on the Sierra Leone project, my current relationship had been going through a traumatic period. A couple of weeks earlier everything had finally come to a head. I was still pretty cut up about what had happened and it must have showed, because after we'd been talking for ten minutes, Paul suddenly said, "What's wrong? Are you all right?" "Not really," I confessed. "I've just split up with my boyfriend."

Paul's face lit up. There was no other way to describe it. Because I thought he was making light of it, I got quite upset. "It's not funny. I'm not very happy about it, you know."

At once he looked contrite. "Oh no, no, no. I'm sure you're upset . . . ," he said. "Look, can we go out to dinner and talk about this some more?"

So that evening we went out to a little vegetarian restaurant in Knightsbridge, where we had a lovely meal and chatted for what seemed like hours. After a while I became increasingly convinced that he was flirting with me. I was a bit taken aback, to say the least, and not at all sure how to respond. Was I imagining it, or had Richard Branson actually been right?

Outside the restaurant he called me a taxi. "We should meet up again," he said as it pulled up. "I'd love to," I said and meant it. It had been fun. As he saw me into the taxi, he gave me a little goodbye kiss on the lips. I thought, *Hang on, is that a northern thing?* Was kissing people on the lips a bit like a handshake in Liverpool? Or had Paul just made a pass at me?

I still couldn't work it out. The obvious conclusion was just too unlikely. A man in Paul's position could probably take his pick from some of the most beautiful and famous women in the world. From the cab I rang Rudi again. She was the only girlfriend who knew I'd been having these business meetings with Paul and I just had to talk to someone. When I told her what had happened, she was in no doubt at all. "For heaven's sake, he fancies you, woman. Just get with the program," she said.

"But I'm just not ready to start going out with someone else so soon," I protested.

Rudi sighed. "Nobody's asking you to marry him, Heather. Just cheer yourself up. Enjoy life again."

I decided to take her advice, and over the next couple of months, Paul and I saw each other secretly several times a week for meals or drives and walks in the country. It was all very slow moving and cautious. Neither of us was quite sure where our relationship was heading, but we were more than happy to take our time finding out.

For me, old-fashioned courtship was a lovely novelty after the whirlwind affairs I had experienced in the past. I had never been wooed so slowly and gently before. And I had certainly never known anyone half so romantic. Every time we met, Paul would bring me small items he had found, often while he was out riding his horse through the countryside. They'd be simple, thoughtful things, like a colorful feather, a shiny chestnut, or a pretty wildflower. Such a nonmaterialistic outlook was quite new to me. Most of the men I knew, especially those working in TV, tended to see beauty in fast cars and fancy clothes rather than in nature. I found it really refreshing. It was too soon to call what we had a relationship. I needed time to recover from my breakup, and Paul was obviously still grieving deeply for Linda. But I really enjoyed his company, and there was no point in denying that I also found him very attractive.

On the whole, the few friends and family members I confided in were supportive. Fiona, especially, encouraged me to enjoy the moment. She revealed that back in July she had answered the phone to Paul, who had chatted to her for a bit and asked which leg was my artificial one and then asked if I had a boyfriend. "I knew straight-away he fancied you," she said. "I can always tell."

When they finally met, Paul and Fiona hit it off straightaway, and talked nearly nonstop about music. I was quite embarrassed to discover how much more Fiona knew about the Beatles than I did. I didn't want Paul to think I was a complete musical ignoramus, so I made sure he was aware that I knew a lot more about AC/DC, Led Zeppelin, and classical music than my sister. I was quite surprised though when I heard her talking to him about films called *Help!* and *A Hard Day's Night.* I thought the only film the Beatles had made was *Yellow Submarine.*

Fiona gave Paul an instant "thumbs-up" after that meeting. "He's the first one who hasn't given me 'the mantelpiece speech,'" she said: Fiona always used to say my previous boyfriends were nervous with her. If I left them alone in the room with her, she claimed they would fidget and look uncomfortable. Then, eventually, they would stand up, put one elbow on the mantelpiece, and start a condescending speech to the "little sister." Fiona felt Paul was altogether more genuine. She also liked the effect he seemed to be having on me. "He chills you out," she said. "You're not so intense since you've met him."

For most of the year I had been working almost nonstop on *That's Esther.* When the series finally came to an end, I arranged to go on holiday with Fiona. I had been suffering from anemia following my bout of dengue fever and felt totally exhausted and in need of a break.

When I told Paul that I wouldn't be able to meet him the following week because I was going away, he laughed. "I was just going to tell you I couldn't meet *you,*" he said. "I've got some business in the States. Where are you going?"

"To the States too."

A smile spread across his face. "Why don't you give us a call? We can arrange to meet up."

I wasn't quite sure if he was teasing or not. America, after all, is a pretty big place. But after Fiona and I had been there for a few days he called me, and it turned out we weren't far from each other.

"Why don't you meet me on the beach next to your hotel tomorrow?" he said. "Tell you what; I'll come and pick you up in my boat." Imagining that all showbiz celebrities did everything in a grand style, Fiona and I were lying on the beach in our bikinis, waiting nervously for a luxury yacht or a cruise liner to appear. I kept looking out to sea, but I couldn't see anything except a tiny little dinghy that kept coming closer and closer until it beached on the sand. At that point, the man sailing it hopped off and walked up to us, smiling. I was pleasantly surprised when I realized it was Paul. He and Fiona chatted for a bit. Then he asked if she'd be all right on her own while he took me off for a sail. She waved us off happily. "Right, climb aboard," he said, holding his hand out to help me. Thank God I'm sporty, because there was no way to climb aboard and sit elegantly on his boat. A Sunfish isn't designed for two. There's just a little hole for one person to sit. I heaved myself onboard, artificial leg and all, and hung on tight with my legs spread out in front of me, balancing the boat as we sailed off. Eventually we landed on a tiny island farther up the coast. There we changed places and Paul taught me to sail the Sunfish myself. I ended up getting thoroughly soaked but I realized that I had enjoyed myself more than I had for years.

It had taken us an hour to get to the island, but it took nearly three hours to return, because the wind was against us. I was glad I'd plastered myself in sunblock before we set off, but I was worried about Fiona. However, when we finally got back to where we'd left her, she was lying under her beach umbrella, totally relaxed, reading her book. As Paul sailed away, Fiona and I packed our things up and hurried off to our hotel. We were late for the massages we had booked and had to settle for a half-hour session instead of an hour, but for me, at least, it had been worth it. I found it really endearing that instead of trying to impress me with a flashy yacht, Paul had wanted to share that cool experience with me. I realized with some alarm that my feelings for him were growing a bit stronger than friendship.

After our sailing trip I met him each day of the brief holiday time that remained. On our last evening, when he'd been working all day, he came out to meet me at eleven o'clock and took me down to the beach. He'd brought his guitar with him and we climbed up to the top of one of the tall lifeguard's chairs where he started serenading me. It was a beautiful clear night with shooting stars everywhere, and people were wandering by on the beach below us. It was just like we were in heaven, and they were back down on earth, because they couldn't even hear him singing. The wind was blowing his voice away. *This is not real,* I thought. *This is every woman's dream.* I think I knew at that moment that my life would never be the same again.

All my meetings with Paul that week had been very correct and aboveboard. But I was now certain that I wanted our relationship to move forward. I knew it was a big step to take. So far we had managed to keep our friendship a secret, but that had been a matter of luck. Sooner or later, if we kept on seeing each other, we would be spotted. I tried to push any misgivings about what people might say to the back of my mind. I told myself I could cope with whatever lay ahead.

I returned from America to discover that at least one person thought differently. My friend Sabrina, a journalist, was one of the most loving and caring people I knew. I had first met her five years earlier, when she started talking to me in the gym. Afterward, while we were having a coffee, she had suddenly asked me what it felt like to lose a part of your body. It turned out she had just been diagnosed with breast cancer and was waiting to have a mastectomy.

Our friendship was cemented when I got an infection in my stump and couldn't use my artificial leg. Sabrina had only just had her breast removed, but she actually came over the day after she was discharged from hospital to bring me some shopping and to take Oliver for a walk because she knew I was pretty helpless while I was on crutches. Since then she'd become one of my best friends. So when Sabrina said, "I don't think it's a good idea," I had to pay attention.

Sabrina's first objection was that she felt that Paul's bereavement would make our relationship very difficult. "I think he will take ages to get over Linda's death," she said. "He may never get over it, and it will be impossible to step into her shoes."

She was the first person I'd heard put my own misgivings into words. It was generally acknowledged that Paul and Linda had enjoyed one of the happiest marriages in show business. As far as I knew, he hadn't been out with anyone else in the two years since she'd died. If that was so, as Sabrina pointed out, the prospect of telling his family that he was dating again would be really daunting for him.

Sabrina's main fear for me, though, was about the publicity our getting together would attract. "I think it'll end up being totally unfair on you when you are someone in your own right and you've achieved so much. If you go ahead with this, you'll just become that woman on the arm of Paul McCartney and you'll get the same sort of hostile press Linda used to get." She was quite adamant. "It's just going to introduce too much pressure and hassle," she said. "You've been through enough in your life already."

Sabrina wasn't telling me anything I didn't know. Like her, I could picture only too well what the future might hold, and it frightened me. I appreciated that Paul was a huge icon, even if I was ignorant about exactly why. Once people saw us out together, I could imagine the press reaction. It would be, *Disabled model goes out with our hero Paul.* My relationship with the media would have to change dramatically. Up until now I had always spoken openly about everything with them, because I knew that reading about someone who'd overcome disability was inspiring to other people in similar situations. But if I started going out with Paul, I'd have to keep myself and everything about our relationship very private. The press wouldn't like that. They might even, as Sabrina predicted, turn against me.

"I know," I told her. "You're absolutely right. I can totally foresee that it could turn into a nightmare. The trouble is, I can't just stop it like that."

Sabrina frowned. "Why not?"

My answer shocked even me. "Because it's too late. I'm in love with him."

# Chapter 25

It was quite a while before Sabrina's fears were realized. For months, whenever Paul and I met, it was in private bolt-holes where we weren't likely to be spotted by the press. In addition, we almost always met on a one-to-one basis, rather than in company. One bonus of this was that we were able to talk and talk. In four months we probably got to know each other better than most people do in four years. I had no idea how creative he was. It came as a total surprise to me that Paul McCartney not only sang and composed but was a recognized painter and poet as well.

I tried desperately to slow the pace. I didn't want to rush into any new relationship, because I'd been so hurt from my last whirlwind romance. But I knew very quickly that I had strong feelings for Paul and he seemed to feel the same way. We just wanted to see each other all the time. By the end of 1999 I had fallen completely under the spell of the most idealistic, sensitive, loving man I had ever known.

One of our favorite meeting places was a certain London hotel, where the staff could be relied upon to be discreet. The first time I arranged to meet Paul there was on Halloween night. I had asked Fiona to drop me off, and because we were a bit early, we parked the car across the road and waited.

"Look at that funny man kicking a can down the street," Fiona said suddenly, looking in her wing mirror.

I turned my head. "Oh my God," I gasped. The man had a scarf wrapped around his face like the elephant man, so he was unrecognizable, but I knew at once that it was Paul. Only Paul could hop, skip, jump, kick a can down the street, and whistle all at the same time.

"So what exactly is the point of the scarf?" I asked Fiona. "Everyone is going to look at him, thinking he's a nutter, and then recognize him anyway."

We were in stitches. He obviously hadn't seen us, so when he walked past, I let the window down and called out in my best cockney, "Hello darling." He turned around, walked back, pulled his scarf down, and gave me a huge kiss through the window.

"Hey," I said, "you're meant to be under cover, remember?"

"Oh," he said like a naughty boy. "Yes, okay." He wound the scarf back over his face. "Right then. Come inside in fifteen minutes, not before." He turned around and danced off again. He didn't seem able to walk normally at all—he was just springing down the street.

A quarter of an hour later I went into the hotel and up to the room and knocked on the door. "Wait one minute," Paul called. There were scuffling noises. Then he opened the door. "Right, you can come in now."

Inside, the room was like a film set. The lights were turned down low and there were cutout pumpkins everywhere with candles burning inside them. To this day I say there were twenty pumpkins, though Paul insists there were only three. The side table was laid for dinner for two, with pumpkin napkins and lots of little Halloweeny things, which he'd brought with him and arranged around the room. I couldn't believe he'd gone to such a lot of effort for me. I felt my heart turn inside out. He was like Peter Pan. A child's spirit with a man's mind. What more could any woman ask for?

Perhaps because he was so young at heart, romantic gestures seemed to be instinctive with Paul. He put more time and effort into making me happy than anyone I'd known. Most days he'd pick me wildflowers or sprigs of rosemary to make my car smell beautiful. He was also a real gentleman, doing all the right things, like opening car doors, fetching my coat, and walking on the outside of the pavement. It was something I wasn't used to and it bowled me over.

Unfortunately, one of Paul's romantic gestures had an unwelcome result. We eventually reached the stage in our relationship where we would spend a couple of days at a time in secluded hideaways. Usually, on these occasions, I'd cook our evening meal and in return Paul would bring me breakfast in bed. The first breakfast he ever brought me was a huge fruit platter of melons, papayas, kiwis, bananas, mangoes, raspberries, and . . . *strawberries.* I stared at them in horror. I'd been allergic to strawberries ever since the episode years ago during the photographic shoot in the South of France. However, I didn't want to spoil the mood, so I ate the lot. Hours later, I came up with great big lumps all over my face. I looked like a spotty teenager. Still I didn't say anything. On our next trip away the same thing happened. It was some time before I felt relaxed enough with Paul to confess my allergy and strawberries were taken off the menu.

Breakfast for Paul was always fruit. He was very health-conscious, which tied in with him being an avid vegetarian. Quite by chance, I had returned to being vegetarian myself in 1999, although at the time it wasn't through any moral qualms about eating meat. My change of diet had been largely due to a medical misunderstanding years earlier.

After I left the Hippocrates Institute I had eaten an almost vegan diet. However, a couple of years later I started getting infections again. Around that time I read a new book called *Eat Right for Your Type* by Dr. Peter D'Adamo. In it he said that people with blood group O should always eat a diet that included meat to maintain their immune system properly. When I'd been given transfusions at Mount Vernon Hospital after my accident, the blood they'd used was labeled O negative, so I assumed that must be my blood group. I decided to give Dr. D'Adamo's theory a try and started to eat white meat and fish again. I can't say my health improved dramatically, but my infections did clear up. It was only when I went in for my cervical operation in May 1999 that Dr. Gordon told me my blood group was actually A negative. Because it is a very rare group I had apparently been given O negative blood—which is known as the universal donor group—in my blood transfusions instead. The instant I found that out, I switched back to a vegetarian diet, which was what Dr. D'Adamo recommended for people with group A blood. Fortuitously, this meant that when Paul and I met, my eating habits were compatible with his, which they wouldn't have been a few months earlier. However, Paul was a lot more careful than I was about nutritional balance, so my diet, which had all too often included chocolate binges, became much healthier after we met. One bonus was that the after-effects of my dengue fever infection, in particular the anemia, quickly disappeared.

It was hard to carry on as normal at work and not let the cat out of the bag, but somehow I managed it. When people in the studio asked me about the rumors they'd heard I just told them to mind their own business. The end of the year was just as busy, workwise, as the beginning had been with lots of public speaking, filming, and counseling. I was also working on a new venture—a CD. In October I'd visited Fiona in Greece for three days and at her suggestion, while I was there, I wrote a song to raise funds for disability charities. I called it "Voice" and in it, I basically said that people with disabilities can speak for themselves and should be listened to. Fiona's record company, Coda, had a recording studio, which she arranged for us to use, and she found someone to help with the electronic side. My job was to find musicians. I decided to do the lyrics myself, but to speak them rather than sing them—I knew my limitations. Piano and strings were sorted. Soon all I needed to complete the lineup were some gospel backing singers. I asked Paul if he could suggest anybody, and he instantly offered to do the backing himself. In fact he insisted, despite my protests that he had done enough for my charity work already. He may have regretted it later, because on the day we recorded, I decided he wasn't doing it exactly the way I needed it. I immediately went into bossy mode, saying, "No no do it higher, do it like this," and telling Paul McCartney how to sing, which cracked everybody up.

I was really happy with the end result. The problem was that when the CD was launched and it was stated in the publicity that Paul had worked on it, the press, who had already been sniffing around, put two and two together. From then on they weren't interested in the CD, only in whether I was Paul's new girlfriend. It meant I wasn't able to promote "Voice" properly and give interviews the way I'd planned, so it didn't do as well as we'd hoped. By mutual agreement, Paul and I denied that we had any relationship other than a professional one. It was actually more my decision than Paul's. I'd rushed into so many things in my life and made some bad judgments. This time I wanted to play it safe. Not all of the press seemed convinced by our denials, but by Christmas the pressure had died down a little.

Soon after he'd recorded "Voice," Paul had to go to New York. One evening, two days after he left, I was visiting Kirsten and her son Alex (who was making great progress after his hip operation) when my mobile rang. It was Paul. "Heather, I've written this song for you." He said he'd been sitting in the hotel thinking about me and missing me. His room overlooked Central Park and he'd looked out of his big plate-glass window at the bare trees all ghostly in the mist and he'd just sat down and written a song.

"I want you to hear it. I'll put the phone down and go and play it." I heard his footsteps going away and then very faintly the sound of a piano playing and Paul singing. When he came back to the phone I had to tell him I hadn't been able to make out the words.

The next thing I heard was a rumbling noise as he dragged the piano across the room to the phone. (Paul told me later the piano was a magnificent black Steinway. I still wonder if it was ever the same afterwards.)

"Right. Hang on a moment. Listen," Paul said. "It's called 'Loving Flame.' " He started playing again, and this time I could hear. "How can I hope to reach your love? Help me to discover what it is you're thinking of. 'Cause when we kiss, nothing feels the same. I could spend eternity inside your loving flame." By the time he finished I was crying like a baby and Kirsten, who had gathered what was happening, was crying in sympathy.

I had hoped to go to Sierra Leone myself that autumn but my blood tests still showed residual effects from the dengue fever so I had to postpone my trip. In the event, fate was on my side because trouble flared up again in the country and the helicopter that James Ruddy and I had planned to travel around in was actually hijacked the week we should have been there. . . . During the fighting, one of the orphanages at Makeni north of Freetown was burned down by the rebels and a lot of the kids were abused and some had their limbs chopped off. Some contacts of James managed to get the orphans out to Freetown but we were desperate to find somewhere safe to put them. I happened to be making a TV appeal that week for more funds to help Ed set up our rehabilitation center. Out of the blue, after the appeal, a woman rang up the TV show and said, "I've two houses in Freetown that I haven't been to for a few years. If you want to use them as your rehabilitation center that would be great."

It was the answer to our prayers. "If you wouldn't mind," I said, "could we use them as orphanages until we get everyone settled, because the rehabilitation centers are important but not as immediately important as having these kids housed somewhere safe." She was quite happy to agree.

James went straight out to arrange it. A couple of weeks later he sent a picture back of all the kids looking really happy outside their new homes, which they'd decided to name the Heather houses.

I was still counseling other amputees and whenever I was in London I tried to visit Sam at the Middlesex Hospital. She was allowed home most weekends, but the news wasn't good. The cancer had not gone into remission and she was starting to look really thin and weak. She was still as cheerful as ever though. In fact she was so brave that I nominated her for an award at the annual Children of

Courage Awards ceremony in December. Unfortunately, the organizers said that because she had just had her seventeenth birthday, she wasn't eligible. I took Sam to the awards ceremony anyway and presented her with a plate I'd had specially painted with a tribute to her courage.

Afterward we went to the House of Lords for a reception and Sam was able to chat with various celebrities. She was bubbling with excitement and really enjoyed it. Her special hero seemed to be Chris Eubank, who spent ages talking to her. After a bit, though, she got very tired. One of her aunties was a black-cab driver, so I called her up and put her back in her taxi to go home.

I was driving off, smiling to myself, thinking how much Sam had enjoyed the day when my mobile rang. It was Chris Eubank. He sounded really agitated. "Where's your friend?" he demanded. "Where's Sam? Where's Sam?"

"She's just left," I told him.

"Oh, no, no," he groaned. "Have you got a number for her?"

"Why?" I was puzzled.

"I wanted to say good-bye to her. I had to nip out and I said I'd come back."

I gave him her mobile number, thinking he was just being polite. Half an hour later the phone rang again. This time it was Sam, almost hysterical. "You won't believe it, you won't believe it," she screamed. "Chris Eubank has arranged for me to spend £3,000 in Harrods and he's wheeling me around in a wheelchair at this very moment and we're eating chocolates and he's getting me a computer."

It turned out that when Chris Eubank had left Sam he had gone off to have "a word" with the owner of Harrods. When he heard about her plight, Mohammed Al Fayed had instantly said, "Take her there and let her choose what she wants." So my idea of giving Sam a day out as a little treat ended up with a huge unexpected bonus.

Christmas that year was magical. Paul was spending the holiday with his family so I wasn't expecting to see him. But on the night of December 23 I was in the kitchen at home when a vehicle pulled up outside. I went out to find Paul unloading a Christmas tree from a van. He had cut the tree down in his forest himself and driven for three and a half hours to deliver it to me. He wanted to plant it in the garden there and then, but it was too dark, so I made him a nice cup of tea instead. It was the first night he'd spent in the barn, and because he'd arrived so late it seemed a bit like a dream, but when I woke up the next morning and there was this tree outside and him in my kitchen, I knew it wasn't. Together we planted the tree and hung it with lights. We were back sitting in the kitchen when the postwoman walked down the drive. I was quite unnerved to realize how close we had come to being discovered.

But for Paul, the time had come to stop being so secretive. By now he had told his family about me and had invited me up to Liverpool to join in the McCartney New Year celebrations. It was an annual pilgrimage for him, and this year was extra special because it was the millennium. The whole enormous family was there and I met the entire Liverpool McCartney clan, who turned out to be the most wonderful, down-to-earth people, who reminded me uncannily of Geordies.

Before the visit Paul had given me a warning. "Whatever you do, when you meet my cousins, clench your teeth."

"Why?" I asked innocently.

"'Cause if you don't, they'll stick their tongues down your throat." Of course, Paul was exaggerating. But I did get kissed quite a lot that New Year! The first time was at the house of one of Paul's cousins. As we walked in, a six-foot-two guy with a great big belly and a warm smile came up to me and said, "All right, love? How's it going?" and planted a smacker on my lips.

It was Ian Harris, renowned as the godfather of the family, who used to send his young cousin Paul on errands to the sweetshop while he was courting his future wife, Jackie. Ian had a wooden-terraced platform in his garden that for some reason was known as the Hugey, and this was the center for family get-togethers. Most nights all Ian's mates and family would come around and drink "beverages" even in the freezing cold because they had a little fire heater in the middle. Next door lived Ian and Jackie's daughter Lizzie and her husband, Ronnie, who had a smaller terrace called the Wimpy. The whole family was very bright, as I found out the second night we were there. It was the "Hugey" quiz night and the quizmaster asked lots of impossible questions, which people were falling over themselves to answer. Any snotty southerner who thinks a Scouse accent means you aren't very intelligent should have a try at the McCartney family quiz night. By the end of the evening while I was shamefacedly adding up my score, I realized they were some of the brightest people I'd ever met.

For me the Liverpool visit was a bit scary because I was going to be introduced to Paul's kids for the first time. It must have been just as scary for them. I tried to remember what it was like for me when I had first met Charles, Mum's new man, and to imagine how they must be feeling. Fortunately, there were no traumas and our first encounter seemed to go well. It was a difficult situation for everybody, Paul most of all, and I knew I would have to tread very carefully. But like most of the world, as the fireworks went up on millennium night I felt very optimistic indeed about what lay ahead.

Straight after New Year, Paul flew off to the Turks and Caicos Islands in the Caribbean with his kids. He wanted me join him in time for my birthday on January 12. I was a bit hesitant because my first introduction to his family had gone smoothly and I didn't want to risk upsetting the applecart. However, he persuaded me that all would be well, and as usual he was right. On January 10 I deposited Oliver once more at his "doggy Hilton" with Mary and James and flew to Miami. After a slight delay caused by bad weather and delayed boats, I finally arrived at Parrot Cay with a few hours to spare before Paul's family left, and was able to meet up with them before they caught their flights home.

We spent an idyllic few days together, staying in a beach villa, sailing, swimming, and scuba diving. I had learned to dive years before in St. Lucia, but to my surprise, Paul had never dived. He took a practice lesson beforehand and, just as I had, fell instantly in love with the sport.

Parrot Cay was a bit of a hideaway for show business people. Aidan Quinn, the handsome actor who starred in *Desperately Seeking Susan,* was there with his wife Elizabeth. In the villa next to us were Liam Neeson and Natasha Richardson. Each villa was very private and we didn't realize who our neighbors were until Aidan put a note through our door saying, *Hey, Paul, I just played you in a film.* The film was called *The Two of Us* and was loosely based on the relationship between Paul and John Lennon. Paul didn't even know about the film, but I had happened to see a trailer for it on TV while I was stuck in a hotel in the Turks and Caicos waiting for my boat to Parrot Cay. Probably because I knew one of the characters concerned very well, I didn't find the dialogue very realistic. However, Aidan's portrayal of a young Paul had quite impressed me.

We decided to invite them around for dinner. All the villas had restaurant service and our cook produced a wonderful vegetarian meal for the six of us. By now, thanks to Paul's influence, I was getting quite zealous about not eating meat and had started to think about the conditions in which food animals were reared. As Liam was an avid carnivore, a very heavy discussion ensued, with Paul and Liam looking all set to have fisticuffs at one point. Luckily, it calmed down as the meal proceeded and at the end everyone, including Liam, agreed it was the best meal they'd eaten on the island. Next day Paul took Liam out and taught him how to sail. The fact that Liam fell in the water an amazing number of times struck me as a bit suspicious, but Paul assured me it was mere bad luck.

We had less than a week together in the Turks and Caicos, but they were some of the happiest days of my life. Paul claimed that he had even missed me in the two weeks before I arrived. One day, as we were walking down the beach, he told me that pirates used to land on the island, which was why it was called Parrot Cay—it was derived from *Pirate* Cay. He said that sometimes if you looked under stones you could find relics the pirates had left. To demonstrate, he walked over to a huge stone and turned it over and there underneath was *Paul and Heather* carved in a heart into the stone. I stood there shaking my head in disbelief. This man was too much. He was just deliciously romantic. Not only that, I fancied the pants off him!

We would soon have known each other for nearly six months, which was my unofficial deadline for being under cover. My closest friends already knew the score, but we had to "come out" to the other people we knew sometime. My belated birthday party, planned for the end of January, seemed as good a time as any to do it. On January 29 I invited about a hundred of my friends and relatives round to the barn, which still had no curtains and looked pretty spartan. The only furniture was my old round terra-cotta table, with its four metal chairs, and my bed. Fortunately the minimalist look was very in that year and most of the guests thought I had cleared the barn out especially for the party. With the help of lots of flowers and hundreds of candles on the windowsills throwing light onto the old beams it became quite atmospheric. Most people arrived soon after seven. I'd left lots of alcoholic fruit punches out for people to help themselves to and soon everyone was chatting. A lot of people from the different branches of my charity work were there, meeting for the first time, so there was some enthusiastic conversation going on by nine o'clock. It was only thanks to Oliver's barking that I knew the chief guest had arrived. I went out to meet him. His collar was turned up against the weather just like any other party guest, so there was no big embarrassing moment of recognition when he came in with me. It was only gradually, as he moved around chatting, that people realized who he was. Thanks to the punch, everyone was already very relaxed and by the time we were ready to dig into the vegetarian supper that Fiona, Sonya, and I had put together, Paul was having animated conversations in the kitchen with TV producers, convoy lorry drivers, and prosthetists.

By the end of the evening as we danced in each other's arms, I realized that Paul's introduction to my friends had not been the ordeal I had expected. I had been far more nervous than he had about this moment. I should have known that he would handle it brilliantly. He can talk to anybody about anything and be really interested in what they have to say. All evening, friends came up and said how happy we looked and how pleased they were for us both that we had found each other.

Naively, I let myself hope that when the rest of the world found out about our relationship, their reaction would be the same.

# Chapter 26

Of course, I was hopelessly wrong. Not that the rest of the world found out about us immediately. My friends were very discreet, so the story of Paul's appearance at my birthday party didn't leak out for quite a while. But once we stopped trying to hide our relationship it didn't take long for the news to spread. The turning point came one Friday evening when we went out to dinner in St. John's Wood with Ringo Starr and his wife Barbara Bach. Someone in the restaurant must have rung the press, because to my horror, as we stepped outside a barrage of flashbulbs exploded in our faces.

Next day Paul and I went for a walk in a London park with his daughter Mary and her baby son. We all had a laugh together, and we were getting into the car when Paul spotted a man with a big press camera watching us from a doorway across the road. "I've had enough of this," he said, and beckoned the man over. He sidled up, and a second man, presumably a reporter, appeared from the doorway and joined him.

"Yes? What exactly do you want?" Paul asked politely.

"We'd like a picture of you together," the photographer said.

"Okay, we'll give you that and then we'll expect you to leave us alone," Paul said.

As the photographer stepped back to take his snap, the reporter asked, "Have you got anything to say about your relationship with Miss Mills?"

"Yes, we're very good friends." Paul said. "She's a very impressive woman. We are an item."

At that, the reporter scribbled away frantically, but Paul hadn't finished.

"What we don't need at this stage is photographers lurking in the bushes. If this is to develop then give us a chance. I'm not a politician and we're not spies. I don't want to be surrounded by photographers, because that could wreck something."

They wanted me to say something as well but I declined to comment. I didn't want to take the smallest risk of upsetting Paul's family. Some time ago I had decided to let Paul do any talking that was to be done about our relationship.

Next day the story appeared in the *News of the World* along with our posed photograph and several others they'd secretly snapped in the park. That night our relationship made the TV news. On Monday all the papers carried the story: not just the tabloids, but the "qualities" too. Mostly, the tone was cordial. Later in the week *Hello* magazine did a lovely article headlined *Why Heather Deserves This Happiness,* but there were one or two sly digs from some tabloids, which seemed more interested in listing my previous boyfriends than in wishing us well. A couple of the papers contrasted Paul's thirty-year relationship with Linda with my "string of failed relationships." Personally, I didn't think having five serious relationships in fourteen years was bad going, but to them it made me a scarlet woman. In their stories my charity work was ignored.

The day the news broke worldwide that Paul and I were "an item," as he'd put it, marked the start of the worst year of my life. Over the next few months, two papers in particular made it their mission to dig out every past boyfriend and pay him to "spill the beans" about me. To their credit, all refused, except one, who was only too happy to oblige. He said some very hurtful and untrue things about me, which to me just confirmed that I had been right to move on. I was only too aware that Paul's children might read the article and would have no way of knowing the things he claimed were a complete fabrication. Only the fear of hurting the parents of the man in question, who were wonderful people of whom I was very fond, stopped me from breaking my vow of silence and retaliating.

After a bit, the stress began to get to me. Every time I stepped out of the door I had a microphone stuck in my face. I was hounded and followed like a police suspect. The phone at the barn went nonstop. Often it was reporters I knew, saying things like, "Come on, Heather, what are you playing at? Talk to us." But I couldn't take the risk. I knew that if I said anything at all it was likely to be misconstrued. In the end I got Fiona to put a message on my answering machine saying, "This is Heather Mills's office. If you're ringing up about her friendship with Paul McCartney she has no comment to make."

Living on my own in a great big echoing barn, I started to get quite scared. When I was lying in bed at night, every time Oliver barked, I imagined he'd heard an intruder. All at once it didn't seem very sensible to be stuck in the middle of the countryside with no security and only one neighbor. I decided to move. Perhaps, I thought, I could find a new, secret address, where I could go to ground. I found a small house quite quickly. It was near the coast, a lot closer to Paul's home, and in a part of the world that I loved. I had spent many happy hours with Grandma in that area as a child and somehow, I felt that her spirit was still there. I planned to do a "moonlight flit" from the barn to my new address so the reporters wouldn't know where I'd gone. I underestimated them. Unfortunately there are some sad people about who will sell any information. The press knew where my new house was even before the contracts were exchanged.

The shadowing continued. Cameras flashed every time I stepped into the street. Reporters followed me around continuously, believing that eventually I would talk. I had known some of them for years and had cooperated with them on a lot of stories, so initially they were friendly but the longer I stayed silent, the more their attitude changed. It was as if they thought, *Screw you, Heather, you've been open with us for seven years, why can't you help us out now?* So they got their knives out. To a certain extent I could understand their frustration but they hadn't for a second considered things from my point of view. Why on earth should I risk sabotaging such an important relationship by talking about it?

One morning, in desperation, I tried to explain my reasons to two reporters who were following me as I did my shopping. "Look," I said. "I'd love to be open with you, but you've got to understand. I'm in love with him. I want to respect his children and the family, so I can't speak." It didn't help. They weren't interested in my reasons. When the story had been *Poor disabled model overcomes adversity* it was fine, but now they had thought of a better story: *You're after our icon, you bitch.* A lot of very nasty things were written. I was called a gold digger, which was really more of an insult to Paul, insinuating his wealth was all he had going for him. Even worse, the paparazzi started to get aggressive in their pursuit of me.

The most terrifying incident came one day when I was going to meet Paul. I came out of the house, got into my car, and spotted a car behind, following me. I stopped; went into a shop; came out; drove off—and it followed me to the next shop. Before I knew it there were three cars trailing me. I felt like a criminal being hunted down. I took refuge in a hairdresser's and asked for a shampoo and blow-dry, hoping the paparazzi would give up and leave, but they didn't. When I peered out of the window after an hour I could still see their cars outside. The photographers were all sitting in the kebab shop opposite, cameras at the ready. *This is ridiculous,* I thought. I called the police and explained the situation. The sergeant who spoke to me was sympathetic, but said his powers to intervene were limited. "We can't arrest them because it's a public space, but I tell you what we will do," he said. "We'll box them in and give you a chance to get away." Five minutes later two police cars drove up and parked tightly in front and behind the photographers' cars. The minute the coast was clear I dashed out, jumped into my car, and sped off.

Unfortunately one of the paparazzi must have parked around the side of the kebab shop because moments later his car appeared in my mirror. I put my foot down. He was *still* following me. Every time I speeded up, he zoomed after me. Then, all of a sudden as I rounded a bend, he overtook and cut in front of me, so I had to stamp on the brakes to avoid crashing into the back of him. I stopped the car, shaking. I'd had enough. I got out and shouted, "Look, here's your picture. Take it and go."

The photographer got out of his car and came toward me looking all excited. It was as if he had a red mist over his eyes. He snapped a few shots, then said, "But I want one of you moving. I don't want a posed picture." In other words, he wanted one of me running away from him looking distressed. I refused to oblige. As he circled around me trying for a "natural" shot, I got back in my car, reversed with a screech of tires, and drove off as fast as I could. When I looked in my mirror again he had gone.

By the time I finally met up with Paul I was pretty distraught. How could people get away with that sort of behavior? No one should be allowed to chase people in cars. It was horrible. Did they have any idea the stress it put on you to be hunted as if you were an animal? I would never have compared myself with Princess Diana. But for a moment I'd had a glimpse of what she must have endured. I hadn't been born with a silver spoon in my mouth. I'd gone through a lot of bad experiences in my life, but out of everything I'd been through—my mother leaving us; the abuse from my father; being homeless; even losing my leg—I'd say one of the most horrible ordeals I'd ever been through was the media harassment that year.

Through it all my friends and family were brilliant. They tried to explain that it wasn't me personally the press were having a go at. In their eyes no woman on earth would have been good enough for Paul. He was their hero. Fiona pointed out that the editors of papers that were being most aggressive were from Paul's generation and to them he was an icon. Some of those editors, she added, trying to make light of it, were women, and might even be jealous.

Unfortunately, the press stories weren't just hurting me. My charity work was being badly affected too. Everyone thought my career would improve because I'd met Paul, but the opposite was true. My income, and therefore the income of the Heather Mills Health Trust, went down by 80 percent. Sponsors pulled out because my image was getting tarnished in the tabloids. In addition there were a lot of things I couldn't do anymore to earn money. I had to think twice about everything. I was asked to sign a million-pound modeling contract with a national clothing company, but in one of the shots, they wanted me to do a bra picture. Although it would only have appeared on the bra tags, I felt I had to turn it down because I knew the press would pick up on it.

Sometimes it felt as if our wonderful holiday in the Turks and Caicos was a hundred years ago. My feeling of optimism on New Year's Eve had certainly been ill founded. So far the new millennium was proving to be pretty horrendous. It wasn't just the hounding by the press that was depressing. Not long after she'd expressed her worries to me about what *my* future might hold, Sabrina had been suddenly taken ill. A scan revealed that the breast cancer had returned. Weeks later she was dead, leaving her teenage son, James, parentless.

Then, in February, despite a last-minute intervention by Mohammed Al Fayed, who offered to fly her to America for treatment, my young friend Sam had finally lost her fight against cancer. We had grown very close and coming so soon after Sabrina's death I found it really hard to cope with. I was both honored and dismayed to discover that in her last wishes, Sam had asked her mum if I would do a reading at her funeral. I stood up in church and gave an address saying how brave and strong and wonderful she was and how she'd never want any of us to cry. And then, on cue, not being nearly as brave and wonderful as Sam, I burst into tears. As it went on, the ceremony became sadder still. Sam had a boyfriend whom she'd known since she was thirteen. He was at the graveside and threw the first handful of soil on the coffin, and the sight of his devastated face was heartbreaking. Sam had just been a young girl with so much to look forward to. Life was so unfair.

The only bright news that spring was that the Heather Mills Health Trust had at last been granted full charity status and Paul's donation was being put to good use. The flare-up of fighting in Sierra Leone meant that Ed Pennington-Ridge's departure had been delayed until February, but now that he was finally out there, he was already helping train local people to make his low-cost limb. Ed had some encouraging stories to tell. One man he'd fitted had been desperate to return to his work as a builder, so was delighted when Ed provided him with an artificial arm. It meant he was able to go back to picking up and chopping up breeze blocks and laying cement. The trouble was, he was so delighted that he didn't come back for his second fitting in case Ed took the limb away from him. Ed finally persuaded him to return by promising that not only could he keep the first limb forever, but he would make the man a second arm, specially adapted for driving so that he could get about in his pickup truck again.

The trouble with Ed was that his brain was so supercharged, he always wanted to move on to new things. After seeing what was going on in Sierra Leone he was now coming up with novel ideas for land-mine clearing devices. But training people to make his limbs was already occupying him full time. "Let's concentrate on doing the limbs first," I told him. "There are lots of people already working on de-mining."

However, I understood Ed's concern. The problem of clearing land mines was occupying my thoughts too. It was disheartening to fit people with new limbs only to be faced with another set of amputees on the next visit. Unless the source of the problem was removed, the job of fitting up amputees would be never-ending. Of course the ideal answer would be to get all governments to agree to ban the use of land mines in all future wars. The Ottawa convention on land mines had been drawn up with just that aim, but although many countries, including Britain, had signed it, America and several others were still refusing to do so. Until they did, any progress made by either the de-miners or limb clinics like ours would be continually frustrated.

Fortunately there were people in America who disapproved of their government's stance. That year we visited John Eastman and his wife Jodie. As John was Linda's brother, I'd been worried how they might react to me, but my fears were unnecessary. From day one all of them, including their sons Lee and Jay, were very warm and loving toward me.

Jodie was very involved in charity work herself and one day she invited Paul and me to a luncheon party for the International Rescue

Committee. Cleverly she had seated me next to William Luers, a former US ambassador, because she thought we might have interests in common. She was quite right. Bill, as he liked to be called, was the president and chairman of the United Nations Association of the USA, which had recently started a campaign called Adopt-A-Minefield. Its aim ultimately was to raise enough funds to clear all the known minefields in the world. Discussing the situation with Bill Luers got me thinking that mine clearance and survivor assistance were so interlinked that it didn't make much sense to fund-raise separately.

After talking to Bill, both Paul and I felt we wanted to get involved with his organization. That September we attended an international conference on land mines in Geneva and had talks with the Adopt-A-Minefield people. Their organization had huge funds compared with those of the Heather Mills Health Trust so I suggested a deal. If AAM donated a portion of their funds to survivor assistance then Paul and I would become goodwill ambassadors for Adopt-A-Minefield. We both believed that most people would gladly have their donations used not just to prevent land mines maiming people, but also to help the survivors when it did happen. Soon afterwards the Heather Mills Health Trust became an official supporter of the Adopt-A-Minefield campaign.

My charity work helped take my mind off the continuing press harassment, but I couldn't escape it. Around this time I discovered that one of the papers was going to publish not only my new address, but also a picture of my house. I took them to court to stop them and won, but then they appealed and the judgment was overturned. It meant they were free to tell every lunatic in the country where I lived, which was pretty scary. The Beatles had some obsessive fans and in the past, several people in their lives had been threatened. It was less than a year since George Harrison himself had been stabbed by a crazed fan.

That judgment plunged me as close to real depression as I had ever come. It was the low spot of the year. Admittedly, the majority of the press wrote great things, but human nature dictates that if people say a hundred positive things about you and one negative, it's the negative you remember. Paul started to get quite worried about me. He did his best to compensate for the effect the stories were having by taking me to new places and introducing me to new experiences.

He started to teach me to ride. I'd only sat on a horse a couple of times before, but luckily, as with sailing, being sporty helped me get the hang of it. I quickly fell in love with horse riding. Usually I'd ride a beautiful horse, which was an unusual, purebred bay Appaloosa with no spots, while he rode his favorite gelding. We'd ride for hours through the forest while he pointed out wild boars and deer and badgers and foxes. I absolutely adored it.

In his efforts to lift my spirits Paul also persuaded me to get out my saxophone again and we started to play music together. We both loved Nat King Cole and often, after dinner and a glass of wine, he'd sing one of the old classics while I accompanied him. Sometimes, I'd say, "Come on, do us some dancing," and he'd get up and dance around the room like Fred Astaire, singing "our song": *"The very thought of you. The mere idea of you . . ."* I loved watching him dance.

Playing the saxophone was a private thing for me and always would be. There was only one occasion when he managed to twist my arm to perform in front of other people. It happened in Liverpool. Ian Harris's daughter Sally was getting married and the whole family was invited along to celebrate. We called in at her house the day before the wedding and I was allowed a quick peep at Sally's dress, which Paul's sister-in-law Rowena had made. It was gold and absolutely beautiful.

"Who's taking you to the city hall tomorrow?" I asked Sally. "Have you got a chauffeur coming?"

"No, of course I haven't," she said. "I'm going to walk down there."

"How far is it?"

"Oh it's just down the road, about half a mile."

"Sally, you are kidding," I said. "Half a mile in your wedding dress? We've got a hire car. Come on, Paul, you be the chauffeur."

"I'd be delighted," he said, giving her a mock bow.

Next morning, while I was having my hair blow-dried, Paul disappeared. Half an hour later he came back with the Jag covered in gold ribbons to match Sally's lovely gold dress. She had nobody to do her makeup so I sat down and did it for her. Then we all rushed off down to the city hall. The ceremony was lovely and afterwards we came back to Ian's house for a party.

The celebrations were in full swing when suddenly Paul turned to me and said, "Come on then, Heather, get your saxophone out." I was terrified, because I'd only just got to know them all, but once Paul had given them the idea they wouldn't let me off the hook. Paul produced my saxophone from the boot of the car where it lived when we were traveling and before I knew it, he had me standing on Ian's "Hugey" playing "Fly Me to the Moon" and "Moon River." I was cheered and kissed and everyone said they loved it. I took that with a pinch of salt. After all, the beverages had been flowing freely all night. But after the battering I'd taken from the press, it was great to be surrounded by people who were so demonstrative and generous, and who made it obvious they liked me. I loved it up in Liverpool.

It was quite a year for weddings. In November my assistant Sonya married a lovely man called David Mills. Bizarrely, it meant that she too became Ms. Mills. "I know I'm training you up to be a replica," I told her, "but there was no need to take it this far . . ."

My thirty-third birthday wasn't until January 12 but Paul had decided to give me an early birthday present. Ever since I'd spent a month working for Roadshow Fashions when I was seventeen, I had dreamed of returning to India. On New Year's Day, while still bleary-eyed from the usual Liverpool New Year celebrations, we flew to Delhi. It was the most incredible trip. We traveled all over Rajasthan, moving on somewhere different every two or three days. We stayed in castles, palaces, and grand colonial hotels and took every mode of transport India had to offer. The highlight of the trip came on my birthday. Paul knew that I'd always wanted to go on a train across India and he had booked a ticket from Delhi to Jaipur on the Palace on Wheels: the Indian equivalent of the Orient Express.

It was incredible—like traveling back in time. As we climbed on board in the blazing sun a smiling gentleman in a white turban and white gloves said, "Welcome, maharaja! Welcome, maharani!" We were garlanded with petals and had a dot of turmeric smeared on our foreheads. Then we were ushered into our carriage and given a glass of champagne as the train drew out. A few hours after we set off, we ate in the paneled dining carriage with the other passengers, who were mostly Americans. The experience I had most been looking forward to was sleeping on a train, but when it came to it I didn't sleep a wink until our morning tea was brought in at seven forty-five. We had a huge double bed that was pushed up right against the window, and because there was a full moon, you could see the scenery outside almost as clearly as in daylight. Beside the track for mile after mile there were people living, squatting around campfires. It was another world. While I stared out into the night Paul picked up his guitar and started composing a song and singing with a Peter Sellers–style Indian accent—*"Riding to Jaipur, riding through the night, riding with my baby . . ."*

In Jaipur we were met and taken up to the Raj villas, where Paul had arranged for us to spend my birthday. Unknown to me he had organized a treat: a private performance by the famous sitar player Nishat Khan. Nishat had been due to play a concert to five thousand people on the night of my birthday, but when Paul contacted him he canceled it. He came up to our private room, bringing his professional dance troupe with him, and all I had to do was to sit there being entertained. Later, I took to the floor with the dancers while Paul videoed us.

By the time we returned home I felt energized and my spirits had lifted completely. The attentions of the press seemed all at once much less important. That was when I decided that the only way to avoid being brought down in future was to avoid reading the papers altogether. I rang up all my friends and asked them never to tell me what had been written. If it was libelous, they could tell my lawyer, but if it was going to hurt me I simply didn't want to know. I reasoned that since everyone who meant anything to me knew who I was and what I was about, it didn't matter what anyone else thought.

If people wanted to believe some of the nasty stuff, then that was up to them. Finally, after a year of being devastated most days, I had found a way of dealing with it.

Maybe because he saw the effect the holiday had had on me, Paul decided to give me another surprise. Two days before Valentine's Day he told me to pick up my passport and pack some nice things to wear and drove me to the airport. A few hours later we were in New York.

On February 14, Paul took me shopping to buy a dress. We spotted a perfect one in red velvet with a slit on the right side—most slits are over the left leg so I can't wear them. In the evening, I glammed myself up and we left the hotel and got into a cab. He wouldn't tell me where we were going and it wasn't until we got out of the cab that I realized our destination was the Rainbow Room where some of the scenes of *Sleepless in Seattle* were filmed.

It was like another era. The dance floor was filled with energetic older women, whom even the youngsters couldn't keep up with. At the end of the night, Paul got the bandleader to play our song "The Very Thought of You" and we put on a little dance performance of our own.

The rest of the day had been equally magical. We had visited the Empire State Building. It was my first trip there but it was a bit disappointing because it was packed with tourists. It meant that we had to shuffle around in the crowd, take a quick look, and move on. Suddenly a big burly security man spotted us and recognized Paul. He put his hand on his shoulder. "If you follow me, we can take you to a level higher up," he whispered. We followed him and were rewarded by a private unhurried view of the amazing New York skyline. All around the edge of the viewing platform, people had carved little graffiti. When he saw them, Paul took out a pen and started to write our names too.

Our escort looked disapproving. "If it was anyone else, I'd arrest you," he said. Then he smiled. "But since it's you . . ."

Thanks to a security guard turning a blind eye, *Paul loves Heather* is now inscribed on the top of the Empire State Building for all time.

# Chapter 27

Only two days after Paul and I left India in January, a massive earthquake had struck Rajasthan, the area where we had been staying. It was hard to believe that the very region we had traveled through the previous week had suffered so horribly. It was only when we returned from New York that the full extent of the earthquake was being recognized. More than thirty thousand people had been killed and at least as many were injured. Among them were hundreds who'd had limbs amputated after being crushed under fallen buildings. When I heard that, my immediate instinct was to get back over there, to see if the knowledge I'd gained about amputees could be of any use.

Paul understood my motives, but he was also worried about the dangers, as aftershocks were still occurring in the region. However, he knew me well enough by now to know that this sort of project was my life's blood, so he didn't try to stand in my way. Paul's donation to the Heather Mills Health Trust was fully committed to the Sierra Leone project, which meant I needed urgent funding for my trip. I contacted *Hello* magazine, which had given me a lot of support in the past, and asked if they would help. My plan, I explained, was to locate the amputees in need of help and try to get them together for a limb-fitting day. The *Hello* team were superb. In return for an agreement for exclusive photographs, they not only agreed to pay for a few thousand limbs but also promised to print an appeal to their readers for more funds when the story was published.

After spending several frustrating weeks waiting for the Bhuj airport to reopen I finally left London for Bombay on March 13. I felt quite nervous about what I would find and was relieved that my traveling companion was Ken Lennox, an experienced war photographer. He had been in Vietnam and the Gulf and so was used to working in disaster zones. We had our initial setback soon after we landed. Back in England we'd been told that we would find our first amputees in Bombay where they had been flown ready to be fitted with limbs. However, we arrived only to be told they had already been discharged and no one knew where they were. Undeterred, we decided to fly on to our next stop, Bhuj—one of the most badly damaged towns—ahead of time. There was no one at Bhuj airport to meet us so I had to quickly find out where to go. About a hundred Indian men stood around me in the rubble-filled street, staring curiously as I made urgent calls on my mobile phone. I was wearing pedal pushers that showed my calves and suddenly one of the men came up to me and gently touched my left leg. Somehow he knew it was artificial, which wouldn't have pleased Bob Watts.

Amazingly, despite the devastated roads, some taxis were still running, and one took us to an emergency Red Cross hospital. It was staffed by volunteer Finnish and Norwegian doctors, one of whom, Dr. Vidar Lehman Bergen, recognized me. He said he had a tent with many child amputees. When I asked if I could speak to them, he looked doubtful, saying that none of the children spoke English. I told him that didn't matter; there were other ways of communicating. The first child they showed me was a ten-year-old boy, Dilip Pranji, who had lost his right arm through the shoulder. A piece of farm machinery had fallen on him during one of the aftershocks in his village and his parents had carried him fifty miles to the hospital. He was still in shock and looked at me numbly when I sat on his bed. I took his hand and got him to touch my artificial leg, and his face changed. When I took it off, so we could compare our amputated limbs, he woke up and got really interested. Even the doctors were impressed. They'd become used to well-known faces visiting hospitals they had worked at, but none of them had come up with a party trick quite like mine!

I spent the rest of the day in the Bhuj area, touring amputee wards in two hospitals fifty miles away from each other and popping off my leg and putting it back again. It was a pretty basic way of counseling, but I knew from experience that it could help people come to terms with their loss and believe that they had a future.

We devoted the following day to finding somewhere to set up a clinic. Ken and I managed to locate members of a Lions Club in Bhuj who said they would help pay for some limbs and who offered their clubroom as a fitting center. It was ideal. The club chairman told us they had worked in previous years with the Jaipur Limb Clinic, coordinating the fitting and distribution of their low-cost limb. I had visited the Jaipur Clinic with Paul back in January and met the doctors there. The Jaipur limb was a really good working limb that only cost £20 to make, including labor, so it seemed the ideal one to use. I rang the clinic and was thrilled when they agreed to come to the Lions Club in Bhuj on May 3, by which time most people's residual limbs should have healed enough for fitting. They promised to get a huge team of people together and to spend the whole day fitting people from the earthquake area with artificial limbs. To fit a Jaipur limb from start to finish would only take them forty minutes, compared with the more sophisticated UK leg which can take one or two weeks. They hoped to fit well over a hundred in that single day. If we wished to organize and pay for further fitting days, they said they would be happy to cooperate. I agreed to keep in touch with them from England and let them know when they would be required again. Over the next year the Jaipur Clinic fitting days provided fifteen hundred earthquake survivors with limbs as well as over six thousand other amputees.

Our main work was now done, but Ken wanted some more photos, so before we left we decided to tour the area that had been closest to the epicenter of the earthquake. The destruction was harrowing. One village, Ratinal, had been razed to the ground by the earthquake, with only the mosque left standing. A mile and a half down the road there was another village that was hardly touched. How could you explain it? If you'd lived in Ratinal it must be hard not to wonder what you had done for God to pick you out. Our photo shoot had at least one positive benefit. In a tented hospital in Ghandidam village we came across a mother of four children, Halima Maagdi. She had been ill in bed when the earthquake came and her house had collapsed on top of her. Her three-year-old daughter was trapped with her, but wasn't badly hurt. Doctors had struggled for six weeks to save Halima's legs but two days before we arrived they'd had to remove one of them below the knee. She was only twenty-six, but looked forty-six after all she'd been through. She had great spirit though and a lot of family support. Often in India, women who lose their limbs are looked down on, but luckily Halima's husband was standing by her. I knew that she might not have healed enough by May 3 to have an artificial leg fitted but it was a possibility. Anyway, it was important for her to make contact with the Jaipur Clinic. I told Halima and her husband all about the fitting day in Bhuj and gave them directions to find the Lions Club. From their enthusiastic response, I was sure they would go.

The whole time that we traveled in India, we slept in the open, on camp beds under the stars. It was a long time since I'd slept outdoors: The last time was when I was living rough under the Waterloo arches at the age of fourteen. On our last night it struck me that I would far rather be homeless in India than in London. The people of Gujarat had nothing, but they'd give you their last rupee. Everywhere we'd been, people had shared their scarce food with us. Potatoes, rice, and dal had never tasted so good. It was a great contrast to the luxury of the "Palace on Wheels" but in a strange way, I had enjoyed it just as much.

Back home in England my charity work and public speaking had expanded to such an extent that it now left little time for anything else. Fortunately I had done my last program for *That's Esther* the previous year. It meant that although I still did one-off programs I no longer had a weekly commitment and could concentrate on charity projects. My main focus in 2001 was now the Adopt-A-Minefield charity, which we were about to set up in the UK. The launch was planned for June and I wanted to make a documentary for the occasion, illustrating the ravages that minefields caused. On April 5 I flew to Croatia and spent three days interviewing land-mine survivors and their relatives. Soon after we finished filming, Paul and I flew to Washington, where Bill Luers had arranged for us to meet Colin Powell, the US secretary of state, for a discussion on the US land-mine policy.

The meeting went well, though Colin and Paul spent the first five minutes talking about the 1960s and the Beatles and singing snatches of "Yellow Submarine," which Colin said had been a favorite marching song with the US and South Vietnamese soldiers in Vietnam!

We got on really well with Colin Powell, who was very supportive of mine clearance, even though the United States was still refusing to support a worldwide ban. One of the sticking points was the so-called smart mines, which had a limited life. The US still wanted to use them, but they were prohibited by the Ottawa convention. However, Colin told us that there were a number of areas where his government could and would cooperate with our campaign. To our delight, he then backed up his words by making a large donation to Adopt-A-Minefield on behalf of the US State Department.

All that spring Paul had been getting increasingly worried about George Harrison. In 1998 George had been treated for throat cancer. At first he seemed to have beaten it, but since he'd been stabbed by an intruder in December 1999 his health had been very fragile, and recently a new tumor had been found in his lung. I'd met George for the first time the previous year in Los Angeles. He had flown us both in his private jet to Las Vegas to see *O,* an amazing theatrical performance involving underwater scenes by the Cirque du Soleil. We had a ball that weekend. Olivia, George's wife, was a very beautiful woman. She also projected amazing mental strength. It was no surprise to me that she had sorted out the guy who stabbed George and had saved his life. Olivia and I got on really well. In fact, we bonded straightaway in the ladies' toilets where she got her skirt zip stuck and I had to rescue her! They were a really loving couple.

George was warm and sweet and they were both devoted to their only son Dhani, who was away at college and whom they talked about all the time.

Soon after we arrived home from LA, George rang Paul up. During their conversation Paul started laughing uncontrollably and looking at me.

"What did he say?" I asked when he put the phone down.

"He told me he thought you were a great girl and I was a lucky, lucky bastard." Paul grinned. I was really flattered.

At the time George was still getting over his stabbing but there was no inkling of any other problem. But now that lung cancer had been diagnosed, he had gone to Europe for surgery. Paul did a short European tour in May, promoting his new CD *Wingspan*, a collection of Wings' greatest hits. After he'd appeared in Milan we both flew on and spent a beautiful evening with George and Olivia. Paul had brought his ukulele along and he and George started clowning around, singing "Something in the Way She Moves" in the style of George Formby. George looked thin but he was in good spirits and we were all hopeful that the surgery had been in time.

On June 4 the UK branch of Adopt-A-Minefield was launched at BAFTA in London. I gave a speech pointing out the scale of the problem—that seventy million land mines were estimated to be still hidden in the ground worldwide. That 26,000 people were being killed or maimed every year, a third of them children. Then we showed the twenty-five-minute documentary I'd made in Croatia. Paul spoke the commentary. "Imagine living in a country during a terrible war and then peace is declared," he said. "You think the killing is over, but when you take your kids to the beach you can't walk on it because your children could get blown up. This is the legacy of the land mine. Land mines take or wreck three lives an hour, every hour of every day of every year. We have to come together now to try to stop that."

We had reasoned that it would help Adopt-A-Minefield's fund-raising potential to have a direct human-interest element. Mines were bits of machinery. The people who stepped on them were real children, men, and women. We were very soon proved right.

Following the link-up with survivor assistance, donations to Adopt-A-Minefield branches worldwide went up dramatically.

At the end of July Paul attended the graduation ceremony at the Liverpool Institute of Performing Arts, of which he is the chief patron. We had visited the institute several times by now. The institute had recently introduced scholarships for students with disabilities and I had met several of them. Paul is very proud of the institute, which used to be his school. It had been closed down and was derelict when he intervened ten years ago and came up with the idea of a school of performing arts. With his help, together with aid from the Liverpool Council, it has become one of the best cradles for young talent in the country.

It had been a busy six months for us both and after the degree ceremony Paul suggested that we should take a few days for ourselves. We booked into a lakeside hotel complex that we'd visited the year before and loved. We had fallen into the habit of giving each other little gifts when we went on holiday, and soon after we arrived I gave him a musical photograph album. It had photos recording our time together with appropriate musical accompaniments for each photo. He loved it. We were just about to walk over to the hotel for dinner when he said, "Oh, wait a minute. I'll just get your present. Sit down again." I sat back on the chair while he ran upstairs. A few moments later he came back down. He was holding something behind his back and had a mischievous look on his face. As he reached me, he suddenly dropped to his knees. I thought someone had shot him in his kneecaps. But no one had. He produced a box containing a ring from behind his back. "I love you, Heather. Will you marry me?" he said.

The room went all fuzzy. I wanted to cry but I couldn't. I wanted to speak but I couldn't.

"Well?" Paul asked.

"Yesss," I squeaked.

Tears were running down his face. That was when it really hit me. I knew he loved me but I hadn't known how much. All the things he'd have to deal with were going through my head at once. Whether the kids would be able to handle it; what the outside world would say about him getting engaged three years after Linda's death. What courage it must have taken him to face all that. *My God,* I thought, *he really, really loves me.*

Later, when we had both recovered, we went in for dinner. In the dining room I kept my hand down by my leg, trying to hide the ring from anyone walking by. I kept playing with it though and sneaking a look. It was a beautiful Indian sapphire bordered with diamonds. Paul told me that he'd bought it when we were in India six months earlier and had kept it hidden all this time because he'd wanted to give it to me on a special occasion.

"You should show it off," he said.

"No. No," I said. "People mustn't know about it. It's secret." I wanted our engagement to be kept very quiet, but Paul disagreed. "No, I'm proud of it," he insisted. "We should make an announcement."

When we got back to his house in London he released a statement to the press. Within half an hour reporters were gathering outside the door. The only way of getting them to go away seemed to be to speak to them, so we went out and posed for photographs. They wanted us to kiss but we refused, saying we didn't do it on demand. It had to be spontaneous. To my relief the response in the papers the next day was overwhelmingly favorable.

We decided to take nearly all of August off to enjoy the moment and plan the future. For four weeks we spent nearly every day swimming and sailing, with me clinging ungracefully to his Sunfish dinghy. Both of us had busy diaries for the next six months and we decided to schedule our wedding for the summer of 2002.

I had envisaged a quiet registry office ceremony, but Paul insisted that he wanted me to have a big wedding. "You deserve a proper wedding," he told me. "This is a serious thing we've got here. I'm moving on and I want people to know that I'm not ashamed of it."

On September 10 I was due in New York to collect an award from the American *Redbook* magazine for my work with land-mine survivors. I was in good company: Sarah Ferguson and Hillary Clinton were also receiving awards that day. Paul came with me and entertained Hillary and other guests with an impromptu jam session while we were waiting.

We had arranged to fly home to London early the next morning. We were actually taxiing along the runway when the pilot's voice suddenly came over the intercom announcing that our takeoff would be delayed because a plane had crashed into the World Trade Center. When we looked out of the window, we could see black smoke rising from one of the Twin Towers. All around us people started dialing up their mobiles, trying to find out what had happened. The captain spoke again, asking us not to panic but to sit tight "until we find out if this thing was an accident or not." We were all talking, trying to reassure each other, when I glanced out of the window again and saw smoke coming out of the second tower. I had a sick feeling in my stomach. Soon afterwards we heard on the mobile that the Pentagon had been hit as well. Minutes later we were rushed off the plane and told that the airport was closed until further notice.

All the roads were cordoned off, so it was obvious we couldn't get back to New York and we decided to head north instead and find somewhere to stay. For the next three days we sat virtually nonstop in front of the telly. Nobody knew what was going on. We didn't know if a war was going to happen. We didn't know if the whole system would close down. Everyone feared the worst. We filled every cupboard with food and rang friends to check if anyone needed help. Several people we knew had friends who'd been lost in the towers but amazingly, no one we knew personally had been killed or hurt.

All flights were grounded for days, but I had some urgent charity commitments in London. I pushed and wangled and eventually managed to get a seat on the first plane back to England a few days later. After doing my work, I flew back to New York to rejoin Paul. During the flights I'd had plenty of time to think. Like everyone else I was still struggling to take in the enormity of what had happened and like everyone else I wanted to do something to help. By the time I got back, an idea was bubbling at the back of my mind. "You should do a charity concert," I told Paul.

At first he was reluctant. He was planning to bring out a new album soon, called *Driving Rain*—his first for many years—and he thought it would look as if he was just cynically promoting it.

"But you wouldn't be," I said. "*You'd* know the reasons you were doing it. That's all that would matter." He still looked doubtful, so I changed tack. We'd spent hours recently watching Mayor Giuliani and President Bush talking about terrorism and freedom on the television. "Why don't you write something instead then?" I suggested. "Write a song about freedom." The same day Paul sat down and composed a song with a rousing chorus. *"I will fight for the right to live in freedom."* It must have inspired him, because a couple of days later he came in after going for a walk on the beach and announced, "Okay. I'll do the concert!"

Immediately we started to look for venues. Radio City Music Hall was available, but not until a week after Yoko Ono did her concert there (she'd just changed it from a John Lennon Memorial Concert to a Twin Towers concert). We were still undecided the following weekend when we attended John and Jodie Eastman's son Jay's wedding to his fiancée Katama at Martha's Vineyard. One of the other wedding guests was Harvey Weinstein, the film producer and head of Miramax. After the wedding he flew us back to England on his private jet and during the journey we started discussing our concert idea. "Funnily enough," Harvey said, "I've been thinking about doing some kind of benefit concert too. Why don't we make a really big thing of it? If you come on board, Paul, then everyone else will come on board."

Before we knew it the planned concert had grown into a huge event. Everyone started joining in: Mick Jagger, Elton John, Keith Richards, Billy Joel, The Who, Eric Clapton, David Bowie . . . the list went on. The head guy of the American TV company VH1, John Sykes, signed up to televise it.

We decided on Madison Square Garden as the venue. Demand was huge and tickets were being sold for hundreds of dollars. I was very concerned that the firefighters shouldn't be overlooked. I found out that many of them hadn't received the free tickets we'd arranged for them to have. I felt direct action would be quicker than going through official channels to put the problem right. Since meeting her during our holiday on the Turks and Caicos, Elizabeth Quinn, Aidan's wife, had become a friend and she'd introduced me to Steve

Buscemi, who was married to her best friend Jo. Steve had been a fireman before he became a director and actor and thanks to his contacts he managed to get us into Ground Zero. It was devastating, like a nuclear site. I spent a few moments quietly paying my respects before moving on to Ladder Ten. There, thanks to the fire chief, I was able to move around illicitly, disguised as an official in the fire chief's own yellow helmet, and hand out tickets.

On the night of the concert, the atmosphere was electric. Behind the scenes, celebrities like Bill Clinton, Meg Ryan, John Cusack, and Jim Carrey dressed down and wandered about like ordinary people. After September 11 fame didn't mean so much. It was as if the stars suddenly felt their own mortality and recognized that however famous they were, ultimately, they were no different from the rest of the world. . . . Every single performer got a rapturous reception. But none got as many cheers as Paul did when he came on and sang his song "Freedom" as the finale. That night raised forty million dollars for the families of those affected: the police and firefighters killed, those in the Twin Towers, and the small businesses around the towers that were damaged or wiped out. It was the concert of a lifetime.

Only weeks after the concert we were back again in New York, but this time for a sadder reason. George Harrison's condition had deteriorated suddenly and he had been getting aggressive chemotherapy. Olivia rang to tell us that he wasn't doing very well and we flew out on the Concorde for the day. As fate would have it, that was the same day that the plane came down in Queens and we were next to land at JFK airport. We saw the plume of black smoke from the air and thought we were having a nightmare. In fact we nearly missed seeing George because of the disaster. Sarah Ferguson was on the plane with us and as a VIP, she had an FBI escort, which was certainly a blessing that day. Everyone else got turned back because it was initially thought to be another terrorist attack, but we managed to follow Sarah and get through the tunnel—there were occasional bonuses to being famous. When we arrived at George's house he was sitting on a couch, looking very weak and not very well. Paul sat down next to him and, taking hold of George's hands, started rubbing them gently. They'd never held hands before or had that sort of emotional intimacy because they were from Liverpool, where guys don't do that kind of thing. But it was obvious it made both Paul and George feel great.

I sat at the other side of the couch and George and I compared notes on our ileocecal valves, on which I felt myself an expert. Mine hadn't worked properly since my accident and George was having problems with his. He kept joking with me and teasing me about it. He still had a sense of humor, even at death's door—he was a gorgeous man. It was a real privilege to meet him. He seemed at peace with himself when we left, hours later.

"Well, you know I'm going to be fine," he told us as we said goodbye with tears in our eyes.

Two weeks later in London we got a phone call in the middle of the night from Olivia with the news we had been expecting and dreading. George had died peacefully in LA, with his wife and son beside him. On December 3 at nine-thirty in the evening, at the same time as Olivia, Dhani, and their friends in LA were holding a ceremony for George, we held a minute's silence for one of the kindest, most talented men either of us had known.

Adopt-A-Minefield was now occupying the majority of our charity efforts. Just before the concert I had done a photo shoot for an American fashion company called INC. At the age of thirty-three I was surprised and delighted when Maryellen Needham contacted me to ask me to model and said she would organize the whole shoot. I agreed to do it provided they gave a percentage of their profits from the clothes I modeled to Adopt-A-Minefield and publicized the fact. Maryellen got them to agree to that and INC also agreed to make lump-sum donations for every store appearance I made. Modeling again was great. The photographer was a brilliant, renowned guy called Walter Chin. With his help and that of the makeup artist Anna Marie Rizzieri, I ended up looking like twenty different people. When the catalog was launched in early February 2002 and I saw the photographs, all together, I couldn't believe it. I was like a chameleon.

I looked back and thought about all the model agencies that wouldn't take me on when I was seventeen and the people who said I'd never make it. And I have to admit I said a quiet *"Up yours."* Because now sixteen years later my picture was in Macy's, one of the biggest stores in America, blown up on ten-foot posters and on huge moving screens outside. I think Paul was more thrilled than I was. He went up to Macy's before me on the morning of the launch and rang me to tell me about the display. Then he started going around telling passersby, "That's my girlfriend up there!" Several newspapers carried the story the next day—he'd been so excited about it. It was a brilliant launch. I signed catalogs and flyers for hours. Lots of British people, both with and without disabilities, turned up to meet me, which was very moving. But most importantly it was all in support of a cause that was now at the center of both our lives.

# *Epilogue*

Looking back on my life you could say it has been a rags-to-riches story. And that's how many journalists seem to have viewed it. But it's not quite as clear-cut as that. Admittedly my life today is often exciting and glamorous, but it also has plenty of occasions that remind me of my roots and help me keep my feet on the ground. Two trips I took recently illustrated the point perfectly.

Going away for my birthday has now become an annual treat and in January 2002, Paul and I went to India again, this time to Kerala, which was exquisitely beautiful, much lusher and greener than Rhajistan. I never know what to expect on the morning of my birthday, but this time Paul surpassed himself. We were staying in a cabin on the edge of a lagoon, and as soon as I woke up, he made me get out of bed, said, "Close your eyes," and led me out of the front door. When I turned around, I saw that the entire cabin was covered in marigolds, lilies, and every kind of flower you could imagine. The smell was incredible. I thought I would never have a more romantic experience in my life . . . until that evening when Paul took me out in a traditional boat with three musicians who played to us as we lay back on cushions drinking wine and eating wonderful Indian food. Eventually the musicians left us to spend the night alone on the boat under the stars. When they'd gone, Paul presented me with my birthday present, a diamond and sapphire bracelet that he'd bought the year before at the same time as the engagement ring and had kept hidden all that time. It was the perfect end to a perfect day.

A week later I said good-bye to Paul at Bombay airport and flew to Vietnam to make a documentary film about the work of

Adopt-A-Minefield. The contrast between this trip and the one I'd just finished could not have been greater. I was back in the real world now. On arriving in Bangkok I had to wait in the airport for seven hours before flying on with Air France to Hanoi. That flight was an hour late, and I sprinted through the terminal to try to get my connection to Hue where I was meeting the film crew. Unfortunately it was very humid; my leg got hot and all of a sudden it started to fall off. Many Vietnamese frown upon anyone who's disabled, so there were some really shocked faces when I pulled up my jeans and popped my left leg off. They watched, horrified, as I dried it off and popped it back on again. In the end I missed the connection anyway. By the time I arrived in Hue the next day, Caroline Goodman, the producer, was panicking because the time was very tight. We started filming virtually straightaway with a young boy called Lai, who'd been blown up by a land mine. He'd lost his right leg above the knee, his left foot and ankle, his right eye, a few left fingers, and his right arm. He was bright, mad about computers, but permanently in a wheelchair because the prostheses he'd been given weren't comfortable enough. We moved on to a six-year-old girl called Suong. She had a piece of shrapnel from a land mine in her brain that her family couldn't afford to have removed because it would cost $2,000.

We carried on filming for several days, during which time I and the rest of the crew stayed in a cockroach-infested guest house and slept on beds like small planks (fortunately with a mosquito net). Supper for me was a bowl of rice, because everything else on offer seemed to have a cow's head or sheep's brains in it. The water that came out of the bath tap was the color of urine, and the rest of the bathroom defied description . . .

When we'd finished our interviews with land-mine survivors we went up to an area called Charlie One in Quang Tri province, which Adopt-A-Minefield was paying to have cleared. It was the homeland of several Vietnamese families who'd been displaced during the war. Their houses are still there and all their ancestors are buried there, but it's never been safe for them to return.

Dave Denman, a de-miner from MAG, the Mines Advisory Group, explained the finer points of the various mines to me on camera. "This is one of the commonest mines," he said, casually picking up a small metal object. "The M14 blast mine. It's also called the toe-popper, because it's designed to injure and take off a leg rather than kill. It's a small US-made mine, diameter fifty-six millimeters, that contains twenty-nine grams of tetro, a highly sensitive explosive. As little as nine kilograms of weight can set this mine off. It has a minimal metal content, which makes detection with a metal detector really difficult."

He picked up another mine. "This is the M16, a bounding fragmentation mine containing TNT. These are even more common in Charlie One. M16s can be detonated either by someone standing on them or by a trip wire. If you were a small child wandering through the bushes you wouldn't stand a chance. It only takes 1.4 kilograms of pull or 3.6 kilograms of pressure for it to jump up and rip your chest open. It would also kill or maim anybody else who was around. Maiming is what the military aim for with mines because it makes the victim become a burden on his country." He shrugged. "If someone is dead you just bury them."

It was a message Adopt-A-Minefield had to get across. I hoped Dave's words would shock a few more people into thinking about the immorality of land mines.

When the filming finished I had to get back urgently to New York for the INC launch. Unfortunately my return flight had been changed because of my late arrival. I'd been told I could pick up the new ticket reserved for me by producing my credit card at Hue airport, but when I got there, they said they didn't take credit cards and I didn't have any cash. There was an hour before my flight left, but it was half an hour to Hue Town where the bank was. I thought quickly. There was no way I could miss this flight because that would mean missing all the other connections and consequently missing the INC/Adopt-A-Minefield launch in America. In desperation

I turned to the Japanese woman standing behind me in the queue and asked her if she'd lend me sixty dollars for an economy ticket to Saigon. I was pretty scruffy after a day filming in the field and she looked at me as if I was mad. I tried to beg from the guy behind her, with the same result. Then, to my relief I saw what I thought was an English face. It turned out to be a Canadian gentleman, with a Vietnamese guy. "Please, please, please," I asked them. "I know this sounds nuts. I'm not a con woman, but all I need is sixty dollars. I'll give you the cash as soon as I get to Saigon. There'll be a bank there. Look, take my Walkman, keep my jewelry." They obviously thought I was crazy too, but eventually got their wallets out. I could have kissed them.

In Saigon, after running around to find the bank and losing my leg in public yet again, I finally stuffed two hundred dollars into my benefactors' hands and ran off to catch my connection. I hadn't eaten anything for five days but rice and tofu. As I sank into the comfortable British Airways plane seat and ordered a big bottle of water, a ricotta and spinach lasagne, and a salad I thought, *Hallelujah.* I realized at that moment that one thing was certain. As long as I stayed involved with Adopt-A-Minefield there was absolutely no danger of me forgetting how the other half lives.

As I write this, it's just a few months before my wedding to Paul and I'm trying to look ahead and imagine what the future holds. I'm already excited about the wedding. I've taken my time about designing my dress and choosing the perfect material and all the little details. I want to relish every moment of the planning, just as I enjoyed our two years of dating and then our long engagement. I've discovered that it's nice, not hurrying into things. Maybe I'm finally learning to slow down.

After we're married, I hope to slow down more. I've been on call twenty-four hours a day, seven days a week for years now. Between my charity work and public speaking, I still work six days a week. I feel it's time to pause and take a breath. I am still deeply involved with Adopt-A-Minefield and always will be. Our current project is to set up a mobile limb-fitting clinic, so that Ed Pennington-Ridge and his team can travel to communities that need their help. However, now that Adopt-A-Minefield works alongside me, there seems no reason to have the Heather Mills Health Trust as well. We can do the same work under a stronger organization alongside the UN Association. As the Heather Mills Health Trust winds down, I can reduce my organizing responsibilities and concentrate on helping amputees and their relatives directly. Counseling and doing goodwill visits will be enough. I've spent a long time rushing around—recently, I worked out that in thirty-four years, I've lived in thirty-seven different houses. Now that I am finally going to settle down with my fella of a lifetime, I want to have time to enjoy it.

In the past I often told people that if my life was like a jigsaw puzzle, there was a whole lot of blue sky still waiting to appear. Today I can say, with my hand on my heart, that I was absolutely right.

# *Afterword*

On June 11, 2002, in the tiny village of Glaslough in Ireland, Heather Mills and Paul McCartney were married. The wedding was a strictly private affair, with just close friends and family present to celebrate the event. From now on, Heather will be known as Heather Mills McCartney. Her work for Adopt-A-Minefield continues.

# *Author's Note*

Adopt-A-Minefield raises awareness and funds to clear land mines and rehabilitate land-mine survivors. It offers everyone an opportunity to give people in mine-affected countries back their lives, return land to productive use, and provide assistance to those who have been injured in land-mine expolsions.

It only costs about $1 to $2 to clear a square meter of land, $30 to help a child walk again. If you'd like to find out what you can do to help, or to learn more about Adopt-A-Minefield, contact:

**In the US:**

Adopt-A-Minefield
UNA-USA
801 Second Ave.
New York, NY 10017
ph: (212)-907-1305
www.landmines.org or info@landmines.org

**In the UK:**

Adopt-A-Minefield (UK)
3 Whitehall Court
London SW1A 2EL
United Kingdom
ph: 44(0) 20 7925 1500
www.landmines.org.uk or info@landmines.org.uk